Successful Real Estate Investing in the '90s

Also by Peter G. Miller

The Common-Sense Mortgage

Successful Real Estate Negotiation

(with Douglas M. Bregman, Esq.)

Buy Your First Home Now

How to Sell Your Home in Any Market—With or Without a Broker

Successful Real Estate Investing in the '90s

A Practical Guide to Profits for the Small Investor

Peter G. Miller

HarperCollins*Publishers*

Library of Congress Cataloging-in-Publication Data

Miller, Peter G.
  Successful real estate investing in the '90s / Peter G. Miller.—1st ed.
    p.   cm.
  Rev. and expanded ed. of: Successful real estate investing. 1st ed. c1988.
  Includes index.
  ISBN 0-06-270123-1
  1. Real estate investment. 2. Real property and taxation. I. Miller, Peter G. Successful real estate investing. II. Title.
  HD1382.5.M565   1994   94-19421
  332.63'24—dc20

94 95 96 97 98 ❖/RRD 10 9 8 7 6 5 4 3 2 1

To Amanda and Samuel

Contents

Acknowledgments

I am deeply grateful to the following people and organizations for their ideas, advice, resources, and assistance. Their willingness to answer questions and discuss a broad range of issues made this book possible.

From Bethesda, Maryland, attorneys Timothy Schwartz and Douglas M. Bregman answered innumerable questions over a year-long period. Mr. Schwartz also read portions of the manuscript associated with tax matters and provided invaluable advice.

The author is deeply indebted to James and Mary Hall of James J. Hall, Inc., Realtors, of Silver Spring, Maryland. Jim Hall is a real estate broker, investment counselor, and educator, while Mary Hall is a property management expert. Our many conversations, dialogues, and debates have honed my ideas, tested my views, and allowed me to consider alternative perspectives which I greatly value and appreciate.

Also, I want to thank Alton Helm, supplements manager at *The Washington Post*, and Edward R. DesRoches, editor and co-publisher of *The Real Estate Professional* for their courtesy and assistance.

Also, Gary Garrity and the American Land Title Association, Robert Engle and Epic Realty Services, Al Lewis, national tax partner with the Washington office of Kenneth Leventhal & Company, Dick Peach of the Mortgage Bankers Association of America, Steve Doehler and the Mortgage Insurance Companies of America, Chuck McManus and the Mortgage Guarantee Insurance Company, Jay Shackford and the National Association of Home Builders, and Steven Wechsler and the National Realty Committee.

Also Bonnie J. O'Dell and Eugene R. Eisman and the Federal National

Mortgage Association (Fannie Mae., John Hemschoot, director of Home Mortgage Standards, Helen Dalton and Jeanette Bernay and the Federal Home Loan Mortgage Corporation (Freddie Mac., and Jack Flynn and the Government National Mortgage Association (Ginnie Mae).

Also, from the National Association of Realtors, Jeffrey DeBoer, Director of Federal Tax Programs, as well as Jeff Lubar, Vice President, and Liz Johnson, Director, Public Affairs Division.

Also, Don Beller of the Office of Economic Analysis, Pension and Welfare Benefits Administration, Department of Labor, Alan Kappelear, Director, FHA Office of Single Family Housing, and Gerald Ference and the Veterans Administration.

Portions of the material in Chapter 11 concerning brokerage, agency, the MLS, and buyer brokers appeared originally in the author's book *Inside the Real Estate Deal*.

The home equity material found in Chapter 6 appeared originally in *The Common-Sense Mortgage*, a finance guide for buyers, sellers, brokers, and investors written by the author and published annually by HarperCollins.

The Appendix material relating to taxes was reviewed by Jeffrey A. Stoltz, CPA, a partner in the Bethesda, Maryland, accounting firm of Osterman & Stoltz, Chartered. While the tax information in this guide was believed to be correct as of the time it was reviewed, readers should be aware that because of changing tax rules, court decisions, and legislative updates the services of a tax professional should be engaged to resolve specific tax matters and to provide current advice and counsel.

The Appendix material relating to seller-paid points, which was originally posted on America Online, was added to the tax material following the review by Mr. Stoltz.

The first investing rule (Chapter 4. was originally self-published by the author in 1981.

The material in Chapter 5, "New Underwriting Standards for Investors," appeared originally in the "Executive Mortgage Report" (November/December 1988).

The description of Ginnie Mae (Chapter 5. originally appeared in *The Common-Sense Mortgage* (1985).

The chart concerning insurance loans (Chapter 7) was provided by the American Council of Life Insurance.

Portions of Chapter 25 are based on material originally published in the "Seller's Perspective," a weekly column written by the author for *The Washington Post* in 1978.

In addition to new material, extensive portions of the glossary originally appeared in *The Common-Sense Mortgage* and *Successful Real Estate Negotiation*. I wish to thank my negotiation co-author, Douglas M. Bregman, for allowing my use of the negotiation definitions in this book.

Preface

The sought-after trinity of wealth, income, and real estate are the central themes of this book, themes which I have attempted to present realistically and in context. I freely admit that in a harsh world prospective investors will have to work and save, and that such success as one may achieve won't come easily or overnight.

Thus this is not a book about instant wealth, guaranteed success, buying property without capital, getting loans without credit, or predatory investment tactics. Nor is this book so generalized that readers will feel compelled to call a toll-free number and buy seminar seats or audio tapes costing hundreds of dollars.

Instead, I have focused on realistic strategies and usable information that readers can employ within the bounds of a meaningful investment program. The idea is that wealth-building is an evolutionary process, one that can be accelerated with information, ideas, capital, and personal energy.

Real estate has always been an attractive investment choice, because it—along with labor, capital, and entrepreneurial efforts—is one of the four classic sources of wealth. It's a commodity that can be rented, traded, sold, subdivided, financed, refinanced, or developed, and because so many ways to manipulate real estate exist, there are numerous opportunities to increase value and create income.

In addition to its basic economic advantages, real estate has been blessed with a variety of tax benefits and preferences. Substantial incentives exist for those with adjusted gross incomes below $100,000, perhaps 98 percent of all households.

This book is based on my experience as a journalist, broker, and investor, and is designed as part of a series of practical real estate guides published by HarperCollins. In form and style it follows *The Common-Sense Mortgage, Buy Your First Home Now, How to Sell Your Home In Any Market—With or Without a Broker,* and *Successful Real Estate Negotiation* (with Douglas M. Bregman, Esq.). Like these texts, the book you now hold can be used as a desk reference, classroom text, or general guide.

To those who read this book I wish every success.

—P. G. M.

Successful Real Estate Investing in the '90s

I

The Quest for Something More

Millions of Americans own investment real estate and millions more would swell investor ranks if they could. Indeed, interest in the subject is so great that real estate has spawned a host of gurus, seers, and oracles, each claiming that real estate—and their secret, inside method of buying property—is the one true path to modern riches.

Unfortunately, the claims and strategies offered by today's TV wizards and seminar seers have distorted the concept of real estate investing. There are profits to be made in real estate, but for most people profits are made buying one property at a time, not four, five, or six houses in a single day. Deals with little or no money down are possible, but investments that require cash and credit are surely more common. And even though tax reform has made real estate less attractive than in the past, significant advantages remain for most investors.

Yet even with the ongoing availability of solid real estate opportunities, most of us are investment voyeurs. We like to watch. We attend the seminars, buy the tapes, check out the books, and hear wondrous success stories on TV. But we don't invest.

We suspect a catch and our hesitation is well-founded. If real estate investing is so simple, if every deal produces great profits, then surely more of us would be wealthy. Given the millions of people who have invested in tapes and seminars, one would expect to see hordes of freshly minted real estate moguls buying great mansions and driving exotic sports cars.

The seductive message offered by various seers and gurus is that through simple techniques real estate investing can lead to a promised land of great wealth and financial freedom. There's hope for those who have never been successful or who now lack cash or credit. The key to your future, say the oracles, is just a seminar away.

What we have today is a kind of populist movement led by motivational speakers and financial evangelists, and the result is that real estate investing now ranks with weight loss, hair restoration, and bust enlargement in the wish books of the innocent, the gullible, and the hopeful.

1

Adventures in the Promised Land

"You can buy real estate now, and you can buy without money up front," said one TV oracle, also known as the "Guru of Ground."

For Granger, an up-and-coming computer technician making $40,000 a year, the TV messenger's words could not be more welcome.

"Our new tapes," said the seer of seminars, "show 845 exciting, powerful, dynamic strategies anyone can use to acquire real estate today and start down that wonderful road to riches and financial independence.

"Let me introduce you to sub-guru Fred," the great oracle continued. "Just 18 months ago Fred was a classic failure. A janitor in a chicken-parts plant, overwhelmed by debt, denied credit everywhere, living in the back of a pickup truck, Fred had no career, no cash, and no future. But then he took my one-day wonder course and now Fred has assets of more than $1 million. Fred, tell us your story."

"Well, master, I was about as low and pathetic as anyone you ever saw. But then your course changed my life.

"I found a house worth $80,000 and bought it for $60,000. I took over the existing $30,000 FHA loan, got a $30,000 second trust from the seller, and had him pay all the closing costs.

"And this is the best part. To hold down costs, the seller agreed that monthly payments on his second trust will only begin three years after closing. With low monthly expenses, my rent today more than covers the mortgage.

"Since that first deal, I've had 14 more, and today I own real estate worth more than $1 million. If I can do it, anyone can."

Motivated, enthused, and all set to go, Granger bought the tapes—and with them the expectation that a real estate fortune was nearly in hand. And when he looked through the Sunday paper, sure enough there were the very ads the wizard had promised. Several homes with 100 percent financing were available in his community.

Granger had heard about such deals. "Motivated sellers," as the guru industry called them, were always in the marketplace, owners who were "flexible" and would sell property for little or no money up front.

Reading between the lines, Granger felt that "motivated" sellers were hard-pressed or perhaps even stupid. To borrow a phrase from English economist Thomas Malthus, motivated sellers were losers in the great lottery of life. "Flexible," to Granger, simply meant "desperate." Implicit in such understandings was the sense that Granger, armed with inside information from the investment oracles, was a success waiting to happen, a winner, an innately superior person.

But when Granger closely examined each ad, he saw the path to great wealth was more treacherous than it looked.

One advertiser had a four-bedroom house in the best part of town, priced at $875,000. The seller wanted a vintage Rolls Royce or a souped-up, 50-foot powerboat instead of cash, but Granger—like most people—had neither.

Another advertiser was offering a three-bedroom house for $120,000. Granger, said the seller, could collect the first and last month's rent in advance, combine that money with the tenant's deposit, and have enough for a down payment. In effect, it was a no-money-down deal, since no cash would come from Granger.

It made sense to Granger until he spoke with a local attorney.

"True," said the lawyer, "you could use the tenant's rent for whatever purpose you like. But there's a problem. You can't use the tenant's deposit for the down payment, in our jurisdiction or in many areas around the country. Here you're required to hold the deposit in trust, or escrow as we attorneys say. Use the tenant's deposit personally, and you could be liable for damages and maybe even criminal charges."

Somewhat dismayed, Granger tried a third ad, this one offering a four-unit apartment building priced at $160,000. If Granger could get 80 percent financing from a lender—in this case, a $128,000 mortgage—the seller would lend Granger the $32,000 balance for ten years at 9 percent interest. In addition, the seller would pay all closing costs.

Ah, thought Granger, if I can find a lender with $128,000 I've got a deal with no money down. No worries here about tenant deposits.

Mr. Kerry, the loan officer, was pleased to meet Granger.

"Yes," said Kerry, "we make investor loans. Our rate is 9 percent a year, somewhat higher than the current 8 percent interest level for personal residences but a competitive rate for investors. And we will make loans up to 80 percent of the property's value, what we call the loan-to-value ratio, or LTV."

Granger told the loan officer about the property and the deal he wanted to make. Kerry seemed interested and suggested they begin the necessary paperwork.

A few days later Kerry called.

"We have a problem," the lender said ominously. "This property won't support the $128,000 loan you're requesting." He explained: "Your credit is fine, but similar properties in the same area are selling for no more than $130,000. If you go through with this deal, you'll pay a $30,000 premium for the privilege of making a no-money-down deal."

By this time Granger was more than disappointed. There were deals out there with no money down, but somehow they always seemed to have a hook. But the oracle said to make phone calls, so Granger tried again.

The fourth ad was a plea: "Help Us Beat Foreclosure." Here was a "motivated" seller!

Granger called, and the seller explained how his business had gone sour, that he hadn't made loan payments in four months, and now the lender wanted to foreclose on his $60,000 mortgage. He had to sell and would take the best offer he could find. The property, said the seller, was worth about $100,000, but there had been no offer in three weeks.

This is it, thought Granger. THE deal. The big one.

Granger made an appointment to meet with the seller, but before going he went to the city records office and checked neighborhood home prices. While there were some $100,000 sales, most were in the $90,000 range.

Granger went to the property and met the seller. As much as he was interested in the house, he was astonished by the owner. Here was a man who stood at least 6 feet 8 inches tall and weighed well over 300 pounds, none of it fat. Granger had never seen a larger human being.

As for the property, it was a good house, probably the best one in the neighborhood.

"I'll make a deal," said Granger. "If you'll hold a $10,000 second mortgage and pay all closing costs, I'll assume the existing $60,000 first trust."

"That's nuts," said the seller. "Anyone can buy this place through the FHA with less than 5 percent down. The loan will be paid off at closing, and I'll get the balance in cash."

"Look," said Granger, "if you don't get an offer soon, the lender will foreclose, and you'll have nothing. I'm saving your credit rating and letting you have $10,000. The lender won't give you a dime."

The seller looked at Granger.

"So you're doing me a favor?" he asked rhetorically. "I can hold off the lender for weeks, maybe months for just a few hundred dollars. That's all it'll cost to tie up the property in a bankruptcy proceeding.

"The lender doesn't want the property. If I list this place with a broker, maybe one recommended by the lender, he'll be happy to settle without a foreclosure on the books. Rather than sell to you with lousy terms and a low price, I can just lower my price to $80,000 or maybe even $75,000. I'll sell at a discount in return for a speedy sale, but I won't just give the place away.

"I may have financial problems," the seller continued, his face red, "but I'm not an idiot."

The seller then launched into a lengthy discussion of his experience as a mercenary in six countries, his belief that Granger's parents were unwed at the time of Granger's birth, and his desire to convert various parts of Granger's body into something resembling the inner workings of a dehumidifier. Fortunately, at least for Granger, there was a knock on the door. Another prospective buyer wanted to see the property.

Granger was happy to leave. The oracle hadn't said anything about unrealistic deals, profiteering sellers, or shady financing. And certainly the guru had failed to mention the possibility of meeting ungrateful sellers, much less unusually large property owners with homicidal tendencies.

Indeed, the more Granger thought about it, the more he realized that much had been left unsaid:

- Sub-guru Fred, for instance, may have assets worth $1 million, but what about debts? For all anyone knows Fred could owe creditors $3 million.
- Fred may not have such a good deal. He claims to have bought an $80,000 house for $60,000, but who knows? The property is only worth $80,000 if it can be sold for that amount or refinanced on the basis of an $80,000 value. The seller, for reasons never explained, couldn't market the property for more than $60,000 but now, magically, Fred says it's worth $80,000.
- Fred claims the rent covers his mortgage, but what about taxes, insurance, repairs, and vacancies? And Fred never says his monthly profit is so great that he no longer lives in the back of a pickup.
- While the seer concentrated on his rise to great fortune, and the rise of several disciples, he never offered credible evidence that a large percentage, or any percentage, of those who bought his tapes or attended his seminars made huge sums of money. Where is the survey or study *signed by a reputable, known polling organization* that half of the seer's

---

The Numbers Game

Three investors met at a bar and each told how $30,000 in cash had been invested.

"I bought property 15 years ago and today I've got a 500 percent profit," said the first investor.

"That's terrific," said the second. "I have a note that pays me $8,000 a year for 15 years. That's a simple annual return of 26.67 percent."

"You fellows have really done well," said their barmate, the third investor. "I have a 15-year note, but it only pays 11.33 percent compounded annually."

Who did best?

The first investor bought property for $30,000 that 15 years later is worth $150,000.

The second investor has a $30,000 note that grows by $8,000 a year. At the end of 15 years the note will be worth $150,000.

The third investor has a bond that pays 11.3264 percent compounded annually. Because of compounding, his $30,000 note will be worth $150,000 in 15 years.

The bottom line: The difference between "large" returns and "modest" returns, before considering taxes and inflation, is often a matter of perception.

---

followers, or even 25 percent, are now rich because the guru's techniques work? Is the percentage of wealthy people who use the oracle's methods larger or smaller than the percentage of wealthy people in the population generally?

- Does not the great success of the guru's tapes and seminars ultimately make student failure more probable? After all, if a seer advises students to be contrarians, to buy when others are selling and to sell when others are buying, then as more and more people follow the oracle, the proper contrarian response will be to buy when armies of go-getters sell and to sell when vast numbers of motivated, goal-oriented zealots buy.

- In a similar fashion, if 300 people attend a seminar together, are they anything other than competitors, people using the same ideas, reading the same ads, and making the same calls to achieve the same results? Would not the seminars be more valuable, at least to students, if only three people attended?

Despite all the contradictions and evasions, Granger realized the guru was right. You can make money in real estate—especially the real estate seminar business.

With 300 people at $295 each, Granger figured the messenger could have gross receipts of $88,500 in a single day—excluding sales from literature and tapes. Even if the seer's overhead for advertising, materials, travel, and renting the seminar hall ate up 75 percent of his total take, the guru could still pocket more than $20,000 in cash for a single day's work.

2
Why Real Estate?

The emphasis on no-money-down arrangements makes enormous sense—at least if you're in the seminar and tape business. Your most hopeful watchers and listeners are likely to be people without sufficient cash or credit to buy property on a conventional basis. Thus no-money-down strategies are essential if your goal is to develop the largest possible pool of tape buyers and seminar attendees. Investing with no money down, however, is less important and perhaps even irrelevant if your central purpose is to find profitable real estate opportunities.

As a matter of random statistical probability, it's not surprising that deals involving "motivated" sellers and predatory terms are made from time to time. Millions of homes are sold each year, and it follows that some tiny proportion of all sales will involve defenseless, ignorant, or desperate owners.

But the fact that something is within the realm of plausibility doesn't assure that it will happen. It's possible to get hit by lightning, but not very likely. It's also possible to buy property with an oracle's strategies, but the odds of finding the correct combination of fire-sale prices, one-sided terms, cash-rich partners, high rents, no vacancies, and few repairs is more remote than winning the state lottery.

Yet behind the hoopla and slick productions of the gurus and oracles is a basic truth: Real estate is a commodity, something of value today and perhaps greater value tomorrow. And compared to other choices—stocks, bonds, mutual funds, gold bullion, commodities, etc.—real estate is an attractive investment vehicle when measured in such terms as inflation and deflation, leverage, risk, yield, control, and opportunity costs.

Whether real estate is "better" than other investment choices is uncertain. One, after all, does not buy "real estate" or "stock" or "bonds" in a general sense. No one calls up a stockbroker and says, "Please order ten shares of each issue on the New York Stock Exchange." We pick and choose, we buy a specific property or a given stock.

Although we can't readily compare real estate with other investments generally, we at least can say whether or not a given property has produced a real profit, profit we can measure with buying power.

INFLATION AND DEFLATION

In the same way that tides constantly erode a beach, inflation continually devalues the worth of currency. Even modest inflation levels, say 3 percent annually, cause cash prices to double every 23.45 years.

Thus, in an environment with 3 percent inflation, a property bought by Mr. Anderson 23.45 years ago for $100,000 should be "worth" $200,000 today. But if it now takes more dollars to buy a given property, and if the buying power of each dollar is worth less, is Anderson ahead?

In economic terms, if Anderson's property is worth $200,000 today, he is merely a survivor. At the $200,000 level, he has managed to preserve the buying power of his assets but nothing more.

If, however, Anderson's property is now worth $250,000, he's a winner. His "real" assets—and ultimately his buying power—have increased by $50,000.

Although inflation constantly erodes cash values, it's not entirely without appeal, especially for borrowers with fixed-rate mortgages.

Suppose Anderson bought his $100,000 house on the following terms: $20,000 down and a 30-year, 7 percent mortgage to cover the remaining $80,000 purchase price.

The very same inflation which erodes property values benefits borrowers. Anderson has a 7 percent interest rate, but if yearly inflation is pegged at 3 percent, then his true interest cost is just 4 percent annually.

We tend to think of inflation as an economic force that erodes the buying power of cash. There's another economic force which can also affect buying power: deflation.

Mr. Anderson the Inflation Beater

Acquisition Cost	$100,000
Inflation Rate	3 Percent
Time Span	23.45 Years
Inflated Value	$200,000
Market Value	$250,000
Increased Buying Power	$50,000
Nominal Interest Rate	7 Percent
Real Interest Rate	4 Percent

In basic terms, deflation means the buying power of currency increases, and in such an environment apparent real estate values may seem to fall, at least in cash terms, since it takes fewer dollars to buy a given property.

Suppose Ms. Adkins buys a home for $100,000, and within a year the country is hit with 5 percent deflation. Now, suddenly, her property has a cash value of just $95,000. She seems to have "lost" money on her investment.

But if the Adkins property is worth $95,000, she has not lost buying power. The property's value is now measured in fewer dollars, but each dollar buys more goods and services. She is essentially even.

In periods of deflation it's actually possible to lose cash values and make a profit. For example, if the Adkins house is worth $97,000 in a period of 5 percent deflation, she's ahead. Her property is worth less cash than before, but more buying power than she needs to break even economically.

LEVERAGE

Leverage is a subject of enormous importance because it's available in every transaction. With $10,000 we can readily buy a property worth $100,000, and if property values rise 10 percent in a year, we'll double our money in just 12 months.

Leverage is only possible in an environment where lenders are willing to make loans and real estate, fortunately, attracts many lenders.

Lenders like real estate because there's little risk, and mortgages have historically offered reasonable returns with few administrative headaches. Real estate loans are rarely delinquent and fewer still are foreclosed, but if foreclosure is necessary, there are buyers in most markets for such properties.

Selling at foreclosure is not attractive to lenders, because it looks terrible and requires a lot of time and money. However, the brunt of a foreclosure—the loss of equity and the cost of legal fees—often involves problems that lenders can minimize or avoid entirely. It's the buyer's down payment, or a portion of the loan insured by a government agency or private firm, that's usually forfeited, not the lender's capital.

The ready availability of financing creates opportunities for investors to multiply both profits and losses. A "conventional" real estate purchase is usually defined as a deal with 20 percent cash from an investor and 80 percent from a lender. Less conservative financing is also available, deals where lenders put up 85, 90, 95, and sometimes even 100 percent of the purchase price.

Suppose Hawkins buys a house for $85,000, and three years later it's worth $100,000.

.We could look at these figures and say Hawkins made a $15,000 cash profit. If he bought the property for cash, his compounded rate of return was 5.57 percent before inflation.

But suppose Hawkins didn't buy for cash. Suppose he used leverage and had a simple, conventional deal and paid 20 percent down at settlement, $17,000 in this case. Now he still has a $15,000 profit but his compounded rate of return jumps dramatically to 23.47 percent before inflation.

Or we could look at leverage somewhat differently. Instead of spending $85,000 in cash on one deal, suppose Hawkins put 20 percent down on five houses priced at $85,000 apiece, and three years later each was worth $100,000. Not considering inflation, he still has a 23.47 percent compounded return. In absolute terms, however, Hawkins has $75,000 in his pocket rather than $15,000.

Examples involving leverage invariably concentrate on the vast profits to be made using other people's money (OPM). Such examples, at least as far as they go, are true. There's no doubt that leverage has the power to multiply financial results.

The problem is that wondrous tales of leveraged real estate profits must be seen in context. The fact is that the very same leverage which multiplies profits also magnifies losses.

If Hargrove bought a property five years ago for $150,000 and it's now worth $120,000, he's lost 20 percent of his equity—if he paid cash. His compounded loss is −4.36 percent per year.

But what if Hargrove financed the deal? If he put down 10 percent when he bought the property, he's now lost twice his entire investment. His compounded loss: −12.94 percent annually.

RENT AND OCCUPANCY AS SUBSIDIES

Rent is an exchange of money in return for the use of property, yet rent can also be seen as subsidy for investors.

The idea of an exchange presumes a trade of values, but investors are in the position of exchanging something they can't use or elect not to use— occupancy of a particular space for a given period of time—for something of value to them, namely cash.

Rent as a subsidy is a concept unique to real estate. If you buy stock on margin, your broker/lender will want to hold the certificates—you won't have their direct use. If you own pork bellies, you must pay someone to move them, store them, and freeze them. But with real estate, tenants pay you.

Not only is rent a subsidy, but occupancy can be viewed as a subsidy also. Given the right tenants—and there are many "right" tenants—your occupants will help maintain the property, protect against burglars, plant flowers in the spring, do some maintenance, and alert you to serious problems.

No one argues that tenants are wonderful in every case, but rather that their mere presence may offer certain benefits, benefits not associated with other forms of investment.

RISK

In a world with no absolute guarantees, real estate is arguably no less, and no more, secure than alternative investments.

Federal bonds, for example, have always been repaid. What could be more secure? But bonds are repaid in dollars, cash which may yield less buying power over time. Just as importantly, owners who need to sell bonds before maturity are often forced to market their holdings at discount because of low yields.

The idea of reasonable risk is not that every property will hold its worth or increase in value, but rather that within the bounds of normal circumstances we can expect that there will always be a market for property, that financing on sane terms will be available, that reasonable profits, benefits, and returns are possible, that the government will not expropriate our property without fair compensation, and that our political and economic environment will encourage private property ownership. In a risky world, no place is safer than our country.

By its nature, the idea of risk is a relative term. What's safe to a skydiver may seem insane to the average airline passenger. And real estate investing has risks which undoubtedly chill the average homeowner. You may not get tenants. The tenants may damage the property. The roof can leak. The washing machine might break. The list is endless.

For investors, risks are part of the game, something that comes with buying, selling, and owning property. What's not acceptable is *undue* risk, risk without limit, risk that results from poor planning or projects with little chance for success.

Risk need not be unbridled, however. Investors can use attorneys, brokers, and structural inspectors to reduce exposure. Prudent business analysis, familiarity with a local community, and common sense can also limit risk.

Besides, if investing is risky, what isn't? Investors are entrepreneurs, people who take risks. Their activities may seem chancy, but at least they have some control over their fate. Who has less risk? The person who works for a huge corporation? He may feel he's without risk, at least until he's laid off, his pay is frozen, the plant closes, or new technology makes both his product and his job unnecessary.

YIELD

Increased buying power is the central purpose of investment, and few commodities offer the potential for appreciation created by real estate. But appreciation alone—buying low and selling high in real terms—is not the sole source of realty benefits.

Real estate owners can create an income stream from rentals. There are tax benefits that effectively raise ownership profits by reducing expenses. There is the opportunity to leverage investments. There is protection against inflation and deflation.

Real estate owners can also profit from fixed-rate financing where true interest costs are often less than zero. A 7 percent loan in a period with 6 percent inflation will have a real cost of 1 percent. Subtract tax benefits worth 1.96 percent for someone in the 28 percent bracket (7 percent × .28), and apparent interest *costs* (7 percent) become real interest *profits*. (The actual cost of this loan, after inflation and taxes, is −.96 percent—that is, 7 percent interest less 6 percent inflation equals 1 percent. One percent less 1.96 percent equals −.96 percent.)

CONTROL

Unlike other investments, real estate owners are in a unique position to influence and direct the value of their property. Invest $100,000 in stock or bonds and no one notices. You're an "owner," but your proportion of ownership is so tiny that it's irrelevant. Buy a house for $100,000, and major decisions that affect its worth—what to fix, what to leave alone, whether or not to expand, how to finance—are yours.

OPPORTUNITY COSTS

Except for property bought with no money down, all real estate deals require some cash up front. And the use of cash has a value or cost, depending on how you view it, which should not be ignored.

Suppose Claxton buys a home for $100,000. A lender provides an $80,000 mortgage at 10 percent interest, and Claxton pays $20,000 to cover the rest of the purchase. What is the value of Claxton's $20,000 investment?

On one side of the ledger, by putting down $20,000, he won't pay 10 percent mortgage interest each year on $20,000. Also, his closing costs will be smaller because he's financed the property with a smaller mortgage. On the other side, he lost the use of his $20,000 (because he spent it to acquire the property) and the income stream it might have produced. These lost options are called "opportunity costs."

Is it better to pay cash or pay interest? The answer, at least in strict financial terms, depends on available alternatives of equal risk. For example, in a market with 16 percent mortgage rates, having a large down payment is likely to make sense because where else can one "earn" 16 percent? If mortgages are 8 percent, small down payments become attractive.

Yet even if Claxton can afford to buy property for cash, it's an unlikely choice.

First, pay cash and there's no leverage in the deal. If Claxton pays $100,000 for one property, he loses the opportunity to multiply his results.

Second, pay cash and purchasing power is limited to the amount of capital on hand. Suppose that instead of the property he bought, Claxton sees a better deal but one that costs $125,000. Without credit and borrowing, the second deal is beyond reach, regardless of its attractive economics.

Third, unless you're very rich, Uncle Sam wants you to borrow.

3

How Others Succeed

One would be impressed with the ideas of various gurus and oracles if they offered solid proof of success among their many followers. But not only is clear and uncontested evidence unavailable, the factual data that does exist paints a far-from-impressive picture. We have seers who are bankrupt, no-money-down organizations seeking protection from creditors, consent arrangements between seers and state consumer authorities, and a host of other problems widely reported in the media.

As an alternative, we have successful investors who have never been on television, never offered seminars, and never been bankrupt. They're quietly at work in every community and many have amassed substantial wealth.

How do they do it? There's no magic formula that works in every situation. All deals are different, and it follows that each property must be approached with a fresh viewpoint to find the most profitable, practical, and coherent investment strategy.

The best answer seems to be that successful investors operate within a series of 14 observations, guidelines, and principles that define their decision-making strategies. Taken together, these considerations define a sensible, low-risk approach to successful real estate investing.

First, the central rule of real estate is that all properties are unique. The idea that no two properties are alike, what the real estate industry calls "nonhomogeneity," means that even properties which look similar—such as identical townhouses in a single subdivision—are actually distinctive.

Property prices are determined at one point in time under specific conditions through the agreement of a particular buyer and a particular seller. At any other point in time, with other conditions, or with different buyers and sellers, values may change. A "good" price today may represent a poor deal tomorrow and vice versa.

Second, the purpose of buying investment property is to make a profit. If an investor can't raise property values or increase income by fixing up, subdividing, expanding, re-zoning, or whatever, a deal won't work. Investing is not a social calling, and the search for profits is not amoral, immoral, unfair, unethical, or unreasonable. Everyone, everywhere, seeks some form of personal benefit, whether or not that benefit is measured in cash terms.

Third, real estate investing is a business. It involves loans, deeds, brokers, lawyers, regulations, taxes, and all the paperwork and headaches found with any business. Unless you're looking for an expensive hobby, investing must be given the time and effort required by every successful enterprise.

Fourth, investing is competitive. There are always players in the marketplace looking for a limited number of prime properties. Because of competition, it's important to be prepared when solid opportunities arise, to analyze deals quickly and to have financing information and sources in place.

Fifth, most deals are made between equals. While seers and oracles search for "motivated" sellers, investors work within the far larger community of people who understand that the purpose of investing is to make a profit.

Sixth, property values do not exist in a vacuum. The market value of a well-maintained property can fall if the biggest employer in town closes, state funds for a roadway are eliminated, or an all-night service station opens next door. Because external influences are important, it's necessary to keep abreast of community changes.

Seventh, there will always be renters. According to the National Association of Home Builders, the homeownership rate in this country stood at 64.6 percent at the end of 1993—down from 65.6 percent in 1980.

Over the past 30 years we have seen a profound change in homeownership patterns. It was once true that with one working adult a family could afford a home. Now it commonly takes two workers in a household. In the future, unless we radically alter our social or marital arrangements, there will be no additional workers within the home who can contribute to its purchase or upkeep. As homes become increasingly difficult to afford, rental demand will rise.

As well, we now have a fundamental economic change with which to contend, the reality that employment is no longer so easy to obtain or so likely to continue. Major corporations have downsized, are downsizing, and will downsize in the future. Even those with advanced degrees face uncertain employment prospects.

According to the House Ways and Means Committee, "1.9 million adult workers (those 20 and older) lost full-time jobs, on average, each year between 1981 and 1988 because their employers closed or relocated, because their position or shift was eliminated, or because of slack work."

"White collar workers," says the Committee, "including managers, professionals, and administrative support personnel, accounted for over 55 percent of all displaced workers. Over 80 percent of workers who were displaced in 1988 had at least 12 years of schooling, and 17 percent had at least a college-level education."

What it means for investors is this: The demand for rental housing has always been present and there is little if anything in the future which suggests that the need for rental housing will significantly decrease.

Eighth, there are times and places where the best real estate deals are no real estate deals. Not every community at every moment offers solid investment opportunities. In such situations it makes sense to invest outside the real estate field. Houston residents who put their money in something as mundane as passbook savings accounts in the mid-1980s made more money than neighbors who invested in local property during that period.

Ninth, real estate investing is not risk-free. Values can go up and they can surely go down, whether measured in cash terms, after-tax dollars, or real terms corrected for inflation. No one can guarantee future values.

Tenth, investor needs change over time. At different periods in our lives we each have different needs, interests, abilities, and concerns—factors that influence investment choices. The deal that makes sense today may be less appealing in the future and vice versa.

Eleventh, leverage is an important investment tool. Investors look for leveraged deals, because they create the opportunity to magnify the impact of investment dollars.

Twelfth, different investors see different opportunities. By definition, because there are different perceptions of value and potential, there is a marketplace.

Thirteenth, investing requires give and take. There are few situations where one side or the other can dictate terms. Real estate bargaining is best seen as a process where all sides must receive some benefit.

Fourteenth, investing is a complex process that requires the use of specialists. When pulling deals together, real estate investors normally work with brokers, lawyers, termite inspectors, loan officers, surveyors, structural inspectors, tax advisers, contractors, and other experts. To be successful, you need the availability of such expertise.

Do these principals and observations absolutely guarantee investor profits? No, but they at least suggest how investing can be approached with minimal risk, maximum sanity, and the most likely chance of success.

II
Money: Raising Cash and Credit

At the heart of every real estate deal is the financial troika of cash, credit, and lenders. Deals become possible with the right financing; without it, investing is a fable, a myth, something from the realm of fantasy and delusion. The best deal in the world doesn't exist if it can't be financed, even if "financed" sometimes means paying cash.

Fortunately, cash, credit, and lenders are everywhere. The phone book and the daily paper are full of institutions and individuals who will happily lend would-be real estate moguls $100,000 or $500,000 or more, as long as the loan is secured by valued real estate and produces real returns.

Real estate deals often involve large sums of money for even relatively small transactions, yet the actual amount of cash needed to buy property is often just a small part of the purchase price. Buy a $100,000 home with "conventional" financing and you only need $20,000 in cash. Shop around and less conservative deals with 5, 10, and 15 percent down are common. In contrast, buy stock worth $100,000, and your broker is likely to demand at least $50,000 in cash, and he'll want it within seven business days.

Lenders are willing to make highly leveraged real estate loans for two reasons.

First, mortgage interest rates have historically ranged from 2 to 4 percent above the rate of inflation. And while a *yield* of 2 to 4 percent may not seem like a large margin, even tiny profits on a huge volume of business produce sizable profits, a fact to consider in light of outstanding real estate loans now worth several *trillion* dollars. After all, if you charge 8 percent interest on $2 trillion, your cash return will be $160 billion a year. If your real profit after inflation is only 2 percent, your buying power will increase by $40 billion in just 12 months.

Second, lenders face little *risk* with real estate. As of the last quarter of 1993, the national rate of "foreclosures in process" was just 1.27 percent, according to Peter Loomis with the Mortgage Bankers Association of America. Most of these properties were never foreclosed. In some cases loans were brought up to date while in other situations properties were sold before foreclosure proceedings could take place.

Foreclosure rates are minuscule because lenders, being rational, play with a loaded deck. Before they'll advance a single dime, they establish terms and conditions to protect themselves.

- Lenders require independent property appraisals, estimates of worth from someone other than self-interested owners or prospective purchasers. Lenders will select appraisers, and investors (typically) will pay for the reports.
- Lenders will want credit checks from credit-reporting agencies. Most likely investors will pay for these reports.
- Loans won't be issued unless the debt is secured with property and recorded in local government offices.
- Lenders won't make 85, 90, 95, or 100 percent LTV loans unless a third party, such as the Veterans Administration or a private mortgage insurer, guarantees or insures a portion of the loan.
- Lenders won't make loans unless the debt is secured both by the value of the property and your willingness to be personally liable for the entire debt.
- Investors won't get lender financing unless they're willing to maintain fire, theft, and liability insurance throughout the mortgage term.
- Lenders won't make a loan on property without clear and marketable title, or on property where title insurance is unavailable. (One exception: The sale of title insurance is prohibited in Iowa. In its place, owners can buy protection from a state-sponsored title guarantee fund or solicit coverage from out-of-state insurers.)

Borrowers often look at lender requirements with disgust, but if you were a lender, wouldn't you make certain that title to a property was good? Wouldn't you want to know if the borrower was credit-worthy? And wouldn't you try to pass the costs of checking and processing to the borrower?

As a borrower you have a choice. You can play by the lenders' rules and gain access to the funds they control, or you can seek financing outside the traditional lending system. Both approaches, as we shall see, have their merits.

And their problems.

4

Outcasts of the Secondary Market

Suppose Henderson buys an investment property for $100,000, puts down $20,000, spends another $20,000 fixing it up, uses his labor and time to make additional repairs, and at the end of six months has a house conservatively appraised at $150,000. Can Henderson now go to any lender in town, have the place refinanced, and pull out the money spent on improvements? Can he capture the additional equity created by his time and labor? Can he get the extra dollars produced by inflation? Can he get 80 percent refinancing, a $120,000 loan in this case?

Don't bet on it, especially if local lenders only make "conforming" mortgages acceptable to the secondary market.

If you wanted a loan in the 1980s, you might have gone to a local savings and loan association or mortgage banker who would take your application, appraise the property, check your credit rating, and respond according to his lending criteria and how much money was on hand.

Today the process is different. The lender still wants an application, a credit report, and an appraisal. And the lender will evaluate the loan according to his lending standards. But, while the lender would have kept the loan in his portfolio in the past, today it's probable that the loan will be sold in what is called the "secondary" market.

The secondary market is nothing more than a glorified system of phones and computers that allows local lenders to sell their mortgages to investors.

The secondary market evolved for a simple reason: Lenders ran out of money in the past. If a lender had $10 million, and 100 people asked for $100,000 mortgages, the lender could help them all. The person who was borrower No. 101 had problems. The lender had no more money.

With the secondary market, the lender takes his $10 million in local mortgages and sells them as a package to such important organizations as the Federal Home Loan Mortgage Corporation (Freddie Mac), the Federal National Mortgage Association (Fannie Mae), and the Government National Mortgage Association (Ginnie Mae). The local lender gets cash in the secondary market for his package of mortgages, money which will allow him to make more loans in his community.

The secondary lenders, in turn, sell bonds, mortgage packages, and certificates to investors such as pension funds, insurance companies, and overseas investors. In general terms, secondary offerings vie with Treasury bonds for investor dollars. Look at ten-year Treasury securities and you can closely track mortgage rates. (Look at ten-year Treasury securities rather than 30-year Treasury bonds because most mortgages only last 10 to 12 years.)

But there's a catch: To have a market where loan packages are bought and sold there must be standardized products, loans that meet certain rules and criteria. When mortgage packages developed by local lenders meet these standards, they're said to contain "conforming" loans.

Who says what's standard and what isn't? The large organizations active in the secondary market.

Are standards used in the secondary market set in stone? No. They can change at any time.

The Big Three of The Secondary Market

Federal National Mortgage Association (Fannie Mae): A publicly held organization that buys conventional, FHA, and VA mortgages plus second trusts. Some loans are packaged and resold to investors, while others are kept in a huge loan portfolio.

Federal Home Loan Mortgage Corporation (Freddie Mac): Operated by the Federal Home Loan Bank Board, the agency that regulates savings and loan associations, Freddie Mac sells mortgage-backed bonds to investors and uses the cash to buy conventional, FHA, and VA mortgages from local lenders.

Government National Mortgage Association (Ginnie Mae): Assembles and guarantees pools of FHA and VA mortgages. Investors may participate in such pools by purchasing *pass-through* certificates on which they receive monthly payments for both interest and principal.

How large are the big three? In rough terms they hold, control, or have financed mortgages worth more than $1.5 trillion.

Do some lenders make both conforming and non-conforming loans? Of course.

Must local lenders abide by the guidelines established by secondary lenders? Absolutely not. *There's no law that says all loans must be "conforming" mortgages.* Lenders can establish their own loan criteria, and fortunately, many do.

But although local lenders are not compelled to accept the secondary market's standards, there's no doubt that ignoring such guidelines makes local loan portfolios less liquid. There's also no doubt that many lenders have simply adopted standards from the secondary market, criteria which make investor financing enormously difficult and largely unattractive.

UNDERWRITING STANDARDS FOR INVESTORS

Among the major secondary lenders, borrowers will discover that the underwriting standards which apply to investor loans are substantially different, and tougher, than the norms established for owner-occupant financing.

Although the rules used in the secondary market represent "guidelines" rather than absolute standards, many lenders choose to interpret secondary criteria as immutable and ironclad rules not subject to exception. Some lenders, in addition, undoubtedly use secondary criteria generally, even for loans they intend to keep in their portfolios. By making conforming loans, they retain the option of selling off portfolio mortgages in the future.

Within the maze of guidelines and standards, there are a variety of standards that should concern investors.

First, guidelines differ among secondary lenders. A loan which is unacceptable to one secondary lender may be satisfactory to another. Thus it pays to shop among local lenders to find loan officers who know how the secondary rules vary, and to speak with "portfolio" lenders—lenders who do not sell all of their loans in the secondary market and thus do not have to follow the secondary rules.

Second, lenders are interested in cash flow. Lenders will take the cash income from a rental property and subtract the cash costs to determine annual cash flow. Unlike on a tax return—where the results are typically influenced by non-cash accounting charges such as depreciation—lenders want to see a positive bottom line when counting dollars.

Third, would-be investors need either a lease to qualify for financing or solid comparables from like properties. With a reasonable rent available as a credit to investors, purchasers will have more monthly income and thus more ability to qualify for loans.

Fourth, you can buy investment property with a regular mortgage loan application. However, in addition to the usual form you will also need to show the operating income for the investment property. Ask for Form 216 from Fannie Mae and Form 998 from Freddie Mac.

Fifth, if you are self-employed, expect to show tax returns and other financial information for at least the past two years. Lenders want to see a solid track record of earnings in the same field.

Sixth, second homes are generally treated like primary residences rather than investment properties. In first mortgages, up to 80 percent LTV ratio is allowed. Time-share units are not recognized as second homes under most guidelines.

Seventh, expect to put down 30 percent when purchasing an investment property under conventional guidelines. In contrast, if you need a mortgage for your own home, you can get conventional financing with just 20 percent down. Better deals with less money down are available for both investment property and personal residences with non-conforming loans from large, independent lenders, but investors should be aware of conventional guidelines because they are used in many loan programs.

In addition, the requirement for great piles of money up front can be offset with the use of private mortgage insurance. Owner-occupants, for example, can readily buy homes with 5 percent down. Some first-time buyers can purchase with as little as 3 percent down. Unfortunately, private mortgage insurance is virtually unavailable to investors.

Eighth, under conventional guidelines, small investors can have a maximum of four mortgages—one for a personal residence and three for investor properties. Each investor property can have one to four units. Note that special rules apply to this numbering system. Commercial and multifamily properties, for example, do not come under the four-or-fewer system. Joint ownership is considered full ownership.

Ninth, with private mortgage insurance, the maximum LTV for properties with two units is 90 percent (versus a maximum of 95 percent for a single-unit property), and for three- and four-unit properties it's 80 percent—provided at least one unit is owner-occupied. These are tough standards, but they still represent a better deal than pure investor loans where the maximum LTV is just 70 percent.

Tenth, those who intend to buy investment property are generally required to hold enough liquid assets to support the property for six months in the event of prolonged vacancies, repairs, or other problems.

Eleventh, if you refinance a principal residence to obtain better rates and terms, loans equal to 95 percent of the property's value are available. If you refinance investment property to get better rates and terms, loans which exceed 70 percent of the property's value are not allowed. "Rate-and-term" refinancing means that no additional cash can be taken from the property other than to pay off existing loans and related closing expenses.

As to new and larger loans whereby owners convert equity into cash, conventional rules allow cash-out refinancing on personal residences for up to 75 percent LTV. For investment property, forget it—cashing out is not allowed under conventional standards.

Is there a way to get cash out of an investment property under these guidelines? One approach seems feasible, though ridiculously complicated and costly.

Go back to Mr. Henderson, our investor from the beginning of this chapter. He bought an investment property for $100,000, put down $20,000, and spent another $20,000 repairing and improving. At this point his investment is $40,000 in cash ($20,000 down plus $20,000 in improvements) plus an $80,000 first trust ($100,000 less $20,000).

If the property's value increases to $150,000 because of his work and improvements, Henderson could borrow an additional $40,000 with a non-conforming second trust—enough to recapture his down payment and repair costs.

Then, after one year, he could refinance with a conforming loan equal to the outstanding value of his first and second trusts plus all closing costs—provided that the LTV ratio at this point does not exceed 70 percent. In this example, Henderson's property will need an appraised value of $171,429 to get a conforming (70 percent) loan for $120,000.

Why bother? Unless Henderson gets a markedly lower rate, he's not ahead. He'll be forced to close out the old loans, hold the equivalent of a new settlement, get another title search, buy more title insurance, perhaps have another survey, and probably pay more points. It's going to take a substantial rate reduction to make such actions worthwhile.

Besides, why should Henderson leave the lender who gave him a non-conforming loan in the first place? By every standard, that lender deserves Henderson's business unless a radically better loan is available elsewhere.

Consider another example. Lanham bought an investment property 15 years ago for $100,000. At the time he got an $80,000 mortgage and repaid it on a 15-year basis. Today the property is worth $350,000. Can Lanham refinance with a conforming loan?

Here, despite the property's value, Lanham is penalized for repaying his loan on an accelerated basis.

The secondary market is designed for the sale and purchase of residential mortgages, and for this reason small investors don't really fit into the system. This situation is not unfair or unreasonable, any more than a car buyer is unfair or unreasonable in selecting one make and not another.

Moreover, it is possible that conventional guidelines may change. Who knows, maybe one day investors will be warmly welcomed by the secondary market, though there are few signs this is likely to happen.

5

Investment Financing's Hidden Barriers

Although the secondary market's terms and conditions tend to limit attractive loan sources, there are lenders who make investor mortgages. And although such mortgages may look just like the type of financing used by regular home buyers, the rules and realities are often different because we are "investors," and being investors makes us different.

If we're buying a home to occupy, we would look for the lowest interest rate and fewest points, among other terms. We know that federal and state regulations require lenders to make certain disclosures and offer special protections.

If we're buying investment property, however, usury limits may not apply. Interest may be calculated on something other than a simple annual basis. Huge prepayment penalties can be buried in loan agreements. We may face higher recordation taxes.

As investors we're regarded as more sophisticated and knowledgeable than the typical home buyer, so there's less need—at least in theory—for public policies to protect our interests. In the real world, whether a small investor can bargain as an equal with sophisticated, multibillion-dollar lenders seems unlikely.

RATES

As investors we represent more risk than home buyers do, a view that's not without merit. If you had enough money to cover only your mortgage or an investment loan, which would you pay? Most people, without hesitation, would opt to keep up their house payments, a fact which means investor loans are inherently more risky than mortgages for owner-occupied property. And more risk, as we know, requires higher rates.

Investors can rationalize marginally higher rates, but such rationalization is not a license for sky-high loan costs. We want the lowest rates possible, but figuring out which rate is best may not be easy.

The humble home buyer can look at an interest rate, say 8 percent simple annual interest, and ask for the true "APR," or annual percentage rate. Because of compounding, the APR will be somewhat higher, say 8.25 percent.

Investors, too, can ask for the APR, but there are several potential problems.

First, investor mortgages may not be protected by usury statutes because they're commercial loans. Rates which are literally illegal for home buyers may be entirely permissible for real estate entrepreneurs.

Second, commercial loan interest may not be computed on a simple annual basis. There are commercial loans where interest is figured on an "add-on" basis that results in substantially higher real costs. Consider a one-year $10,000 loan with 8 percent interest. Monthly payments on a simple basis would amount to $869.88, or a total of $10,438.62.

An add-on loan with the same apparent terms would work like this: $10,000 in principal plus interest worth $800 produces a total debt of $10,800. The monthly cost, $10,800, divided by 12: $900. The true interest rate: 14.45 percent!

Another unpleasant interest formula: the rule of 78s. This formula produces higher expenses than simple interest, and much of the cost is bunched up front. For short-term loans, say one to five years, it's not a major problem. With longer loans, however, the difference can be substantial. Several states ban loans with interest formulated under the rule of 78s while others allow it only for loans with terms of four years or less. However, because investors are not consumers, such bans may not apply to them. *Always ask if interest is computed on a simple annual basis and avoid loans which are not.*

Third, if paying loan costs entailed no more than writing out monthly checks for principal and interest, comparing mortgages would be fairly simple. Unfortunately, borrowers must also look at closing fees and points.

CLOSING FEES

Lenders can raise loan yields by charging for expenses they might otherwise incur, such as surveys, credit reports, and title examinations. There's an argument to be made that borrowers actually save when lenders purchase these services, because lenders buy in bulk and can obtain discounts. Whether such discounts are passed on to borrowers is a different issue.

Another cost faced by both buyers and investors is the so-called loan origination fee, a charge for mortgage processing generally equal to 1 percent of the entire amount borrowed. For example, the loan origination fee for a $100,000 mortgage will total $1,000. A loan origination fee largely represents a payment to the lenders or loan officers for their work to secure the loan, make a commitment, check credit information, prepare loan documents, obtain an appraisal, and so on.

Another expense is the "lock-in" fee, a charge paid by some borrowers to assure that a given interest rate will be available at closing. Lock-in rates are usually good for 45 to 60 days, but such agreements can pose problems. For example, in the fine print of such agreements, the lender may reserve the right to change the lock-in rate if market "conditions" evolve—in other words, if interest levels change. Obviously a lock-in agreement that becomes void if rates change is worthless.

Lock-in agreements also have another problem. What if the term of the lock-in agreement passes? Since the lender controls the loan application process, he's in a perfect position to influence whether or not processing will be completed within the allotted time frame. The Maryland Court of Appeals, in a case that may serve as a national precedent, ruled in 1986 that lenders must use "reasonable care" to assure that lock-in agreements are kept. Without reasonable care, the lender may be considered negligent and liable for damages.

Another way lenders can bend lock-in agreements is to leave interest rates alone and simply raise the number of points required to close the loan. A good lock-in agreement should address *both interest rates and points* to protect the borrower.

POINTS

As investors we're concerned not only with the total cost of a loan, but *when* expenses must be paid. A seemingly high-priced mortgage may actually be cheap if we properly structure its costs.

In today's marketplace, lenders typically offer a combination of rates and points. If we pay one point for a $100,000 mortgage, the lender will receive $1,000 in the form of cash or credit at closing.

For example, if Mr. Larkin borrows $100,000 at 8 percent interest plus 2 points, the lender will receive $2,000 at closing. Larkin only has the use of $98,000, but he's expected to repay $100,000 plus interest on the loan's full value. In effect, the lender has discounted the loan.

If the Larkin loan is outstanding for 30 years, he will pay $733.76 a

---

Basic Questions for Lenders

1) Do you make investor loans? If not, can you tell me who makes such loans locally?

2) What is your current interest rate for investor financing? Is interest computed on a simple basis or in some other manner?

3) How many points are required?

4) How long does it take to process a typical loan?

5) When are interest rates locked in? At the time of application, at the time the loan is approved, or at settlement? Can I lock in rates by paying an additional fee? How much is the fee? How long does the lock-in agreement last? Is the lock-in agreement an absolute, ironclad guarantee of *both rates and terms?*

6) Do you charge an application fee? If so, how much?

7) Do you offer both fixed-rate and adjustable-rate mortgages (ARMs)?

8) For ARMs, what is the initial interest rate, and how long does it last? On which index are future rate levels based? What is the margin above the index? Is negative amortization allowed? Are there yearly and lifetime interest caps? Are there yearly and life-time payment caps? Can I convert from an ARM to fixed-rate financing?

9) Can I prepay any loan with your firm, in whole or in part, at any time and without penalty? Is this clearly written into the loan agreement?

10) Will the loan officer provide a letter confirming both answers to the questions above as well as the officer's authority to make a clear commitment concerning points, fees, rates, prepayments, and other terms?

---

month, and the lender will receive $100,000 in principal as well as interest worth $154,155. However, since only $98,000 was ever given to the borrower, the lender's real interest rate is 8.2 percent.

The catch is this: Most of us don't repay mortgages over three decades. Suppose Larkin's loan lasts 10 years. The monthly cost is the same, $733.76, the number of points is the same, 2, but the lender's return—and Larkin's cost—is far higher. After 10 years he has made 120 payments

($733.76 x 120 = $88,051), but the remaining loan balance is still $87,873.46. The effective interest rate: 10.33 percent.

Suppose we had a somewhat different situation. What if Larkin bought property, fixed it up, and refinanced after three years? Given the same $100,000 loan with the same interest, points, and monthly payments, Larkin now has an effective rate of 9.4 percent.

We could go even further. What if Larkin has the property for just one year? He's borrowed $100,000, received $98,000, and paid points worth $2,000. Now his rate is 11.85 percent.

Larkin will find that lenders offer an array of loan choices, usually different combinations of points and interest. In the usual situation he will be faced with a choice of points plus a low rate or no points plus a higher rate.

Which is best?

Oddly enough, higher interest rates can sometimes be a bargain.

Suppose Larkin considers two loans, both for 30 years and both for $100,000. Lender Able wants 7.5 percent interest plus 2 points while Lender Baker wants a flat interest rate of 8 percent.

- If Larkin holds the property for one year, the Baker loan will be far less expensive.
- If Larkin holds the property for three years, the Baker loan is less expensive.
- If Larkin holds the property for ten years or longer, the Able loan is a bargain.

For investors who intend to fix up, repair, and refinance over a short period, higher interest rates are often cheaper than lower rates plus points.

For investors who want to hold for the long term and don't expect to refinance, lower rates plus points can be a good deal. To figure out which loan arrangement is best, you've got to "run the numbers" and see how each deal compares for a given number of years, as we did with Mr. Larkin.

When considering the cost of points, be certain to look at the tax consequences as well. Points paid to acquire a prime residence are deductible for the year in which they are paid, provided they are reasonable and consistent with the marketplace. Points paid to purchase or refinance an investment property can be deducted only over the term of the mortgage. If you borrow $100,000 over 30 years for an investment property and pay one point, then the yearly deduction is just $33.33. Because of occasional changes regarding how points are treated for tax purposes, investors should check with a tax professional when planning a points strategy.

PREPAYMENT PENALTIES

Another way that lenders raise interest costs is to have a penalty for paying off loans early, say six months' interest or a specific amount, perhaps 1 percent of the original loan principal.

Prepayment fees are a juicy benefit for lenders, especially since lenders might logically be expected to encourage fast payoffs. We know that lenders get a large portion of their profits from fees and charges collected at settlement, and the faster they get their money back, the faster they can generate new loans which produce more high-profit points, fees, and charges. Considering the benefits involved, perhaps lenders should offer a bounty or discount to thrifty borrowers who prepay.

It can be argued that although lenders may want loans prepaid, pension funds, insurers, and other investors do not. They want a steady income stream and for them, it's claimed, prepayment penalties help assure regular income at known rates of return.

In our precise world, where pension and insurance actuaries calculate everything, someone has surely noticed that few people hold mortgages for 30 years. Pension funds and insurance companies can undoubtedly plan their affairs with statistical certainty, knowing when mortgages are typically repaid and adjusting their portfolios accordingly.

So we have a curious paradox. Borrowers may be assessed a penalty for prepaying a loan, even though prepayments demonstrably benefit lenders and do no harm to well-managed pension or insurance funds.

Among the big secondary players, Fannie Mae does not require prepayment penalties to create conforming loans. If a lender inserts a pre-

Mr. Larkin's Loan Choices

	Lender Able	Lender Baker
Loan Amount	$100,000	$100,000
Loan Term	30 Years	30 Years
Interest Rate	7.5 Percent	8 Percent
Points	2	None
Monthly Payment	$699.21	$733.76
Cost for Points & Interest After:		
1 Year	$8,849.01	$7,308.24
3 Years	$23,579.09	$23,046.61
10 Years	$72,157.64	$75,190.90
30 Years	$153,721.98	$164,160.47

payment penalty in a loan agreement, however, Fannie Mae will enforce it. Fannie Mae applies the same prepayment rules to both owner-occupant and investor financing.

Freddie Mac does not require prepayment penalties for loans to conform and does not distinguish between owner-occupant and investor loans on this issue. When Freddie Mac buys a loan with a prepayment rider, however, it will not enforce such a clause—good news for borrowers.

How do you avoid prepayment penalties?

- Look for FHA and VA loans. Prepayment penalties are not permitted under these programs.
- Try adjustable-rate mortgages, or ARMs. These mortgages usually allow prepayments without penalty, but check the small type to be certain.
- Bargain with lenders. More than interest rates and points are negotiable. Look for a lender who wants to close a loan and will agree *in the loan documents* to eliminate prepayment penalties.

DUE-ON-SALE CLAUSES

Virtually all conventional loans contain so-called "due-on-sale" or "alienation" clauses, mortgage language that entitles a lender to full payment of the entire outstanding loan balance when title to the property is transferred.

Without due-on-sale clauses, loans would be freely assumable; anyone could sell a property, and purchasers could take over existing financing without lender approval.

Unlike prepayment clauses, due-on-sale language is within the realm of reason. If you were a lender, you wouldn't want loans to be freely assumable. You'd want to know something about the new borrower and about the borrower's ability to repay the debt. In addition, to raise your yield from the loan, you'd want the right to charge an assumption fee and the right to change the interest rate, if possible.

But you're not a lender, you're a borrower, and you have a decidedly different outlook. You want to avoid due-on-sale clauses, especially when combined with prepayment penalties.

When mortgages contain both due-on-sale and prepayment clauses, loans can't be assumed, and owners can't sell before the loan ends without setting off the prepayment clause. The effect of such dual clauses is to magnify lender profits.

What to do?

First, look for loans which say in effect that they "may be prepaid, in whole or in part, at any time and without penalty." Beware: Oral commitments are worthless!

Second, consider FHA and VA financing. Such loans can be pre-paid without penalty and they are assumable in most instances.

Third, examine ARM financing. Such loans can usually be prepaid without penalty.

Fourth, beware of owner financing. Regulations which apply to people in the lending business may not affect individuals who make a single loan here or there.

6

Where to Find Investor Financing

Having looked at the size, barriers, and formality of the traditional lending system, it's obvious that conforming loans are not particularly attractive even when available. But the traditional lending system, those lenders geared to the secondary market, is not the only mortgage source in town. Many lenders offer investor financing without the secondary market's strictures and rules.

How do you find investment lenders?

- Dig through the phone book, call each lender, and ask if they offer investment financing.
- Check real estate and business sections in local newspapers. Look for ads that mention investor financing and non-conforming loans.
- Speak with brokers, lawyers, appraisers, and other real estate investors.
- As you speak with various contacts, develop a file that lists loan sources and their phone numbers, addresses, and the names of individual loan officers.

NON-CONFORMING BUT TRADITIONAL LENDERS

Non-conforming but traditional lenders are a major source of investor financing and include such providers as mortgage bankers, certain savings and loan associations, lenders who make both conforming and non-conforming loans, captive subsidiaries of conforming lenders, and insurance companies.

These specialized lenders are largely indistinguishable from conforming lenders except for two major differences: They frequently offer higher

LTVs, and they ignore no-cash-out limitations. These distinctions, in turn, are extremely important.

For example, suppose Mr. Wilson bought property five years ago for $125,000. He put down $25,000 in cash and took out a $100,000 loan. Today the property is worth $260,000, and his loan balance is $97,000.

With conforming loans, the most Wilson can get is the value of his outstanding debt plus closing costs—say about $100,000. With a non-conforming loan, Wilson can refinance and receive a mortgage with an 80 percent LTV ratio—in this case, $208,000.

The first choice makes no sense for Wilson, the second puts more than $100,000 in his pocket after the existing mortgage is paid off. Wilson, and most investors, thus make a point of finding lenders who offer non-conforming loans.

Wilson will have little difficulty finding a non-conforming loan because non-conforming investor financing produces higher interest rates and yields than regular mortgages.

Like conforming mortgages, however, non-conforming loans often make little sense when short-term money is required. Non-conforming but traditional lenders are apt to charge the same fees, points, and charges up front as their conforming brethren, costs that make mortgages exceedingly expensive when money is needed for six months to a year—enough time to fix up, repair, and sell a given property.

COMMERCIAL LOANS AND BANK CREDIT LINES

Unlike conforming lenders, commercial banks are a good source of interim financing. Bankers don't want long-term mortgages; they deal regularly with business people, and they have cash. But dealing with a commercial bank may not be the panacea investors seek.

Banks will want to know something about you and how the loan will be repaid if the deal sours. They'll also insist on the protections any mortgage lender will require—a survey, title insurance, plus fire, theft, and liability coverage.

Complicating bank financing even further is the idea that you don't see commercial bankers pushing short-term real estate loans. Such financing is available, but not if you just walk in from the street. You need a "banking relationship"—a history of doing business with the bank, knowing its officers, and borrowing money in the past. This intricate dance between banker and borrower can take months or years to develop; yet once established it represents an immediate source of capital on a large scale.

"Doing business with the bank" is an expression that has changed over the last decade, as the services offered by commercial bankers have expanded. Now doing business means keeping both personal and business accounts with one lender, having a home equity loan with the same company, and even getting credit cards from the same source.

Bank deals usually look like this: interest at 1.5 to 2 points above the prime rate. The loan is secured by the property, and a survey, insurance, and title search are required. The loan will be a first trust, and the LTV ratio will not exceed 90 percent. Points, rare in the past, are becoming more common, and one point may be charged. Monthly payments will be interest-only, so when the loan ends the entire principal amount will be due. Loan size: $100,000 plus.

To get this loan, borrowers will need all the paperwork required for lenders generally, a banking relationship, plus an interview, cover letter, or both, explaining why the property is being bought, how they intend to raise its value, and how the loan will be repaid.

Bank loans, for all their attractions, still have problems. First, you may need a speedy response to close a deal, and some banks are notorious for the length and exactitude of their loan approval process. Second, your application could be denied.

These difficulties can be avoided by establishing a commercial line of credit. With a credit line, the bank checks your finances, qualifies you for a given amount of credit—say $100,000 to start—and when you need interim financing, you merely write a check. Credit-line borrowers usually pay a charge up front equal to 1 percent of the entire line of credit, whether or not funds are actually used, and then a rate that is 1.5 to 2 points over the prime rate.

The advantage of a credit line is that a current application is unnecessary because you're already a qualified borrower. A second advantage is that as money is paid back, the amount of credit available is restored up to the original limit.

Bankers, as you may imagine, are not thrilled at the prospect of giving credit lines to everyone. Yet if you need short-term financing, credit lines are terrific. How, then, do you reconcile the banker's reluctance with your needs?

One approach is to establish an informal line, an ad hoc arrangement that will lead to a credit line.

Tell the banker you want a line of credit (and you do) and why. Explain further that you realize credit lines are valued, standards are tough, and perhaps for the first one or two deals it may be best to have a restricted arrangement with the following understandings.

First, you will supply all the data required by the lender for a typical business loan or line of credit—assets, debts, income, etc.

Second, the lender will review these materials and determine in general terms how much credit might be made available. However, you will not receive a formal line of credit. You will also not pay an up-front fee.

Third, the lender will be kept up-to-date. You'll write to the lender when there are significant changes in your financial status.

Fourth, when a deal comes into view, you'll immediately give the lender a written account of the property.

Fifth, if a purchase opportunity comes up, the lender will give final approval on the financing *within a few days.* To do this effectively, you'll have to give the lender a letter showing why the property is a good deal, why its value is likely to increase, what rentals might reasonably be expected if you intend to lease, and how the property will be refinanced or sold, whichever is appropriate.

Sixth, the lender will provide a written loan-commitment letter if the deal is acceptable. The commitment will outline the basic loan terms and conditions: interest rates, fees, settlement date, repayment schedule, liens, etc.

Seventh, *if you're relying on an ad hoc line of credit, you cannot sanely offer to purchase real estate without a financing contingency.* When you submit a purchase offer, the deal must be contingent on your ability to get a written financing commitment within a short period, say seven to ten business days. Your contingency must provide that if the financing you want isn't available, the deal is off, and your deposit will be returned in full.

What will bankers think of an ad hoc credit approach? They should be more than happy. They'll have a chance to review individual deals before making a commitment, and if the purchase looks good, they'll be able to make a significant commercial loan.

From the investor's perspective, after one or two ad hoc deals bankers will want your business. You'll be seen as a valued customer, and a regular line of credit should be readily available.

SELLER TAKE-BACKS

One of the best financing sources, and one frequently mentioned by various gurus, oracles, and seers, is the simple seller take-back, sales in which the seller actually lends money to a buyer.

In general terms, there are two ways to create seller take-backs.

First, the seller can supply 100 percent financing. If Gardner sells his home for $100,000 and agrees to hold a $100,000 first trust, we not only have a deal with no money down, we have a situation where outside lenders are not involved, a deal without points, fees, or application forms.

Second, a seller can offer partial financing. If Tabbard has an existing VA loan with a $50,000 balance and sells his home for $100,000, a buyer can assume the first trust, Tabbard can take back a $30,000 second trust, and the buyer can pay the $20,000 balance in cash.

Seller take-backs are clearly feasible and since there must be a seller with every sale, there's no shortage of prospective lenders. But while seller take-backs are logical in theory, in practice they're often unworkable and undesirable. Not only can they cause problems for sellers, but investors may also face tax problems as a result of such financing.

For instance, seers often suggest that sellers accept financing where buyers have the right to substitute collateral—that is, use something other than the property to secure the loan.

The problem here is the question of what will be used for security other than the property. To you, and to me, an adequate substitute might be something of equal or greater value and liquidity. But a blanket right to substitute is unlikely to mention such concepts; instead, sellers may discover that the new collateral is nothing more than a few beads (described as "jewelry") or an old car (a "valued antique" to some eyes).

If new collateral is used, sellers must ask, How do you know it has enough value to cover the loan in the event of a default? The answer is, you don't, and the risk of default is effectively transferred from borrower to lender.

Still another idea from oracle-land is that sellers should allow their loans to be subordinated to any other financing a buyer can arrange. For instance, if you sold property worth $110,000 and took back a $90,000 first trust with a subordination clause, a buyer could later refinance with another $90,000 loan on the property, and your note would then become a second trust. If there was a foreclosure, your note would be repaid only after the first trust holder received his entire $90,000. If the property was sold for only $90,000, your note would be worthless.

Why would sellers agree to subordination or substitution clauses when they take back financing? One answer is that such clauses are rarely publicized by purchasers; usually they're buried in lengthy contract forms. Another point is that even if they know about such terms, sellers who agree to subordination and substitution clauses probably don't understand the impact of such legal language. Alert sellers, when they see offers containing subordination or substitution clauses, undoubtedly have such proposals reviewed by the most exacting attorney they can locate.

Even if a loan proposal does not contain subordination or substitution clauses, the deals proposed by gurus are critically deficient in another area as well: seller risk.

Seers, after all, are looking for deals with no money down. And if someone buys your property with no money down, if he or she has no cash or credit, if he or she has no assets, how are you protected in the event of default? Yes, you can get the property back, but time-consuming and expensive litigation may be required. Meanwhile, who pays the property taxes? What if the place is ruined? Why should sellers take such risks when buyers with financing are in the marketplace?

In addition, sellers who take back financing may also find themselves in a strange position if a purchaser/borrower elects not to make monthly mortgage payments.

Suppose Wilkins sells his property to Danforth and takes back a $100,000 first trust. What happens if Danforth doesn't pay the mortgage, but instead claims that Wilkins misrepresented the property's condition by hiding certain defects?

Wilkins may not be able to foreclose until the buyer's claims are settled, something that will probably require a lawsuit, expensive attorney fees, and several years of litigation—all without monthly payments from Danforth. If there was a regular lender involved, the probability is that the claim would never arise, because a third-party lender isn't normally responsible for the property's condition or the seller's representations.

Seller take-backs also involve so-called "at risk" rules. In general terms, you can have deductions that exceed income only when you're personally at risk for a debt. Suppose Tanner borrows $200,000 to finance a store and the debt is secured by the store's assets. If Tanner has no personal liability for the debt—what's called a non-recourse loan—his deductions cannot exceed his income.

In broad terms, using a third party to finance a deal—say money from a mortgage banker, S&L, or other non-seller—will produce recourse financing. If a sale is financed by an owner (or a relative of the seller), it's possible that it will be considered a non-recourse loan.

Suppose Courtney buys an investment property for $250,000, puts down $30,000, and the seller takes back a $220,000 note. Suppose further that Courtney has no personal liability for the loan. Suppose also that the property must be sold for $210,000—a $40,000 loss.

How much can Courtney claim as a loss?

Just $30,000. Why? Because non-recourse loans may not be regarded as qualified financing under at-risk rules. (See a tax attorney, CPA, or enrolled agents for the latest information and complete details.)

Thus seller financing, which looks alluring and has been attractive in the past, should now be viewed with caution. Because of the various tax rules, especially those concerning recourse financing, both buyers and sellers should speak with a tax attorney or CPA before making deals with owner take-backs.

PRIVATE INDIVIDUALS

Sellers may not always be in a position to finance real estate deals, but there are private individuals who lend money, especially when that money is secured with property. In return for the use of their cash, such folks look for better interest rates than might be available through other low-risk investments, such as money market funds, savings accounts, or municipal bonds.

Private money is rarely available for a 30-year period because few people have such capital to set aside. Instead, investors are likely to find individuals making real estate loans for one to five years. Such short-term financing, however, is not a handicap for many investors. If you have a project to fix up and sell, short-term financing is fine. If you intend to hold for a longer period, short-term loans allow you to acquire property, improve it, raise both rents and values, and then refinance on a long-term basis.

Borrowing from individuals is not the same as dealing with traditional lenders. There are no forms, loan committees, cash-out rules, or mortgage-amount limitations. Private individuals rarely charge points, and application fees are unknown.

There are also no standards for approval or rejection. Each deal is entirely dependent on whatever criteria the lender elects to use, whether rational or not.

Investors will have the best chance of obtaining private funds if they suggest a well-structured, conservative deal. A model loan might include the following terms:

- The borrower will provide a survey, title examination, and termite inspection at settlement.
- The borrower will purchase title insurance with at least full lender's coverage.
- The loan will be recorded in local government offices upon settlement as a first trust or second trust, as appropriate.
- The interest rate, monthly payment, and loan term will be clearly stated.
- Interest will be computed on a simple, annual basis.

- The borrower will have the right to prepay the loan, in whole or in part, without penalty at any time.
- There will be no points or origination charges.
- The loan shall not be assumable, assignable, or subordinated. The borrower will not have the right to change collateral or sell the property "subject to" the lender's note.
- If the loan is a "trust" and not a "mortgage," the lender will have the right to name the original trustees. The lender will also have the right to substitute trustees at any time with notice to the borrower.
- The borrower must maintain fire, theft, and liability insurance equal to at least the value of the loan as long as the debt is outstanding. The lender will receive a copy of the paid-up insurance policy at settlement.
- In the event of a late payment, the borrower will be liable for a 5 percent penalty, if allowed by local regulations.
- The full loan agreement will be written in a form satisfactory to the lender or the lender's attorney.

The arrangement outlined here represents a reasonable balance between lenders and borrowers. It lacks tricks and traps, has no hidden clauses, and presumes that both lenders and borrowers are rational. Such thinking may not appeal to seers and oracles, but it will make immediate sense to prospective lenders.

Finding private individuals with cash to lend is more difficult than locating traditional lenders. Cash-rich individuals don't advertise or hand out loan applications, and even with capital in hand they may not want to be lenders.

Some individuals with money advertise in the papers ("Capital Available"), but investors should use extreme caution here. People who advertise, by definition, are in business, yet they may be entirely unregulated. Their "standardized" loan documents can contain a variety of "killer" clauses and bizarre interest formulas.

An alternative choice is to contact a mortgage broker, someone who charges a fee to locate attractive financing. Such brokers, however, are most likely to work with institutions and organizations rather than individual lenders.

Lawyers and accountants are the best sources of private capital. Speak with local professionals, explain what you need, and ask if they can help. Many will contact selected clients who might be interested.

There are several attractions to working with professionals.

First, they know who has money.

Second, they can present investor ideas to clients without revealing individual client names, thus protecting client privacy.

Third, lawyers and accountants are business people. If presented with a deal that can benefit one of their clients, it's in their interest to notify those clients because additional legal work, accounting services, or whatever may be required.

Fourth, it's not uncommon for attorneys and other professionals to act as intermediaries and introduce clients to each other.

Family members are another source of private funds. There's no question that families often pool money to invest jointly or that rich uncles often make loans to impoverished nephews and nieces.

Family loans are attractive because you at least know the lender. But knowing the lender is not a substitute for solid business deals or clear terms. Family loans, like all mortgage financing, should be in writing with a complete list of terms and obligations and filed with the government records office where the property is located. Written documents will quiet potential family squabbles before they arise and affirm the loan's business nature.

As tempting as family money may seem, borrowers should recognize that the cost of such financing may include more than interest. Social and psychological debts may also be incurred, a heavy price within some families.

PARTNERS AND PARTNERSHIPS

Although there are individuals who make real estate loans, such financing is not particularly common, especially on a long-term basis. Those with cash have many options, and interest-paying real estate loans are just another ho-hum choice.

Some people with capital want more than interest. They want participation. A piece of the action. Equity. They want a stake in the property as partners. The question is: Do you want them?

Partners can bring in money as well as skills and the idea of a partnership should not be overlooked. Giving someone an ownership interest in exchange for work, capital, or risk may be a sound strategy, particularly for first-time investors.

But what if you want to control your property? Partnerships, by definition, mean control is diluted. Your freedom to act quickly and independently may be lessened—if not ended.

Partnerships represent relationships with other people and in the short term such relationships may be workable. But for long-term investments, partnerships can pose difficulties. Individual interests diverge. You want action, a partner wants inaction. You want to sell, a partner wants to hold. You want to refurbish, a partner wants a bigger dividend check.

But what if you need money? Can you just turn down an investor who wants participation?

It's going to be tough to ignore demands for a partnership if you depend on a single investor. The investor will know that his capital or talent is crucial to the project, and your bargaining position will be demolished.

The way to avoid unwanted partnerships and still raise capital is to deal with more than one funding source. Then, when the question of equity participation arises, you can always say, "Well, I can get money, funds are available from several investors. The only question is where I can find the best deal. If you want to go ahead with a loan, I can offer a top interest rate. If not, I'll understand."

For more information concerning partnerships, see Chapter 16.

CREDIT CARDS

An offshoot of the no-money-down oracles are various sub-gurus who claim that you can buy real estate with credit cards. In essence, you apply for as many credit cards as possible—several hundred might work—and then buy real estate at little or no cost. And, it's been suggested, you can get credit cards even if you lack a job.

How, you may wonder, can you possibly use credit card money at no cost?

The system, at least in theory, might work this way. Some credit card companies charge borrowers only when a statement is issued rather than when purchases are actually made. Some credit cards also lack an annual fee. If credit from dual-value cards—those which neither charge an annual fee nor begin interest charges until the end of the month—can be withdrawn in the form of a check, then a slick borrower can supposedly draw funds on credit cards and amass enough cash to buy property.

The cards—each with a credit line of several hundred dollars—can be repaid, one assumes, by constantly borrowing and repaying from a succession of cards before interest charges are assessed or by reselling the property at a profit with enough speed to pay off all debts.

You probably suspect there are some problems with this system, and you're right.

First, credit card companies are in business to make money. Few offer cards without annual fees, few fail to charge interest when money is withdrawn, and fewer still have neither an annual fee nor an immediate-interest policy.

Second, the sheer labor involved in finding and applying for hundreds of cards should not be discounted. Juggling payments is a massive headache and an administrative nightmare—especially for people who already have trouble paying and tracking monthly bills.

Third, what happens if the property can't be sold quickly? Or can't be sold at a profit? Or can't be sold at all?

Fourth, where do you find a mailbox large enough to hold all the bills, coupons, premiums, ads, and offers which result from being on several hundred mailing lists?

Fifth, if postage costs $.32 per letter and someone has 100 credit cards, his or her postal cost is $384 a year (12 × $32). With 300 cards, he or she pays $1,152 annually. Where do people without cash, credit, or jobs get stamps worth nearly $1,200?

Although gathering hundreds of credit cards to buy real estate is ridiculous, card accounts *can* be used to acquire and repair property.

For example, if Tilden has four cards, each with a $2,500 credit line, he can quickly amass $10,000. Can Tilden get four cards? Can Tilden have a $10,000 credit line or more? Judging from the mail, if Tilden is employed, lives in the right zip code, and subscribes to the right magazines, he might acquire both cards and pre-approved credit within a few weeks—all without an application of any kind.

Whether such credit is used for a trip to Tahiti or to buy real estate is irrelevant as long as the money is repaid. Also, if the four cards have a $25 annual service fee and postal costs total $1 per month, the annual expense to obtain such credit is just $112—a not unreasonable cost for increased financial flexibility.

Tilden can use his credit to acquire property—$10,000 is a fair down payment for a property worth $100,000—and for fix-up and repair costs. If the property needs a new dishwasher, no problem, just put it on a credit card.

Credit cards are readily available, because they represent big business and large profits to card companies. Credit card interest typically ranges from 13 to 21 percent, an unusually high figure when compared to mortgage rates, inflation levels, and so-called prime rates.

How can such high rates be justified? It does take a certain amount of time and personnel to service credit cards—but that's also true of other loans. People will pay more for convenience, and credit cards are surely convenient. But the real reason credit card rates are high is simply that few consumers object. People blithely pay their card bills each month and as long as few complain, lenders will rightfully charge whatever the market will bear.

Not only are credit card rates stratospheric, but repayment plans are steep.

Suppose you borrow $10,000 and have a choice of three loan sources: a 30-year mortgage, a 10-year second trust, or a credit card. How will each source compare if mortgage rates are set at 8 percent?

- With the 30-year 8 percent mortgage, our benchmark, you'll pay $73.38 a month over 30 years, and the interest bill will total $16,412.
- The 10-year second trust will have a higher interest rate than a 30-year mortgage, say 9.5 percent in this example. Monthly payments will then be $129.40, and interest will total only $5,528.
- A credit card company might require monthly repayments equal to 3 percent of the outstanding balance, $300 for the first month of a $10,000 cash advance. The monthly payments will decline in size with each monthly payment and after 15 years a 19.8 percent loan will have a remaining balance of $1,335.15. Interest in the first 15 years totals $12,870.

These figures show that credit cards are entirely unattractive as a substitute for long- or medium-term financing. On a short-term basis, however, *modest* credit card borrowing can make sense.

If Hopkins, for example, needs $5,000 for a contract deposit but must wait seven business days before cash from a stock sale will be available, there's no reason why an advance from one or two credit cards should not be used.

If Hopkins borrows from credit cards, even for a short period of time, such debt must be reported to lenders. If the debt is repaid during the loan application process, the lender should be made aware of the entire transaction—how much was repaid, where the repayment money came from, etc.

Less appealing, however, are deals where the potential for repayment is questionable. If Hamilton buys property to fix up and immediately resell, credit cards can be used as a down payment, to underwrite repair costs, and to finance appliance purchases. However, if the property is not sold quickly or Hamilton runs out of credit before the property is refurbished, he can face major financial problems.

Hamilton could be in even greater trouble if he attempts to finance property *entirely* with credit cards. Suppose he uses cash advances worth

$100,000. In the first month such debt is outstanding, he will need at least $3,000 to keep his account current—more than four times the monthly payment for an 8 percent, 30-year mortgage of the same size. Indeed, in six months he'll need nearly $18,000 to keep up payments.

Credit cards are designed to encourage borrowing, and there's nothing innately wrong with using credit cards as one of many financial resources. But investors should realize that credit card financing is a high-cost financing option with steep up-front payments, an option that should suggest care and restraint.

In addition, the credit card industry is changing because of tax reform. More and more cards will be secured by real estate so borrowers can deduct interest. But with cards secured by property rather than personal credit, the penalty for default is no longer limited to nasty letters or court suits. In the new world of credit cards tied to real estate equity, foreclosure is entirely possible.

PERSONAL CREDIT LINES

While credit cards have their place, personal credit lines may be more interesting to investors.

One type of personal credit line is the simple overdraft protection offered on most checking accounts. The idea is that if the value of your checks exceeds the amount you have on deposit, the overdraft line will prevent checks from bouncing. Overdraft credit lines typically require no annual payment and, in some cases, offer interest rates which are well below prevailing credit card levels.

Someone, invariably, will suggest that investors go out and start 50 checking accounts, each with a $2,000 overdraft allowance. With such credit in hand you can—at least in theory—underwrite a property purchase.

Although mathematically correct, the idea of having 50 checking accounts is not plausible. Banks and savings and loan associations are not likely to give overdraft allowances without restriction, especially if they see that you just happen to have 49 other accounts—each largely inactive and without significant deposits.

And while it's true that depositors do not pay annual fees for overdraft credit, monthly service charges are normally required for checking accounts. With a $7 monthly fee, someone with 50 accounts will pay $4,200 a year ($7 × 50 × 12) in account charges before a single check is written. If we assume that each account contains $100, it means that

$9,200 must be set aside to obtain such credit ($50 \times \$100 = \$5,000$ plus service charges worth $4,200).

There's another type of personal credit line, however, that's particularly attractive to investors. Offers of personal credit lines from $5,000 to $50,000 appear regularly in the mail, including some with these worthwhile features:

- Pre-approved credit, not credit subject to verification or qualification.
- A substantial line of credit, not less than $5,000.
- No annual fee or a modest annual fee, say $15 to $25.
- Low interest rates.
- Credit lines that are signature accounts unsecured by property.

Some credit-line offers are good deals. For instance, at a time when mortgage rates were above 10 percent and credit cards hovered at 18 percent, one lender offered a $10,000 credit line at 9.5 percent with no annual fee.

Such accounts are worth opening, holding, and placing in a file. If you ever need a few thousand dollars to close a deal, immediate cash will be available at reasonable rates.

Repayment terms vary, but a typical credit-line account might work like this: 5 percent per month for the first $3,000 and 3 percent a month for higher balances. Such lines thus require the ability to make large payments, a situation which might be attractive for a few months in connection with the right deal.

HOME EQUITY MORTGAGES

Real estate has traditionally been considered a non-liquid asset, property that can be converted to cash only by selling or refinancing—two very expensive and time-consuming ways to raise capital. But the old image of real estate is now changing. Today property can be converted to cash immediately through the use of a home equity loan secured by real estate—a matter of substantial interest to investors.

Credit is the great wonder of American society. You can be born on credit, live on credit, and probably die on credit. Like gravity, credit is silent, invisible, and with us every moment.

While credit is all around us, all forms of credit are not identical. Consumer credit differs from traditional real estate financing, another form of credit, in three ways.

First, the credit represented by hundreds of millions of flat plastic cards is unsecured debt. When you make a credit purchase the card company advances money to a gas station or department store on the theory that you will repay. Real estate debt, in contrast, is secured by the value of your property. If you don't pay, the property will be sold to pay off what you owe.

Second, real estate debt traditionally has been advanced at one time. Consumer debt is usually a revolving line of credit. You may have the right to borrow $5,000 from a single credit card company but you don't have to. If you borrow only $150 you pay interest only on the outstanding debt. Moreover, once you pay back the $150 you can again borrow up to $5,000. With most real estate loans, it's understood that once you pay back any portion of the principal the lender is not obligated to loan to you again.

Third, there are few if any charges to get consumer credit. Companies will gladly send you credit cards with the fervent hope you really do buy now and pay later. Real estate lenders will not only charge a fee to apply for financing but they also have a variety of closing costs which the borrower must pay.

Home equity mortgages are hybrid loan products that take features both from traditional mortgages and consumer credit practices. A real estate loan with a line of credit can work like this:

The Taylor house is worth $125,000 in today's market and has a $40,000 mortgage balance. The Taylors feel they may need some ready cash in the next two years to start a small business and send Junior to college, so their lender suggests a credit-line arrangement.

The lender says the Taylors can borrow up to 70 percent of the equity in their home and values their equity like this: 70 percent of $125,000 equals $87,500, less the remaining mortgage balance, $40,000, equals $47,500.

The lender tells the Taylors that the minimum home equity loan is $5,000 and the minimum loan advance is $1,000. Since they have equity worth $47,500, the Taylors elect to get a $25,000 line of credit.

To get this loan the Taylors pay for a credit report, title search, and other closing expenses. Their application costs are figured on the basis of a $25,000 loan but they do not, however, pay any points. While interest rates for second trusts at the time of their application average 8 percent, the Taylors pay 1.5 percent over the prime rate charged by a major bank, or 7.5 percent in this case. The lender has the right to change the rate of interest every three months. In contrast, the current cost of consumer credit in this example ranges from 16 to 24 percent.

The lender explains that the Taylors may select any loan term they choose, from 1 to 30 years. They select 15 years and make their first draw, $12,000, eighteen months after their application is approved. Thus they have a maximum of 13.5 years to repay the $12,000 debt. The Taylors can repay the loan in advance, however, without penalty.

How do the Taylors withdraw their money? The lender offers four choices: a check mailed to their home or business; a deposit in a savings or checking account maintained with the lender or at another financial institution; a telephone transfer; or, most interestingly, a book of blank drafts which the Taylors can use up to their credit limit.

After six years the Taylors have paid down their debt to $7,000. Because of the revolving nature of the credit-line system, the Taylors can still borrow $18,000 ($25,000 less $7,000). In effect, by making their monthly payments they have raised their available credit line from a low of $13,000 ($25,000 less $12,000) at the time they made their first draw.

Home equity loans are attractive to lenders because they can often collect processing fees up front even though actual monies may not be advanced for months or years—or at all. Also, such loans are commonly adjustable-rate mortgages, so lenders are largely protected against inflation.

Investors like credit lines because they have the ability to instantly convert bricks and pipes to cash with relatively little cost up front and far lower interest than they would normally pay for unsecured consumer credit. The access to such credit may prove extremely valuable. For instance, if they wish to buy an investment property, the Taylors can just advance the money they get from their credit line, as long as they are able to make the proper payments. If they combine a credit-line loan with a freely assumable mortgage, the Taylors will be able to buy without taking a dime from their savings account.

Home equity loans also have several features that should concern potential borrowers.

Since a home equity loan is a second trust, a borrower who defaults can be foreclosed. The difficult issue here is this: Suppose a homeowner has a $10,000 credit line, becomes unemployed, and for some reason borrows $500 on a credit-line mortgage which is not repaid. Can a lender foreclose if only $500 is outstanding? Absolutely. Will a lender necessarily foreclose? The answer depends on the facts and circumstances in each case and the lender's policies. As a matter of good public relations it seems likely that most lenders would try to work out some arrangement before seeking foreclosure.

Another potential problem may seem somewhat contradictory. Home equity loans may be too accessible for certain borrowers. Many otherwise responsible people overextend themselves with unsecured credit card loans, and it is probable that some homeowners will do the same with credit lines secured by real estate.

As this is written, for example, lenders often permit the withdrawal of relatively small sums, say $300, $400, or $500. To prevent frivolous expenditures that can result in foreclosure, lenders may set higher minimum draws, say $1,000, as they gain more experience with this type of financing.

HOME EQUITY LOANS AND SPECIAL RULES

On November 7, 1989 the federal government issued rules that significantly changed the home equity lending game.

One rule that clearly benefits borrowers is that so-called "call" clauses are no longer permitted. With a call clause, a lender had the unilateral right at any time to seek full and immediate repayment of the entire loan—even if loan payments were up-to-date and the borrower had fully honored all terms.

A second pro-borrower rule eliminates the use of internal indexes. For instance, under the old rules a lender could raise its prime rate, thereby causing home equity costs to go up—even if interest rates generally were falling.

A third provision of the new rules says that lenders cannot reserve the right to change fixed rates. It may seem as though a fixed rate should be, well, fixed, but in the wonderful world of lending, some institutions created home equity loans with a fixed rate and then reserved the right to change that rate later.

Along with three pro-borrower rules, the government also created new regulations that make home equity loans less certain than they were under the old guidelines.

Under the new guidelines, lenders *may* unilaterally prohibit additional withdrawals under several conditions:

- If the value of a principal residence used to secure a loan is "significantly less than the original appraisal value of the dwelling," then lenders can freeze withdrawals. In areas where home values have dropped, this rule can cover large numbers of homeowners.
- If the lender has "any reason to believe that the consumer will be unable to comply with the repayment requirements of the account due to a material change in the consumer's financial circumstances," lenders can stop further home equity withdrawals. Surely if someone has filed for

bankruptcy this rule makes sense. But what happens if borrower Langston is hit by a bus, the accident is reported in the local paper, and a lender stops home equity withdrawals because one can "reasonably believe" that Langston's financial circumstances have changed? This scenario seems possible under the new rules, though not fair or equitable.

The "financial circumstances" regulation raises an important question: How can a lender know when a borrower has financial problems? The answer is that many home equity agreements now permit lenders to make regular credit checks.

Not only can lenders make credit checks, but other lending regulations virtually insure that such checks will be made. New rules require lenders to reserve relatively large amounts of capital for home equity loans, but reserve requirements drop substantially if lenders have the right to limit withdrawals and if they make annual credit checks.

If a home equity interest cap is less than prevailing interest rates, then lenders can freeze withdrawals. Since home equity loans often have caps set at state usury rates—more than 20 percent in many cases—the possibility of hitting this cap is remote. Conversely, if a cap is hit, not too many people will want to make withdrawals anyway.

INSURANCE LOANS

Millions of people own life insurance policies and for many policyholders insurance can be a substantial source of credit, including credit to purchase investment real estate.

Life insurance policies are attractive because interest and appreciation earned during the policy's term are not taxed, in effect giving upper-income policyholders as much as a 33 percent investment advantage. "Whole" life policies, in particular, are noted for fixed benefits, fixed premiums, and the matter that interests us, fixed cash values.

As premiums are paid into whole life policies, cash values rise. The longer the policy is held, the greater the cash value buildup.

Not only do whole life policies offer a cash buildup, but that money is accessible to policyholders. The usual provision of a policy is that cash values, less one year's loan interest, may be withdrawn with appropriate written notice.

"Borrowing" is a term which suggests the usual array of application hassles and monthly payments, but with whole life insurance such matters are handled somewhat differently.

- When whole life policies are first issued, policyholders receive a schedule showing future cash values. These cash values reflect the amount that can be borrowed. Be aware, however, that insurance companies may restrict cash withdrawals in some cases. For this reason, *if a deal is dependent on insurance money, you'll need a financing contingency in your offer*—language that says if the money you expect cannot be obtained by a certain date, the deal is off and your deposit will be returned in full.

- The application process typically consists of little more than simple written notice to the company 31 days before the money is required. Check individual companies and policies for specific information. Note that if funds are needed for settlement, say by September 15th, it's wise to have the money in hand well before closing.

- Loan interest is usually pegged at the most recent monthly composite rate for corporate bonds. This rate is typically 3 to 4 percent less than investor interest levels—say 5 percent in a market where investors pay 8 percent for real estate loans.

- Monthly payments are unnecessary! If you don't make payments, the loan's value simply increases (because you've taken out cash and interest is being charged on the amount withdrawn), and the remaining policy value declines. If the policy value reaches zero, there's no more to withdraw and the policy ends.

- Interest on insurance loans may or may not be taxable, depending on the purpose for which the money is used. If the money is used for consumer purchases such as a new car not used for business, then the interest is not deductible in the usual case. If the money is used for a business purpose, such as buying investment real estate, interest should be deductible. See a CPA, tax attorney, or enrolled agent for full details.

- Borrowing from an insurance policy will not create a lien against the property. With whole life insurance, the loan is secured by accumulated value in the policy, not the value of your real estate investment.

As to how much you can borrow, that will depend on the policy's age, your age when the policy was first established, the policy's size, and how it's written.

When considering the use of money from whole life policies, investors should carefully review the tax consequences with a knowledgeable CPA, tax attorney, or insurance broker. For instance, if your policy has a gross *cash value* of $50,000, and you've paid in *premiums* worth $20,000, then $30,000 might be regarded as taxable income if the policy terminates. To prevent untimely terminations, consider policies that automatically pay premiums from accrued cash values.

In addition to whole life policies, there are other forms of life insurance that also offer cash value benefits. For more information, ask an insurance broker about universal life, excess-interest whole life, and variable life insurance plans.

7

Pensions: Special Money for Investors

In the past decade a new source of investor financing has emerged, one which is nationwide, well-funded, and outside the secondary loan system. Known broadly as Keogh Plans, HR 10s, and simplified employee plans, these retirement programs for individuals and small organizations represent one of the largest investor financing pools to be found.

According to the Labor Department, by 1990 more than 659,000 small organizations (those with 100 or fewer participants) had retirement plans, plans which held assets worth $242 billion. In many cases, the trustees for these smaller plans are local doctors, lawyers, accountants, and business people whom investors know and deal with every day.

Among larger organizations, those with more than 100 plan participants, there were nearly 53,000 retirement programs. The assets held under these plans totaled almost $1.4 trillion!

Okay, so there are a lot of private pension systems. And they have a lot of money. How can investors use these funds?

Private pensions are interesting because each plan has a trustee who runs it, typically the owner of a small business or company. Being a trustee is a serious responsibility; the person who administers a pension has a fiduciary obligation to assure that plan money is safely invested and the interests of beneficiaries protected.

Trustees can elect to place pension funds in money-market funds, stocks, bonds, or whatever investment they choose, as long as they invest with care.

According to the Labor Department, a pension trustee must "discharge his duties with respect to a plan with the care, skill, prudence, and diligence under the circumstances then prevailing that a prudent man acting in a like capacity and familiar with such matters would use in the conduct of an enterprise of a like character and with like aims."

Real estate is a reasonable investment choice, and pension trustees could conceivably buy property with retirement funds if allowed under the rules of their particular program. But although large pension funds with enormous assets do buy real estate, property is not a good choice for small pensions.

Small pensions have a problem when dealing with real estate. Because they're small, a large portion of their assets may be required if just one person leaves or retires. If assets are placed in relatively illiquid investments such as real estate, it may be tough to quickly raise cash when needed.

Real estate ownership also presents another problem to small-pension trustees. A large portion of the account may be required to buy even a single property. Committing a significant part of pension assets to a single project is something most trustees want to avoid.

But if outright ownership is unattractive, real estate financing is not, especially short-term loans—*precisely the type of mortgage many investors need.* Pensions are well-positioned to make short-term loans: They have funds, they don't want capital tied up on a long-term basis, and loans can be arranged in a prudent business manner.

Suppose Kingston finds a property that can be acquired for $100,000 because it needs extensive repairs. Suppose further that the property is in a subdivision where similar homes typically cost $125,000. Kingston figures $10,000 will be required for repairs and refurbishing.

The problem, however, is that if Kingston gets a conforming loan, the maximum LTV will be 70 percent. With a conforming mortgage he'll need more than $40,000 in cash—$30,000 for a down payment plus $10,000 for repairs.

But a more galling problem is that Kingston must pay points, perhaps two points—$1,400 in this case. Then, when the property is repaired and fixed up, Kingston will have to pay points again when he refinances. If the second loan—which might be made within six months of the first one—brings in $100,000 (80 percent of $125,000), and if it also requires two points, then Kingston will be out another $2,000.

Thus to finance and refinance his property over a very short span of time, Kingston might pay $3,400 in points. In addition, he may face two sets of application charges, credit-report fees, survey costs, and settlement charges. By the time all the charges are added together, Kingston may pay $4,000, $5,000, or even more just for the privilege of borrowing money.

Kingston, however, can cut his financing costs significantly with the use of pension funds.

Instead of financing the property twice with regular lenders, Kingston can take a different approach. He can obtain interim, short-term financing from a small pension and then, when repairs are completed, borrow money on a long-term basis.

Where does Kinston find pension money?

Every self-employed person and every small business can be seen as a potential lender. Look for pensions with sizable deposits in money-market funds or other liquid assets. Ask accountants and attorneys if they know where such funds can be found.

Many professionals will help locate pension money if your deal can benefit the fund. Professionals know about pensions because they're specifically entitled to charge "reasonable compensation" for their services, even if they're so-called parties in interest—that is, trustees or beneficiaries of the plan or fund.

To approach pension fund trustees, as well as their lawyers and accountants, investors must have an attractive, coherent, and prudent business proposal in mind. A workable deal might look like this:

- The loan will pay a premium interest rate, something above what the fund is currently earning. How much higher is a matter of negotiation.
- The loan will be for two years.
- To encourage work on the project, and to raise yields, trustees might require a two-tier interest program—say, 8 percent simple annual interest for the first 12 months and 10 percent for the loan's last 12 months.
- The investor must make a capital commitment. This commitment can be in the form of a down payment, money for repairs, or both.
- The loan must be secured by the property as a first or second trust and recorded in local government offices.
- There must be a title examination, survey, and termite inspection satisfactory to the lender.
- The investor must buy lender's title insurance.
- The investor must have the right to prepay the loan, in whole or in part, without penalty.
- The loan shall not be assigned or assumed, nor shall the property be sold subject to the loan. The pension shall have the right to name and substitute trustees at will.
- No funds will be used to acquire or improve any real estate except the property for which the loan is specifically intended.
- All loan documents will be in a form satisfactory to the pension fund.

In essence, the deal looks very much like the one outlined with private individuals. There are, however, five important differences.

First, if you get money from individuals, if they simply hand you a check, that's fine. Individuals have the right to handle their money any way they choose.

Trustees have a higher level of responsibility. The dollars they control are not theirs, and for this reason a trustee would be foolish if he or she merely gave checks to an investor.

The problem with handing over a check is this: If Bill Parson, the trustee for Parson Plumbing's Pension and Retirement Fund, makes out a check for $50,000 so Kingston can buy a particular property, what's to prevent Kingston from cashing the check, not settling on the property, or buying something else? Such switches have been known to occur.

A better idea is to make the check payable to the party conducting settlement, such as an attorney or title company, and *give no money whatsoever directly to the investor.* This approach provides the investor with his loan, assures that the money is actually spent for its intended purpose, and provides a clear paper trail showing who got the money and when.

Second, there may be situations where the trustee will want not only a credit report, but also a cash deposit from the investor equal to the probable cost of all repairs and improvements. The money can be held in an escrow account and disbursed as repair bills are presented. The attraction of this approach is that the trustee is not dependent on the investor's credit to assure the project's completion.

From the investor's perspective, the creation of an escrow account is not a hardship because the money will be required at some point anyway.

Third, trustees may require an appraisal, but the value of an appraisal should be seen in context. We can assume that investors who seek trust funds are often looking for short-term, interim financing and that the property they're buying will require repair and renovation. In such situations, it's probable that the property will appraise poorly because appraisers cannot give credit for repairs not yet completed.

Fourth, the note will be repaid on an interest-only basis. Monthly payments will be equal to $1/12$ of the interest due on the outstanding balance of the note.

Since we are dealing with a short-term note, there's little advantage to amortizing the loan, especially on a 30- or 40-year basis.

Fifth, a special requirement for pension trustees is evidence that they have made a prudent business decision. This evidence can include copies of all settlement documents and loan agreements, plus materials associated with the deal and recorded in local government offices.

Part of the trustee's evidence should also include a letter from the investor, clearly describing the project, its potential, and the risk involved.

A MODEL LETTER FOR PENSION TRUSTEES

A letter to pension trustees should carefully outline how much cash is needed, how the money will be spent, a general time frame for the project, and a listing of all major loan terms. A letter might follow the pattern used by Mr. Kingston when he contacted Bill Parson.

> October 15, 1995
> 123 Main Street
> Anywhere, U.S.A. 00000
> 555-123-4567

Mr. Bill Parson
Trustee
Parson Plumbing's
Pension and Retirement Fund
5000 West Street
Anywhere, U.S.A. 00000

Dear Mr. Parson:

A property known as 567 Smith Street in the Eastwick area of Anywhere has become available, a property which we feel has excellent potential.

The property, which we would describe as a Cape Cod style, is a two-story home with a front brick facade and aluminum siding. The first floor includes an eat-in kitchen, dining room, living room, entry foyer, half bath, laundry area, and pantry off the kitchen, as well as an attached two-car garage. The second floor contains a large master bedroom with a full bath and walk-in closet. Also, there are two additional bedrooms and a central bath on the second floor. The basement contains a finished recreation area with a fireplace, walkout access to the backyard, full bath, and an unfinished area.

In addition, the property has a large rear deck, storm windows and doors, central air-conditioning, many trees, and a lot that measures 100 × 200 feet.

The property is now available for $100,000 in its current condition. The property has been used as a group house for several years and suffered substantial wear and tear. Problems with the property include, but are not limited to, a broken central air-conditioning system, an unusable kitchen oven, an outdated refrigerator, an outdated clothes washer and clothes dryer, water damage beneath a second-story bath, water damage from frozen pipes, damage to concrete sidewalks and driveways, poor paint throughout, and rotted decking.

Repairs, according to a report by a structural engineer (see attached copy), will require estimated work worth approximately $10,000. Thus it's possible to acquire and refurbish this property for about $110,000 plus monthly carrying costs. Similar homes in the neighborhood, according to two area brokers (see attached letters), are now priced in the area of $125,000 to $130,000.

It's possible, however, to have lower repair costs if we do some of the work ourselves.

The property will also be more attractive economically if we could obtain interim financing until repairs are completed. Once the property is refurbished, it could then be sold or refinanced on the basis of its new and higher value.

We would be interested in the following arrangement:

We will put down 10 percent of the sales price.

We want 90 percent interim financing, for a total loan of $90,000. To close the deal before December 31, and to avoid onerous application fees and two sets of loan charges (once when acquiring the property and once again when it's refinanced), we are willing to pay a premium interest rate on a loan secured by the property.

The loan will have a maximum term of two years and a simple annual interest rate 2 percent above the return of a given money-market fund on the first business day of each month for the loan's first 12 months. In the second year, the margin will be a simple annual interest rate 3 percent above the return for a given money-market fund. The loan may be prepaid in whole or in part without penalty at any time. Your loan will be secured by a first trust on the property and recorded in local government offices. We will make monthly payments equal to $1/12$th of the interest due on the outstanding balance of the note.

With such financing, the situation will work like this:

1) We will acquire the property.

2) We will immediately begin needed repair work. Hopefully exterior painting and concrete work can be started before settlement.

3) Repairs should take from two weeks to six weeks, depending on how much of the work is done professionally and how much we do ourselves. Once repairs are substantially completed, we will then seek a tenant. Rentals in the area range from $700 to $1,300 a month. We think a rental of $900 will be reasonable, especially once the property is repaired.

4) With a lease in hand we will obtain permanent financing. We will refinance the house once repairs are completed on the basis of its new and higher value. If the property is worth $125,000, and we obtained 80 percent non-conforming financing, we would receive $100,000—enough to repay the interim financing as well as much of the repair bill.

5) At the end of this process we will have a leased property in excellent condition, and the pension will have received a high rate of interest on a secured mortgage.

In terms of having a valid economic loan, our arrangement will produce a higher rate of interest than is currently available from a money-market fund, security in the form of a recorded lien against the property, security in the form of our 10 percent down payment, security in the form of our repairs and improvements, plus our personal liability to repay the loan.

It should be recognized, however, that our project entails risk, including, but not limited to, the following concerns: Repairs may be more costly than anticipated, and necessary work may require more time than we project. Rentals with good tenants at the $900 level cannot be guaranteed, nor can we warrant the availability of money to refinance the project. A list of neighborhood rentals for similar properties is attached.

The idea of making a loan is always a difficult judgment, and we're talking about a substantial sum of money. It's entirely appropriate and understandable to review the ideas above from a prudent business perspective, to check with your lawyer and accountant to assure that all applicable rules and regulations are met, and to see if this proposal makes sense within the context of your needs and interests. If it does, let's do business.

Sincerely,

William G. Kingston

It's worth noting that the model letter is very precise in certain areas (the pension *will* get a recorded first trust) but less specific elsewhere. For instance, several risks are listed, but the letter clearly states that there may be additional risks as well ("our project entails risk, including, but not limited to"). From the investor's perspective this is a good approach. If something goes wrong in the future, with this language you won't be in the position of having to explain why an unforeseen risk was not mentioned.

Also, the letter provides supporting documentation for projected repairs, sales, and rentals. Such documentation creates justification that a "reasonable man" can use when making a loan decision as well as evidence, if needed in the future, that the decision was well-founded.

GETTING PENSION APPROVAL

The usual loan review process can take weeks or even months with conventional lenders, but pensions offer the possibility of quick responses—a day or two with trustees you know, to not more than a week or ten days with others.

To speed the process, investors should provide not only a letter outlining their project, but also two identical copies of a letter approving the plan that can be signed and dated by the trustee. One copy can be returned to the investor, and one can be sent to the party holding closing.

Such a letter might read as follows:

October 15, 1995
5000 West Street
Anywhere, U.S.A. 00000

Mr. Philo P. Reynolds, Esq.
555 Main Street
Anywhere, U.S.A. 00000

Dear Mr. Reynolds:

With regard to our loan arrangement concerning 567 Smith Street in the Eastwick area of Anywhere with William G. Kingston, please note the following terms and conditions.

1) There will be a first deed of trust on the property of $90,000 due in two years with a simple annual interest rate 2 percent above the annualized return of the Silver Slipper Money Market Fund on the first business day of each month for the first 12 months of the loan term. In months 13 through 24, the margin will be a simple annual interest rate 3 percent above the annualized rate of return of the Silver Slipper Money Market Fund on the first business day of each subject month.

2) The loan can be prepaid, in whole or in part, at any time and without penalty.

3) We shall have the right to name one or more trustee(s) and to substitute trustees at will and without notice.

4) As the lender, we shall be formally named in all documents as "Parson Plumbing's Pension and Retirement Fund."

5) The note shall be made in a form satisfactory to us and supplied to you by our attorney, Mr. Harold T. Cranford, Esq.

Property		1401 Benton Ct.			
Owners		Charlotte & Ed Wilson			
Social Security #		000-27-8484			
Loan Amount		65,000.00			
Interest Rate		8.5 Percent			
Monthly Payment		$505.00			
Payment Start Date		Sept. 15, 1997			

#	Date	Interest	Payment	Balance	Check Number
1	Sept. 14	460.42	505.00	64,955.42	3140
2	Oct. 14	460.10	505.00	64,910.52	3304
3	Nov. 11	459.78	505.00	64,865.30	3314
4	Dec. 14	459.46	505.00	64,819.76	3370
	1997 Interest		**1,839.76**		
5	Jan. 11	459.14	505.00	64,773.90	3417
6	Feb. 12	458.82	505.00	64,727.72	3467
7	March 12	458.49	505.00	64,681.21	3525
8	April 14	458.16	505.00	64,634.36	3537
9	May 10	457.83	505.00	64,587.19	3572
10	June 10	457.49	505.00	64,539.68	3676
11	July 12	457.16	505.00	64,491.84	3734
12	Aug. 10	456.82	505.00	64,443.66	3779
13	Sept. 15	456.48	505.00	64,395.13	3827
14	Oct. 14	456.13	505.00	64,346.27	3867
15	Nov. 11	455.79	505.00	64,297.05	3951
16	Dec. 14	455.44	505.00	64,247.49	4059
	1998 Interest		**5,487.73**		

6) Settlement shall be held on or before December 15.
Please advise us well in advance concerning the actual date of settlement so we can deliver a certified check.

Sincerely,

Bill Parson,
Trustee

cc: Mr. William G. Kingston

The response letter drafted by investor Kingston and signed by the pension trustee confirms the loan and outlines its terms. Since the loan is to be in a form "satisfactory" to Parson, it means that Parson can dictate such issues as assumability and assignment. From Kingston's point of view, major issues—the loan's length, amount, rate of interest, monthly payments, and the right to prepay without penalty—are all cited in the acceptance letter.

The huge size of the small-business private pension system, and the vast number of trustees, suggests that investors should have little trouble finding short-term capital, provided sound business procedures are followed. Perhaps the best part of pension financing is that having successfully worked with one pension, others will look at you with greater acceptance. After all, experience has merit in the eyes of a "prudent man."

KEEPING THE PENSION HAPPY

Once you have a loan from a pension there is the very important matter of assuring and reassuring the pension trustee that you are working in good faith to keep up your end of the bargain.

One of the best possible practices is to make full and timely payments, and to include with each payment a complete loan history.

Suppose you have a $65,000 note at 8.5 percent interest. Suppose as well that monthly payments are set at $505 a month—a little more than the $499.79 that would normally be paid with a 30-year schedule. A borrower in this situation would want to show each monthly payment, the amount credited to principal, the monthly interest cost, the remaining principal balance, and the check number for each payment.

Using a basic computer and a simple spreadsheet, it is an easy matter to construct and update an appropriate statement for the lender. It can show the amount of interest paid each month, and it can show as well the interest paid for the year—important information for tax purposes. By including check numbers, it is a simple matter to track payments, should that be necessary.

CONVERTING TO LONG-TERM FINANCING

Investors who use pension funds to finance and refinance real estate investments should be aware that such funding is not without potential pitfalls.

First, since conforming lenders routinely want 30 percent down, investors will have to work harder to find money sources with better LTV ratios, say 80 percent LTVs rather than 70 percent.

Suppose a property is bought for $100,000 using a $90,000 pension loan. After being fixed up, the property is valued at $150,000, a situation where an 80 percent LTV loan will provide $120,000 in financing while a 70 percent LTV mortgage will yield only $105,000. If the cost of acquiring and fixing up the property exceeds $105,000, an investor without a better loan will not be able to get his or her money out at the time the property is refinanced. A worse example would be a situation where the value of the property does not increase enough to refinance the original loan. If the value of the property went from $100,000 to $120,000, a 70 percent LTV loan would yield only $84,000—not enough to cover the pension debt.

A second concern for investors is the issue of "seasoning." Those lenders who refinance investment property typically prefer a history of ownership, say one to three years. The seasoning concept, however, raises a problem for efficient investors who buy property with pension money, fix it up within several months, and then turn around and try to refinance. Having quickly overhauled the property, such investors may find that lenders now want them to own the property for at least a year before seeking a new loan, a requirement which may doom a short-term deal with a pension.

A third issue revolves around "cashing out," taking money out of a property through refinancing. Lenders are wary of deals where owners can cash out, especially investors. Thus investors may be able to get enough money to pay off their pension debt, but nothing for repairs or acquisition costs paid above the old loan's current balance.

In some cases, the best choice for both pension and investor might be a five-year agreement that works like this: The pension will loan money to the investor at acceptable rates and the money will be repaid over a five-year period. Monthly payments, however, will be calculated on the basis of a 30-year loan schedule. At the end of the five years, the loan will be due and payable and the investor will have a balloon payment to make.

For example, a $100,000 loan at 8 percent interest amortized over five years will require monthly payments of $2,027.64. A loan with the same principal amount and interest rate will cost just $733.76 a month if payments are made on a 30-year basis. At the end of five years, the investor owes $95,070.21, an amount that can be repaid through the sale of the property or refinancing.

Five years is not a long time in the lending game and many pension funds, if given sufficient security and interest, will find such deals attractive. Investors also may prefer longer loans, especially when refinancing is not available without seasoning.

The use of loans with longer terms may help with seasoning but they do not resolve the problem of getting cash from the property. If recapturing cash is important, and it usually is, then second trusts should be considered. Second trust sources can include pension funds. In fact, there are situations in which one pension fund might first provide the initial loan used to acquire the property and then a second trust once the property has a new and higher value. When it comes time to refinance, both mortgages—being seasoned debt—may be refinanced with a single new loan.

Because of the frequent guideline changes, it is important for investors to check with lenders and determine what is and what is not allowed with regard to investor refinancing. Be aware that loan guidelines are always changing and that different lenders have different underwriting standards. As a defensive strategy, structure pension loans to meet conservative refinancing standards in case nothing better is available.

8

How to Finance Investment Property

Financing investment property is somewhat like running in a marathon with high hurdles. We have conforming-loan boundaries, the prepayment hurdle, the points impasse, and then the loan-source obstacle. Having gone this far, we now run into a new type of mortgage problem: the multiple-choice barrier.

Real estate financing is marked by a surplus of choices, and although we want the largest possible menu of mortgage options, we're not buying everything on the menu. We only need one or two loan products for each deal.

Because there are so many loan choices, investors can customize borrowing to maximize profits. We can search for the one loan that produces the best results for a given deal. What we can't do is find one loan that always works. Since each deal is different, no mortgage is right in every case.

CONVENTIONAL, 30-YEAR, AND 15-YEAR FINANCING

Virtually all homeowners are familiar with the basic "conventional" mortgage, financing in which investors put up 30 percent of the purchase price and a lender supplies the balance. Conventional loans typically offer 30- or 15-year terms, equal monthly payments, and self-amortization. Such financing is easy to understand, avoids negative amortization, and never requires a balloon payment.

Conventional loans work not only for home buyers but also for investors. Conventional mortgages are acceptable, conforming financing in the secondary market when used to acquire real property, whether that property is bought by a prospective owner-occupant or investor.

But whether acceptable to the secondary market or not, a mortgage that requires 30 percent down doesn't offer much leverage. Moreover, even if a transaction with 30 percent cash up front is attractive, it may consume so much capital—particularly for first-time investors or those with little cash—that additional deals are impossible.

Also, even though the latest secondary guidelines allow borrowers to input income from properties which have yet to be rented, some lenders still require a signed one-year lease before they will make a mortgage commitment, a condition which raises difficult problems for investors:

First, because financing is not assured, investors can offer only contingent contracts if they're buying with conventional mortgages—that is, no lease, no loan, no deal.

Second, leases must also be conditional. If you're dependent on conventional financing, and you can't obtain such financing without a lease, then it follows that you can't be obligated to lease property you don't own. A lease under such conditions must provide that if the purchase falls through, the lease is void, the prospective tenant's deposit will be returned, and you won't have any further obligations.

Third, to get a lease, you must be able to show the property to potential tenants. However, in deals that depend on conventional financing, you may be in the position of trying to lease something you don't actually own. You'll need the seller's permission to show the property before closing, to post a sign, and to advertise—all matters which should be included in your offer.

Fourth, if an investor buys a property to fix up, having a tenant can be a major hassle. Who wants to move someone else's furniture when a floor needs to be refinished? Repairing is a far easier process when properties are vacant.

High interest costs are also a problem with conventional loans. Borrow $100,000 at 8.5 percent interest over 30 years and the interest bill will total $176,809.

We can lower that interest cost, however, if we change the loan term from 30 to 15 years. Now we have a loan that still offers equal monthly payments, self-amortization, plus two extra benefits: a lower interest rate (because of less lender risk) and a far smaller interest cost, just $77,253.

And while the monthly payments for a 15-year loan will be higher, such additional payments can be seen as a kind of enforced savings plan—one that cuts mortgage expenses by nearly $100,000 in this example.

Conventional loans are a perfectly acceptable form of financing, though not one which investors generally prefer. Here are several cases, however, where conventional loans might be considered.

- Mr. Angelo buys a property to fix up and repair. He expects to hold the property less than a year. He's wealthy and can afford to hold the property for as long as necessary to get a good price.

  Conventional financing is an option for Angelo, but not a first choice. Unless interest rates are unusually high, Angelo is better served with a smaller down payment.

- Ms. Franklin buys a property to repair, rent, and retain. She expects to hold the property for at least five years. Rental rates in the area are rising, but the property will still produce a negative cash flow for at least two years. Franklin can afford a large down payment because of a recent business success, but worries about ongoing negative cash flow.

  Franklin is a good candidate for a 30-year conventional loan because she has money available for a large down payment, and a large down payment will reduce monthly cash expenses. Also, rising rentals will gradually relieve her negative cash flow problem.

  Franklin, however, should avoid 15-year financing. Although she has adequate funds for a big down payment, she has cash flow problems that will be aggravated by the high monthly costs associated with a 15-year loan.

- Mr. Gordon bought property six years ago for $115,000. Today he still owes $90,000 on his original mortgage, but the property is worth $200,000 and produces $1,400 a month. He wants to refinance and is looking at both 15- and 30-year loans.

  Gordon can't refinance with an 80 percent LTV loan that conforms to the secondary market. However, many lenders make non-conforming loans that will allow him to borrow $160,000, less closing costs and the repayment of his existing $90,000 loan balance.

  Gordon has no problem with a down payment because his equity in the property will satisfy a lender. He expects monthly rents to rise over time and is willing to carry a small negative cash flow.

  With 8 percent interest, a $160,000 mortgage will have a monthly cost of $1,174.02 over 30 years, a figure that leaves almost $226 a month for taxes and insurance at current rents. On a 15-year basis, the same loan will cost $1,529.04.

  Gordon elects the 15-year mortgage. He knows this loan will create a negative cash flow for several years, but as rents rise, monthly losses will diminish. Also, he'll have almost $70,000 ($160,000 less $90,000) to offset minor monthly losses.

  In addition, Gordon's overall interest bill will total just $115,228 for the 15-year loan versus $262,648 with 30-year financing, a savings of almost $150,000. The faster payoff has another benefit as well: Because the loan's principal balance is being repaid so quickly, Gordon will have enough equity to refinance again within several years.

- Mr. West lives in a town which has grown little in the past decade and shows little potential for change. Rents and prices have been stable in cash terms and have actually been declining when inflation is considered. He has a chance to buy a $100,000 investment property but only with conventional financing. The property rents for $500 a month, and the cost of taxes, insurance, repairs, and a provision for vacancies is expected to raise monthly expenses by another $100.

For West to buy the property on a conventional basis will require at least $30,000 down plus monthly loan payments of $513.64 for a $70,000 mortgage at 8 percent interest over 30 years. West must also consider the money he is not earning on his $30,000 investment. At 4 percent interest per year, he has lost the opportunity to earn $100 per month ($30,000 × 4 percent = $1,200 yearly).

With little prospect of higher rents or rising values, West cannot buy this property for $100,000 and prosper. His best choices are to buy for a substantially lower price or not invest in this property. In any case, the best financing in the world won't perfect an innately bad deal.

Since not everyone can afford 30 percent down, there must be alternatives. For homeowners, alternatives that feature low down payments include FHA mortgages, VA loans, and private mortgage insurance (MI).

FHA LOANS

For many years FHA financing was a useful and valuable investment tool. And while those days are not entirely over, use of the FHA program by investors is severely limited.

FHA financing is particularly enticing because such mortgages are available with modest down payments. Rather than 20 percent down, the FHA down payment schedule, as of this writing, is 3 percent of the first $25,000, 5 percent of the next $100,000, and 10 percent of any higher amount. Other FHA advantages include liberal qualification standards and the right to prepay without penalty.

The catch is that such financing is not available to investors buying single-family homes. Only owner-occupants are able to purchase single-family properties with FHA financing, a prohibition that leaves pure investors out in the cold.

But investors should still know about the FHA program because there are instances where it may be useful.

To start, the first property purchased by many investors is simply their own home. The idea is to buy today, build equity, and sell or rent sometime in the future. Since FHA financing can be used to purchase a prime residence, the program is clearly open to would-be investors who need financing for the home in which they live.

If you buy with an FHA loan, as much as 29 percent of your gross monthly income can be used for housing expenses—mortgage principal, interest, property taxes, and insurance (PITI). Within the guidelines, up to 41 percent of your income can be devoted to general monthly costs such as PITI, auto payments, credit card debt, etc. The 29/41 ratios available through FHA are far more liberal than the 28/36 ratios associated with conventional mortgages. In effect, the FHA allows you to borrow more with a given level of income.

Buying a home requires the payment of closing costs, but with the FHA program allowable closing costs can be financed and added to the principal balance. Not all costs are "allowable," so be certain to check with lenders to determine how much you will be required to pay at closing.

Little down and liberal qualifications are the good news. On the other side of the ledger, FHA is an insurance program and loan amounts are limited.

Because the government insures loans made by private lenders under the FHA program, it follows that borrowers must pay an insurance premium. As an example, in 1995 the up-front premium is set at 2.25 percent of the mortgage amount plus a monthly fee of .50 percent. The up-front fee can be added to the mortgage amount, a strategy that saves cash up front but results in a larger mortgage. (When you sell you may be entitled to a partial refund of your up-front insurance premium. Such a refund, if available, is far in the future and not assured.)

A second FHA hurdle concerns the amount that can be borrowed. In 1994, for example, the largest FHA loan available for the purchase of a single-family home under the 203(b) program (the most common FHA loan format) in the lower 48 states was $151,725. (The figure is 50 percent higher in Alaska, Hawaii, and Guam.)

The maximum loan amount under the FHA program varies according to where you live. If you are buying in an area with lower housing prices, such as a rural state, then the FHA loan limit is reduced. Because the FHA loan limit varies, borrowers should always check with lenders to find the local limit before house hunting.

We know that you cannot use FHA financing to buy a pure-investment property, say a single-family home that you intend only to rent. However, in the eyes of the FHA, if you purchase property with the intent of living in it, you're an owner-occupant. If you buy a property with two to four living units, occupy one, and rent the rest, you still qualify for owner-occupant financing. The results can be highly profitable.

When Brown bought a four-unit building last year, he paid $200,000 for the property. Income from the three rental units totaled $1,800 a month, just enough to cover mortgage payments, taxes, and interest. The fourth unit, which Brown occupied, was essentially his on a rent-free basis.

Brown did his own maintenance and as many repairs and improvements as possible. Rather than raise rents directly, he instead converted to separate electric meters for each unit, making tenants individually responsible for the energy they used.

At the end of a year, Brown had a building that was in far better condition than when he first bought the property, and in addition his operating costs were reduced.

As tenants moved, Brown gradually raised rents. After three years, his rent roll reached $2,100 a month, and his expenses had been reduced because the cost of electricity was now paid by the tenants—a savings of $150 a month. Considering that Brown paid $9.25 for each $1 in income produced to acquire the property, on the same basis it's now worth $249,750 ($2,100 + $150 × 12 × 9.25 = $249,750).

As the deal with Brown shows, financing small, multi-unit properties can be attractive for owner-occupants. And to make the concept even more interesting, maximum FHA loan limits in the lower 48 states are set at the following levels as of this writing:

Duplex property: $194,100
Three-unit property: $234,600
Four-unit property: $291,600

When considering the loan limits above, it's important to recognize that the limits are subject to change, and that they are revised periodically. Another point is that maximum FHA loan amounts are only available in high-cost areas. Thus if you live in a community with low housing prices, the maximum FHA loan amount available to you may be significantly less than the amount available in areas with expensive housing.

Another way to use FHA financing is by purchasing a home and assuming an existent FHA mortgage.

Historically, FHA loans have been freely assumable—that is, anyone could assume the loans without going through a formal loan-qualification procedure. Combine free assumability with an outright ban on prepayment penalties, and FHA loans were attractive both to owner-occupants and investors who assumed such financing.

Now, however, the rules have changed. In capsule form, FHA assumption rules look like this:

Loans made before December 15, 1989 may be assumed by anyone. Loans made after December 15, 1989 may not be assumed by investors. Fortunately, there are great numbers of older FHA loans still on the books.

FHA assumptions are most interesting when associated with second trusts and wraparound financing. For example, if North buys a $130,000 property with a $95,000 assumable FHA loan in place, he needs another $45,000 to close the deal. But if the seller will take back a $35,000 second trust, North's cash requirement drops to just $10,000 and the deal becomes more interesting.

By assuming an FHA loan, someone—North, the seller, or North and the seller together—must pay the $500 assumption fee. But $500 is a lot less than the cost of the points, fees, and charges usually associated with a new loan.

Refinancing is another area where FHA financing may interest investors.

The deal with an FHA "streamline" refinance works this way: You can refinance an FHA loan to obtain a better rate and terms. If you refinance with an appraisal, and the property appraises appropriately, then questions regarding income, assets, and debts need not be answered. If an appraisal is not used, then a full application is required.

In effect, even if property values have fallen, it may be possible to go from a 9.5 percent loan to an 8 percent note. The theory here is that while the debt has not changed, a lower interest rate will make ownership more tolerable.

If you refinance with FHA be aware that new loan documents will be required. A major point in such new documentation is that investors cannot assume your refinanced mortgage.

Although the FHA program should be regarded as attractive for owner-occupants and owner-occupant investors, FHA loan terms change with some regularity. As this is written, for example, there are proposals in Washington to raise the FHA loan limit and reduce down payment requirements. Because the FHA program is often in flux, investigate with care before considering it as a financing vehicle. In particular, determine loan limits for your community, insurance premiums, and investor restrictions.

REHAB LOANS UNDER FHA 203(K)

Many real estate investments are three-stage deals where money is need-ed to buy the place, more money is required to fix it up, and still more money is needed to refinance the first two loans once the property is in top condition. Making matters worse, each loan is likely to involve a variety of fees, charges, application forms, and possibly even points.

In the usual case, developers use a two-step process. They get 75 per-cent interim financing to acquire and improve the property and then per-manent or "takeout" financing once repairs are made. With two-step financing there is one less loan to open and thus fewer fees, points, and charges.

Even better are deals with combination financing, loans that join inter-im and long-term mortgages into a single package. Now we have not only fewer fees and charges, but also a commitment for long-term financing from the day we acquire the property.

The federal government has a program which parallels combination mortgages, FHA 203(k) financing, loans which can be used to purchase one to four units. Like other FHA loans, these mortgages are assumable and can be prepaid without penalty. Unlike 203(b) loans, however, 203(k) loans can be used by investors. In addition, the program has other specifics of interest to investors.

- A 15 percent down payment is required from investors. This is half the amount sought by conventional lenders, but not as good as the FHA deal available to owner-occupants.
- If a 203(k) loan is assumed within 18 months by a first-time purchaser—generally someone who has not owned a home within the last three years—there is no down payment requirement.
- With 203(k) financing, there is no up-front mortgage insurance premi-um—it's paid out over the loan term.
- Because the loan is more complex than standard financing, interest rates tend to be a touch higher.
- The 203(k) program can be used to purchase or refinance a home.
- The amount that can be borrowed is limited to the same levels offered under the 203(b) program.
- Not all lenders make 203(k) loans, but around the country several hun-dred offer this mortgage product. To get a list of area lenders who offer 203(k) financing, contact the HUD field office for the community where the property is located.

Under 203(k), investors can borrow an amount equal to the property's purchase price in "as is" condition plus the value of improvements, or an amount equal to 110 percent of the anticipated market value when all repairs are completed—whichever is less.

If Drover buys a shell, a property with little more than four walls, for $25,000 and expects to make improvements worth $40,000, he can get a 203(k) loan for $65,000, less 15 percent down. Alternatively, if the property is worth only $55,000 when he's finished, the maximum loan size under the 110 percent rule will be $60,500, again less 15 percent down.

Under 203(k), investors can never get more than the property's acquisition price plus improvements, and they can't get that amount if it's more than the loan limits under 203(b). In effect, the FHA program works especially well for small properties where improvements create not less than dollar-for-dollar increases in value.

FHA financing under 203(k) can be used to expand a dwelling, finish an attic or basement, refurbish plumbing and electrical systems, install solar energy units, fix up kitchens, and replace or improve such basic necessities as walls, floors, and ceilings.

Getting a 203(k) loan, however, may not be easy. Not only do investors need to provide the usual information required by the FHA, but they also need contractor estimates (or bids) for proposed improvements and repairs.

When the loan is granted, investors do not receive all the money. That portion of the loan assigned for repairs is placed in an escrow account and paid out as work is completed and there, for lenders, is the catch. No work, no money.

Unlike typical loans, which are largely wrapped up once the money is disbursed, under 203(k) lenders must determine when each work stage is completed before they can release funds. This is extra work, so the FHA allows lenders under 203(k) to charge an additional 1.5 points for the rehab portion of the loan.

FHA 203(k) loans can also be used in situations where a property has been purchased and an investor needs second-trust financing to complete repairs. Since the loan can only be insured once all repair work has been completed, lenders will again hold money in escrow and release it as repairs and improvements are completed.

The 203(k) program, despite its limitations and complications, can be attractive to certain investors. The program can cover acquisition and repair costs, and it may be a better financing choice than having two or three conventional loans for a single property. These mortgages are available through FHA-approved lenders, who can give full details.

FIXING UP WITH TITLE 1

Another approach to fixing up under FHA is the Title I program, a mortgage option for which investors are generally eligible.

Under FHA Title I, you can borrow as much as $25,000 for such selected improvements as building materials, architectural fees, storm windows, built-in ovens, or a new heating system. Luxury items are prohibited, so pools and saunas will have to be financed from other sources. Also, Title I can't be used to finance work already completed.

Title I funding is available to both owner-occupants and investors. In the case of investors, however, two special rules stand out.

First, you must have at least a 50 percent ownership interest in the property.

Second, if the Title I loan amount exceeds $15,000, your equity must equal or exceed the amount borrowed.

Title I is interesting for a number of other reasons, as well.

- It's easy for homeowners to get. Investors, however, need a long-term (one-year or longer) lease and evidence that they can repay the loan.
- Since HUD insures 90 percent of the loan, lenders have little risk.
- Loan terms can be as long as 15 years.
- If you borrow $5,000 or less, a lien is generally not recorded against the property.
- If you borrow more than $5,000, the note is recorded as a lien against the property—say as a first, second, or third trust. However, Title I loans are recorded behind existing liens, so if you have already financed the property but need still more cash to make improvements, Title I can provide the money without disturbing other loans.
- Contractors used under Title I must be approved by the lender, a not inconsiderable protection against unscrupulous repair firms.
- Because the loans are so small, fees and charges are minimal.

The Title I program is quick, easy, and available nationwide. It's open to investors, and there's no reason why Title I financing should not be considered, especially by investors who intend to fix up property.

The only catch to the program is the requirement for a long-term lease. The difficulty is that owners won't be able to get maximum rents leasing unimproved property. One solution to this dilemma is to create a long-term lease with escalating monthly payments based on completed improvements.

For example, if King buys a unit that needs central air-conditioning plus storm windows, he can lease the property to Hughes for $600 a month, but with a lease that raises the rent to $650 when the air-conditioning is in place and $675 when the storm windows are installed. This arrangement gives King a lease to show lenders plus an incentive to complete the work. As for Hughes, if the work isn't done, he properly pays a lower rent.

VA LOANS

In addition to FHA-backed mortgages, the federal government sponsors another major loan-insurance program of possible interest to investors.

The VA loan program, now under the authority of the Department of Veterans Affairs, is designed to benefit military veterans, certain spouses, and others who have served the federal government, such as officers in the Public Health Service. Under the VA program, there's no down payment requirement, and substantial loan amounts—as much as $184,000 at this writing—are available.

Every vet has an "entitlement" equal to $36,000, a figure that means lenders will routinely provide up to $144,000 in mortgage debt for financially qualified individuals. In addition, the VA will guarantee 25 percent of any mortgage debt above $144,000 up to $10,000. Since lenders like to have a ratio of 1 to 4 when it comes to guarantees, the additional VA backing translates into another $40,000 in borrowing power for financially qualified individuals. Adding the entitlement and extra loan guarantees together, a financially qualified vet can borrow up to $184,000 under the program.

As with the FHA, the VA does not lend money directly, but instead insures private lenders. The cost of VA insurance, a so-called "funding fee," varies according to the amount down. The fee schedule currently looks like this:

5 percent down or less: 2 percent of the loan amount
5 to 10 percent down: 1.5 percent of the loan amount
10 percent down or more: 1.25 percent of the loan amount

There are also special funding fees for vets who refinance to get a lower rate (.5 percent) or who reuse their eligibility (3 percent). National Guard and reserve personnel who qualify for the VA program pay the usual funding fees plus a .75 percent surcharge.

The VA offers no special programs, incentives, or inducements for investors. Indeed, VA loans are for owner-occupied housing only, and the purchase of investment property is generally prohibited. There are two exceptions, however.

First, qualified vets may buy duplex, three-unit, and four-unit properties with VA funding, provided they live in one unit.

Second, VA loans are assumable at their original rates and terms. However, if the loan was made after March 1, 1988, only qualified buyers may assume. There's a processing fee which cannot exceed $500 plus a .5 percent funding fee. Loans made before March 1, 1988 are freely assumable at their original rates and terms.

VA loans should not be overlooked by investors because it is often possible to assume a VA loan with extremely attractive terms.

To see why, imagine that Kaplan—someone with active-duty military status—buys a home for $150,000 with nothing down. Three years later Kaplan retires and elects to move out of state. He places his home on the market for $165,000.

Imagine also that when Kaplan bought his home he obtained a 30-year mortgage at 7.5 percent interest. After three years his outstanding loan balance is $145,660.

Now we have a situation where the difference between Kaplan's loan balance and his asking price is roughly $20,000. But an asking price is not necessarily a sales price, particularly in a slow market. In addition, Kaplan may want to take back a small loan in the form of a second trust to make the sale work.

The result is a situation where a buyer may be able to assume Kaplan's VA loan and, with some negotiation back and forth, acquire the property with 10 percent down or less. Considering that no points are involved to assume Kaplan's loan, this may well be an attractive deal.

The millions of existing VA-backed mortgages represent a huge pool of assumable financing, loans available to both vets and nonvets, owners and investors. Thus while VA loans cannot be *originated* by investors, VA loans can often be assumed—a worthwhile financing tool in many cases.

PRIVATE MORTGAGE INSURANCE

Because of their restrictive nature, FHA and VA programs necessarily limit investor activity. As an alternative to these federal programs, private mortgage insurance (MI) can be used to offset down payment requirements.

Private mortgage insurance is nothing more than a guarantee by an insurance company to cover a certain portion of a borrower's debt in the case of foreclosure. In a sense, the private mortgage insurer is a kind of co-signer, and with such strong and well-qualified support *residential* buyers can get loans with 5, 10, or 15 percent down.

The attraction of MI financing is that many restrictions found in the FHA and VA programs are eliminated. You don't have to be a vet, and loans up to $500,000 can be readily covered.

But although MI is a form of insurance we could discuss at some length, such discussion is unnecessary because MI is virtually unavailable to investors buying property with 30 percent down or less, and it's unnecessary for investors who pay more up front.

Rather than getting MI, buyers should look for lenders who compensate for the greater risk investors represent with marginally higher rates. Typically the best sources for such loans are portfolio lenders, and mortgage brokers with access to portfolio lenders. Also, consider pension loans and assumptions that offer low down payments when compared with new conventional financing.

ASSUMPTIONS

Like good wine, there are mortgages which improve with age, especially those with low interest rates and high amortization rates. And such financing is sometimes assumable, much to the lending industry's chagrin.

Although the term "assumption" is widely used in real estate, it's actually a special word with a specific meaning. When a loan is "assumed," it means both seller and buyer remain fully responsible for repaying the debt. In contrast, when property is sold "subject to" the mortgage, the buyer takes over monthly payments, but the *seller* remains responsible for the mortgage if the buyer defaults.

Not all assumable loans are equally assumable. For example, VA loans made before March 1, 1988 were (and are) "freely assumable." For a minimal fee you can assume such loans without marathon mortgage applications or processing hassles.

Many conventional loans, if assumable at all, are "qualified assumptions"—that is, the loan may be assumed if the borrower is qualified. Who determines if the borrower is qualified? The lender. What standards does the lender use? Whatever standards he likes.

Thus if the decision is up to the lender, a 10 percent mortgage may be instantaneously assumable in an 8 percent market. A 6 percent loan in a period when lenders can get 8 percent interest might be assumable only if buyers are willing to pay high assumption fees.

When available, assumptions are attractive for three reasons.

First, assumable loans may have below-market interest rates.

Second, assumable loans—especially those backed by the VA and FHA—have limited assumption fees.

Third, the mix of interest and principal with assumed loans is better than with new financing. For example, if Rowan borrows $100,000 at 7.5 percent interest over 30 years, his monthly payments are $699.21. In the first month just $74.21 is principal; the rest—$625.00—is interest. If Sanders assumes the loan after five years, payment No. 60 is still $699.21, but now the interest cost is down to $584.43 while the principal reduction totals $114.78.

Oddly enough, some people argue that it is good to have the higher interest costs associated with a new loan because then a borrower has a larger tax deduction. This reasoning is simultaneously correct and irrelevant.

If you have $1 in income and pay a 28 percent tax, then 72 cents is left over for your use and enjoyment. If you pay $1 in interest, $1 goes to a lender and your taxes are reduced by 28 cents. In effect, your 28 cents has simply moved from Uncle Sam's account to a lender's, and nothing is left in your pocket.

SECOND TRUSTS

Even when assumable financing is present, such loans may be unattractive. The problem is usually not the interest rate or assumption fees, but rather that little principal remains.

What often happens is that a huge gap exists between the price sellers want and the existing mortgage balance. If Merton has a $95,000 assumable mortgage at 8 percent interest but wants $150,000 for his property, a buyer will need $55,000 to cover the difference.

To fill this gap investors can simply pay cash, but this isn't a workable solution in most cases, because many investors lack cash and even if they had it, they would prefer a deal with more leverage.

But the money gap can be bridged with a second trust supplied by a seller or conventional lender.

To understand how a second trust works, consider the idea of a line at the movie theater. The theater will sell tickets until the last seat is gone. The next person in line, though having waited patiently, can't get in.

In real estate, claims against property are entered in local records, and the order of recordation establishes the priority of repayment—sort of first recorded, first paid. The initial loan is a first trust or mortgage, the next loan is a second trust or second mortgage, etc. Note that the order of repayment is not based on which loan is bigger. Also note that tax liens may come first, regardless of when private claims are established.

If there's a foreclosure, the first trust holder must be paid in full before the second trust holder receives a dime. As with the line of people snaking around the theater, if you're one person too late, you don't benefit.

Because they represent more risk, second trusts command a higher rate of interest. And because second trusts traditionally have short terms—three to five years, and usually not more than 10—they often have balloon payments.

Despite high rates and the possibility of balloon payments, second trusts are a common investment tool because they can bridge the gap between assumable loan balances and seller prices. Merton, our seller with the $150,000 property, might take back a $45,000 second trust if a buyer will put up $10,000 in cash—a deal with 6.6 percent down ($95,000 from the first trust, $45,000 from Merton, plus $10,000 from a buyer equals $150,000).

Second trusts, especially when held by sellers, are also attractive because they typically involve no points or fees. Even when second trusts are borrowed from conventional lenders, points are rare and fees are low, in part because the loan's size is often small.

If you hold a second trust as lender, be certain the note cannot be assumed, assigned, or the property sold subject to the note. Allow prepayments at any time without penalty (because second trusts are riskier than first mortgages). Require the borrower to maintain what you define as adequate fire, theft, and liability insurance. If you sell property and take back a second trust, be sure the buyer is obligated to get enough title insurance so that both the first trust and your note are protected in the event of a title claim. Make the buyer personally liable, both for tax reasons and for your protection.

In addition, to protect against unjustified warranty claims after closing, have the buyer complete a property inspection at the time of closing, which states without reservation that the property's physical condition is acceptable and that all mechanical systems are in good working condition. Ask an attorney for advice to assure that the buyer's inspection and remarks "survive" closing.

There's also a form of financing related to the second trust, a note farther back in line, the third trust. It's the exact same idea as a second trust, only riskier. The NAR investment survey shows that third trusts are involved in 2 percent of all commercial deals.

BALLOON NOTES

The short terms typically found in second trusts often create huge balloon payments when such loans end. If you borrow $20,000 at 8 percent interest but only pay $146.75 a month, at the end of five years you'll still owe $19,014.17.

For investors, however, balloon notes are often irrelevant. Yes, a loan may have a balloon payment, but that payment can be unimportant when investors have no intention of holding property until the loan terminates.

If Turner buys a $200,000 property by assuming a $130,000 first trust and getting a five-year, $50,000 second trust at 8 percent interest, he'll have a balloon note if he pays $333.33 a month. When the loan ends, Turner will owe the entire $50,000 because he's created an interest-only loan ($50,000 × 8 percent = $4,000 annually, or $333.33 a month).

This isn't a problem for Turner, because he plans to fix the property and sell it within eight months. What he's really done is to rent $50,000 for $2,666 ($333 × 8 months), not a large carrying cost in the context of a $200,000 deal.

Although Turner did well with his balloon payment, some investors aren't so lucky. They don't have a coherent investment plan, and they're not prepared to sell, refinance, or otherwise make full payment when the balloon payment is due. The result is foreclosure, loss of equity, and sometimes bankruptcy as well.

WRAPAROUND LOANS

First mortgages serve as a sort of building block when properties are financed with second trusts, but there's a different way to use first mortgages, to make them into income-producing assets for sellers with a technique called wraparound financing.

When deals involve assumable first trusts, it's possible for investors to take over such loans. If additional financing is required, a seller or third party can then provide a second trust.

But if a second trust is used to finance the deal, it means the buyer gets the benefit of the assumable loan's rates and terms. If the first trust is a fixed-rate loan that can be assumed at 8 percent, that's great for the purchaser.

What about the seller? With an assumption, the seller gives up such advantages as the first trust may offer. Rather than pass so many goodies to the buyer, however, we may prefer a deal where the owner can both sell the property *and* benefit from the assumable loan's attractive terms.

Wraparound financing provides such an arrangement, as McHenry demonstrates.

Suppose McHenry has an assumable 7 percent VA mortgage with a remaining loan balance of $100,000. Suppose also that he can sell his property for $145,000 and that investor financing is now pegged at 9 percent interest.

If Wilkens wants to buy and has $20,000 for a down payment, McHenry can make this deal:

- McHenry will get $145,000 for the property.
- McHenry will provide a wraparound loan for $125,000 at 8.5 percent interest.
- McHenry will be responsible for paying off the existing VA loan.
- Wilkens will provide a $20,000 down payment.
- The wraparound's term will be equal to the remaining term of the original VA mortgage, say 25 years in this case.
- Monthly payments for principal and interest on the wraparound note will be amortized over 25 years.

This deal has attractions for both McHenry and Wilkens.

McHenry, the owner, is marketing his property at full value, joyous news for any seller. He also makes a substantial profit on the financing. He earns 8.5 percent on $100,000, money that costs 7 percent. He also earns 8.5 percent on $25,000, the wraparound's additional value.

In total, McHenry earns interest worth roughly $10,625 in the first year after the sale. Of this amount, $7,000 must be used to cover the VA mortgage. The remaining $3,625 is the return McHenry earns for providing credit worth $25,000 and holding on to the VA mortgage. McHenry's true rate of return is 14.5 percent ($3,625 compared to $25,000).

Wilkens also saves because the deal involves no points. McHenry, who might otherwise pay a portion of the points, also benefits from this situation.

But as good as a wraparound deal may seem, there are several problems for both buyer and seller to consider.

First, McHenry can't create a wraparound note unless he can afford to take back financing, something not every seller can do.

Second, Wilkens is dependent on McHenry to pay off the VA loan. A better situation would work like this: Wilkens will deposit each month's mortgage payment in an escrow account. Funds from that account will automatically be credited to the VA lender and only then will any remaining balance be available to the seller.

Third, since McHenry is holding a loan and he's the seller, the loan may not be regarded as qualified financing under at-risk tax rules. Check with an accountant or tax attorney for details.

Fourth, if you're the investor, you'll do better if you assume the VA first trust and have the seller or a third party take back a $25,000 second trust. If you paid 9 percent on a second trust, or even 12 percent, those figures are still less than the 14.5 percent McHenry earns in this example.

NO MONEY DOWN

No discussion of investor financing is complete without an exploration of deals with no money down. Usually, when investors talk about no-money-down sales, they don't mean VA loans or deals with almost no money down, such as mortgages guaranteed by FHA.

Investors—especially those inspired by a variety of TV gurus—want deals where the seller takes back so much financing that the buyer doesn't need cash. It's the seller who invariably must take back financing because no lender will allow 100 percent financing except with strong VA guarantees.

A no-money-down deal might look like this: Barkley offers to sell his property for $100,000. However, because he needs to raise cash quickly, Weber talks him into selling the property for $75,000. Weber also gets three other concessions from Barkley. First, Barkley will take back a $15,000 second trust. Second, Weber will assume an existing $60,000 FHA mortgage that's more than two years old. And third, Barkley will pay all settlement costs.

So here we have a fictional situation where Weber has purchased a home for no money down. Most such deals are fictional because few people are so desperate, or so stupid, that they will sell property at a deep discount and then hold the financing needed to make a bad deal possible.

In addition, deals without cash raise other issues and concerns:

- In a no-money-down deal the seller receives no cash. How then can he purchase another property after his is sold?
- A deal with no money down requires the largest conceivable mortgage the property can support. Monthly mortgage payments, even when offset with rental income, may still mean Weber pays out more than he takes in.
- A deal with no money down typically means deferred obligations. In exchange for no money up front, money is required later in the trans-

action. In this case, Weber has a $15,000 second trust which must be paid off.

■ A no-money-down deal that involves seller financing may run into the at-risk rules limiting investor tax write-offs.

Certainly investors want discounted property, and the fewer dollars required up front, the better. But real estate deals must have an exchange of value; both buyer and seller must get something. In a situation where a seller is offered a discounted price and asked to take back financing as well, there's nothing in the deal for him, so he's not hurt if he simply holds onto the property and waits for a better offer.

Predatory no-money-down deals are sometimes justified by claims that buyers in such situations are heroes. They save the seller's credit rating, we're told.

But it's difficult to imagine that an owner who's selling at a discounted price and accepting ridiculous terms has a wonderful credit history to protect. A more likely situation is that by the time a seller is so desperate he's willing to consider a predatory offer, he has financial problems on so many fronts there's no credit rating worth saving.

CASH-PLUS DEALS

Even more enticing than deals with no money down—at least from the investor's standpoint—are transactions that give both title *and* cash to a purchaser at settlement.

Carson offers to sell his home for $100,000. Thorens likes the property and makes the following offer: He'll buy the property for $90,000 with a $10,000 down payment. He'll take over a freely assumable $30,000 first trust and the seller will take back a $70,000 second trust payable over 20 years at 8 percent interest. If this arrangement goes through, the property will be sold for $90,000 and buyer Thorens will receive $20,000 at closing. Here's how:

Thorens paid $90,000 for the property. He put down $10,000 plus he got loans worth $100,000, a total of $110,000. Subtract $90,000 from $110,000 and there's $20,000 left over, money which goes back to buyer Thorens. In effect, Thorens gets back his $10,000 deposit at settlement plus an additional $10,000. As for the seller, he gets paid $90,000 for his property, but then lends $70,000 to the buyer. In the end, the buyer walks away from settlement with $20,000 in cash for a $90,000 property.

Cash-plus deals are even more outlandish than sales with no money

Mr. Thorens's Cash-Plus Deal

Purchase price	$90,000

Money In

Down payment	$10,000
First trust	$30,000
Second trust from seller	$70,000
Total financing	$110,000

Money Out

Total financing	$110,000
Payments to seller	$90,000
Cash to buyer	$20,000
Payments to seller	
Total	$90,000
Note from buyer	$70,000
Cash to seller	$20,000

down. Here we have a situation where the seller not only gives up title to his property, but the *buyer* walks away from closing with cash.

The deal has so much inherent risk that few lenders will even consider the small first trust sought by Thorens. Although the first trust will be well secured in this example, the buyer has no reason to pay the mortgage. He's already cashed out in the most flagrant manner possible.

The seller has virtually no security within this cash-plus arrangement. If the property is foreclosed, the first trust holder gets $30,000 while anything above that price goes to seller Carson. Carson, in turn, has a $70,000 note, which means that for his entire note to be repaid the property must sell for $100,000 at foreclosure. Surely, if Carson believes his note is secure, he must think his property is worth $100,000—and if he thinks it's worth $100,000 he has no reason to sell for $90,000.

While a cash-plus deal is possible in theory, investors should be warned that if a lender is involved in the deal, and the lender is not told about the cash-plus arrangement in the loan application, then the transaction will be regarded as a fraud. In turn, as soon as a lender sees that a cash-plus deal has been arranged, the loan will be declined because the property cannot be sold at the inflated price required in a cash-plus deal.

In addition, of course, if there is a cash-plus deal and the buyer collects money at closing and then fails to make required mortgage payments, you can bet that all parties will soon be in court. The buyer/borrower will require the services of an esteemed criminal attorney while any sellers and lenders caught in this mess will have a property that must be foreclosed.

The bottom line is that cash-plus deals should be avoided; the mere suggestion of a cash-plus deal should set off alarm bells.

ADJUSTABLE RATE MORTGAGES

Mortgages have always represented a contest between borrowers and lenders to see who could get the best rates and terms, a contest which has taken on a new twist. While interest rates are set in stone when a fixed-rate mortgage is established, they can float up or down with adjustable rate mortgages (ARMs).

With an ARM, rates are pegged to an index such as one-year Treasury issues. A "margin" is then added to the index, say 2 points, so that if the index stands at 4 percent, the actual interest rate will total 6 percent.

Floating interest rates are not the only feature which make ARMs unique.

- Because interest levels can change, mortgage payments are adjustable. Depending on the program, payments can be adjusted monthly, every six months, annually, every three years, or every five years.

  Many borrowers believe that as payment intervals become longer, ARMs become more secure, but longer adjustment periods may not always produce better rates. For example, a loan with monthly adjustments pegged to the 11th District Cost of Funds may have far less movement than an ARM which uses Treasury securities as an index.

- ARMs have caps to limit monthly payments and lifetime caps that prohibit interest above a certain level.

- If an ARM has a monthly payment cap—say a rise of not more than 7.5 percent a year—but interest rates rise steeply, it's possible for some ARMs to have "negative amortization." For instance, if the monthly payment for a given year is capped at $750, but $800 a month is required to pay off the loan in 30 years, then $50 a month will be added to the loan balance. Lenders won't allow loan balances to grow forever, and they usually have the right to call the mortgage on 30 days' notice if the principal amount reaches 120 percent of the original loan.

If a borrower had 80 percent ARM financing, then 120 percent of the original loan equals almost the entire purchase price. Even if the owner could sell and settle on the property in 30 days, and even if he received the property's original purchase value (something not likely because of the need to sell quickly), by the time the note and closing costs were repaid, there would be little if anything left for the owner.

A piece of good news: Many ARMs prohibit negative amortization.

ARMs present special problems for both investors and lenders. From the lender's perspective, investor loans are already risky and ARMs simply increase the level of risk.

From the investor's viewpoint, unpredictable mortgage costs can play havoc with budgets and projections. Worse yet, while mortgage costs may rise, rentals may not keep pace—especially in areas with rent control. In addition, while fixed-rate loans have been a source of inflation protection for borrowers, ARMs shift that advantage to lenders.

Yet while not as predictable as fixed-rate loans, ARMs can be attractive to investors.

Suppose Williams is buying property in a market where interest levels for fixed-rate investor financing start at 7.5 percent plus 2 points. Williams certainly won't accept an ARM with similar rates, so he shops around and here's what he finds.

- Brown Mortgage offers an ARM with an initial rate of 4 percent plus 4 points.
- Smith Mortgage offers an ARM with an initial rate of 4.25 percent plus 3 points.
- Jones Mortgage offers an ARM with an initial rate of 4.5 percent plus 2 points.
- Green Mortgage offers an ARM with an initial rate of 4.75 percent plus 1 point.
- Blue Mortgage offers an ARM with an initial rate of 5 percent and no points.

The initial rates quoted by each lender are good for six months, after which rates float. If Williams borrows $100,000, here's what each deal costs in the first six months with interest calculated on a 30-year schedule.

- Brown Mortgage: $5,992.76
- Smith Mortgage: $5,117.65
- Jones Mortgage: $4,242.55
- Green Mortgage: $3,367.49
- Blue Mortgage: $2,492.45
- Standard deal at 7.5 percent with 2 points: $5,742.99

In the best case, Williams can save $3,250.54 ($5,742.99 less $2,492.45) in the first six months of ownership. With the first ARM, built-in costs are actually higher than fixed-rate investor loans over six months. Higher costs plus unpredictable rates make this loan a remarkably bad deal.

The Blue Mortgage deal makes sense for several reasons.

First, cash-poor investors can use the $3,250 they save in lender fees.

Second, one would expect that ARM interest levels would rise above the "teaser" rates used in the first six months. However, at least for the first year, it's unlikely that ARM rates will top fixed-rate financing. It's even possible that ARM rates could fall.

Third, with no points up front, if interest rates decline, an investor can switch to fixed-rate financing with little penalty.

Fourth, if Williams is only going to hold the property for a brief period, the ARM with no money down is a far better deal than the fixed-rate loan with high up-front costs.

Note that in our example, we're assuming that investor Williams will pay all points. The results will change dramatically if Williams negotiates well and gets the seller to pay one point, two points, or more.

Because ARMs are a good deal for lenders, investors can often get attractive terms. LTV financing of 80 percent and refinancing coverage are often available, and cashing out is possibe with some lenders. Prepayments without penalty are usually encouraged, as are qualified assumptions. Indeed, because interest flexibility is so good for lenders, investors have leverage in the marketplace and should be able to get better terms than fixed-rate lenders might accept.

As an alternative to a straight ARM, investors may want to consider convertible loans, mortgages which start out as ARMs and can then be converted to fixed-rate financing.

Convertible loans sound good in theory and there are situations when they can be attractive. If you buy property in a 10 percent market, ARMs might be available with start rates of 7 to 7.5 percent. This may be good not only in terms of interest costs, but also because buying when interest rates are high often allows purchasers to obtain lower prices and more concessions. Later, if market rates decline generally, you can convert to fixed-rate financing if you wish.

The question with convertible financing is this: Convert to what? Many convertible loans allow conversions for a small fee ($250 to $500), an expense that represents far fewer dollars than a new closing with its assorted insurance fees, legal bills, inspection costs and tax payments.

Conversion, however, may not be a good deal when rates and length of ownership are considered. Suppose a loan can be converted to fixed-rate status at a rate equal to a particular price plus five-eighths of 1 percent, or what lenders call 62.5 basis points. Now a loan in a 7 percent market costs 7.625 percent and for a 30-year, $100,000 loan that's a difference of $42.49 per month ($665.30 versus $707.79).

If you're going to own the property for a short time, it may be best simply to continue with adjustable payments because they may be lower than current fixed rates and also because there is no conversion fee to pay. If you're going to own the property for a few years, then a conversion may be justified. But if you expect to hold the property for the long term, then it may be cheaper to obtain a fixed-rate loan at the current market rate rather than pay a premium interest cost through conversion.

III

In The Arena

Unlike professional sports, real estate investing is not a spectator activity. To get the most out of it, you have to invest. No substitutes allowed.

For most people, investing will not be a large-scale activity. It's unlikely that an entry-level investor will start with a 100-unit apartment complex or a regional shopping mall. A more reasonable approach is to expect that starting and small investors will buy one property at a time, learn from the experience, and develop a real estate portfolio over a period of years.

Although a gradual, evolutionary approach to building real estate assets contradicts the "instant wealth" formulas which come into vogue every few years, it's the strategy that most nearly parallels the interests and financial resources of typical investors. It takes time, patience, and work—words which may not be dynamic, powerful, or exciting, but which nevertheless define the real-life experiences of most investors.

9
Building a Team

Much of history and literature is filled with stories of lonely underdogs who overcome great odds to succeed. David beat Goliath, Dorothy went back to Kansas, and Lindy crossed the ocean.

Real estate has its stories as well, many featuring individual entrepreneurs who fight the world for profit and advantage. And while going it alone sounds great, it's a mythic ideal, a fantasy that denies societal complexity and interdependence.

The reality is that few of us have *all* the skills needed to be successful investors. We're not simultaneously brokers, accountants, lawyers, contractors, engineers, plumbers, electricians, insurance agents, or financial counselors. The good news is that we don't need to be trained in every field.

Professional help is widely and readily available, but to have value, our team of advisers must be assembled *before* we begin making deals. Searching for an inspector, lawyer, accountant, or whoever once a deal begins is cumbersome and may force us to take the first available person rather than the best.

Lawyers play a crucial role in the purchase, sale, and leasing of real estate. It's not so much that attorneys find property, manage investments, or locate buyers, but rather that lawyers are crucial at several points in the investment process.

Real estate deals must be in writing and so-called standard real estate forms can be found in every locality. The problem is that most areas have several "standard" forms, some favoring buyers while others give an edge to sellers. As an investor, you want to be familiar with local forms *before entering the marketplace,* and you want to use that form which favors your interests and requires the least amount of revision. In effect, you want a standardized contract that's pro-investor.

Forms can be obtained from local brokers and lawyers, read at home, and then discussed in detail with an attorney, broker, or both. As you read through a standardized agreement, you can find numerous concessions hidden in small type and vague language. But even though these concessions are in print, they can be changed or modified.

For instance, a form might require purchasers to pay transfer taxes, perhaps thousands of dollars. There's no law that says the purchaser must pay transfer taxes, but let's say it's a local custom. Why should you, as an investor trying to make a profit, give up a large sum of money because of someone else's tradition? *The fact is that all elements within the real estate agreement are negotiable.* The document can be changed so that the seller pays the transfer tax or perhaps splits it 50/50.

Lawyers—trained in the art of legal writing—can perfect contract forms with "contingencies" or "addenda." These provisions—such as who pays the transfer tax or your rights to a structural inspection—must be carefully phrased to be worthwhile.

One contingency can actually involve lawyers. You might offer to buy property, but only with a legal review "satisfactory" to your attorney. If you don't like the deal, your attorney—being your agent—can be directed to find the contract "unsatisfactory." The same clause, if properly written, will assure the full return of your deposit if the deal is called off.

Attorneys are also important in the settlement process. Lawyers can conduct the closing, recommend title insurance, and provide legal advice. After closing, if you decide to rent, lawyers can help perfect lease agreements consistent with local regulations.

How do you find a lawyer?

As an investor, you want someone familiar with the nearby community, because real estate regulations are often a product of local interests. Look for attorneys who specialize in real estate matters, not patents, divorces, or malpractice claims. Get names by speaking to brokers, accountants, and other investors, and then call and ask each prospective lawyer about the services he or she offers, their experience, and their fees. Beware of lawyers too busy to handle your business or too expensive. Settlement attorneys are often a good choice.

No less important than a lawyer is a knowledgeable tax authority, someone who can tell you what the tax codes say and help you complete various forms and documents. Look for CPAs, tax attorneys, and enrolled agents to help with taxation issues.

If you intend to buy and fix up property, then the key person you need to know is a good contractor, a combination craftsman, handyman, and all-around mechanic who can help turn run-down properties into desirable gems.

For your protection, contractors must be licensed, bonded, and adequately insured.

A written agreement should govern relations between investor and contractor, something to be reviewed by an attorney before signing. Look for agreements with a variety of understandings.

- A clear payment schedule that shows when money is due according to how much work has been completed.
- The right to hold back payment for work not completed.
- Provisions that employees be covered by worker's compensation.
- Contractors who are bonded so you have leverage if promised work is not completed.
- A time-completion schedule that requires the contractor to do work at a given pace. Note that time-completion clauses are unbelievably difficult to enforce because they usually contain wording that allows contractors more time in the event of poor weather, supply problems, or labor difficulties—situations which are impossible to define.
- Binding arbitration to avoid elongated and costly court battles.
- A deal where contractors pass through material costs instead of charging on a cost-plus basis.
- A completion penalty clause to assure compensation if the work isn't finished on time. There's little possibility of getting this clause for small jobs.
- Wording which makes the contractor responsible for obtaining all licenses and permits needed for the job.

Contractors can be found by checking local papers, but individual recommendations are best. Ask brokers, attorneys, and other investors for their suggestions.

Once you have several names, have each contractor show you one or more current projects in progress. Ask to speak with several past customers. Key issues include pricing, timeliness, payment schedules (how much is due before the project begins, how much when it's partially finished), and the contractor's materials policy.

The use of contractors is not an all-or-nothing deal. If you want to fix up yourself but lack certain skills or equipment, get a professional for some of the work. Maybe you can paint, and the professional will add a deck or refinish the kitchen.

In addition, the contractor should know a variety of specialists such as plumbers, electricians, gutter specialists, roofers, and trash haulers.

At first the idea of needing a trash hauler may seem ridiculous. But if you're going to buy and fix up property, you or your contractor need to know where to send the garbage—not just a few bags every week but several tons at one time.

It might seem as though a property purchased "broom clean" would have few trash problems, but fixing up a home can yield an enormous volume of debris, especially when kitchens are remodeled, concrete is replaced, or decks are re-planked. The dump load can be reduced by burning wooden and paper leftovers in a fireplace (if there is one) and breaking up large items so the regular trash collectors will remove them. But trash crews often refuse to take appliances, furniture, or construction materials—the very stuff you're likely to toss out. That's when haulers become important.

Although people sometimes buy property sight unseen, it's a remarkably bad idea, something on the level of investing in swamp land. If you don't physically examine a structure before buying, you might discover anything from rotted wood to a leaky roof, or worse.

The trouble with looking at real estate is that the average person can't identify every defect or estimate repair costs. There are people who specialize in such work, experts known generally as "structural inspectors" who can tell what's broken, what's about to break, what may need to be fixed in the next several years, and what repair costs you should anticipate.

When looking for a structural inspector consider the type of report the inspector typically offers. Is it just a series of checklists, or is there also a written report detailing specific problems? Is the inspector available for telephone consultation once the property has been examined? How quickly can an inspection be arranged once the inspector is notified?

Property inspectors can have experience as builders, architects, engineers, contractors, or used-car salesmen. Inspectors are licensed in only two states as of this writing, so in most places anyone can hang out a shingle and proclaim great expertise. But you're likely to do best with inspectors who belong to the American Society of Home Inspectors (ASHI), a nationwide professional organization. Look in the phone book under "Building Inspection Services" for members of this group. Ask about prices, the type of report (simple checklist or something more substantial), the inspector's experience, and his or her availability on short notice.

It's often asked, why use a structural inspector at all when you already know a contractor? Contractors can be used to inspect property and estimate repair costs, but they have a built-in conflict. They're paid for the work they do, not for providing estimates. Inspectors receive the same fee whether or not you buy a property or take their advice, a payment scheme that gives inspectors independence.

Investors should make a point of going along with inspectors during the examination process. You're paying for expert advice, so ask questions. Also, the inspection process is a good time to obtain detailed property photographs. If you decide to buy, you'll then have a record showing the property's condition at the time of sale. If the screen door was in one piece when you bought the place and by settlement the screening is torn, pictures will demonstrate that it's the seller's responsibility to make a repair or provide compensation. Without pictures there's only an irresolvable debate.

Satisfactory inspections, like legal reviews, can also be used as a contingency. A deal might depend on a structural inspection satisfactory to you. If you don't like the deal, the inspection can be declared "unsatisfactory."

It's not uncommon for investors to buy a variety of new applicances when upgrading property, relatively large items that, one would think, stores would be happy to sell. But somehow, finding a reliable and reasonable appliance dealer is often ridiculously hard.

You may find stores that sell electric clothes dryers or stoves, but cords are extra. How you can possibly use such appliances without a cord is difficult to understand. Next, perhaps, some marketing genius will want to sell stoves without burners or clothes dryers without doors. If the trend keeps up, we won't buy finished appliances, we'll buy kits.

Delivery practices are even more irritating.

"When can you deliver my washer and dryer, Mr. Cutler?" you might ask.

"We can schedule you for Wednesday."

"Wednesday is a 24-hour period. *When* on Wednesday can you deliver?"

"We might be able to get it there by noon. It depends on the driver."

"You're selling me $600 items. If I'm forced take a day off work to wait in a vacant house, this stuff will suddenly cost a lot more money. Can you at least assure me that my goods will be your first delivery that day?"

"We can't promise, but we'll certainly try."

"Tell me, does the word 'yes' ever leave your lips?"

"No."

If you can nail down a delivery time, you must then negotiate the exact terms of installation.

"Mr. Cutler, now that we've agreed on a delivery schedule, can you put the washer and dryer in the basement, hook them up, remove the old appliances, and take away the large cardboard and wooden cases used to hold my new appliances?"

"Our usual delivery practice," responds Cutler, "is to deliver from our door to your door. Now, if you want the washer and dryer taken inside, there's an extra cost of $10 per item. If you want them taken down a flight of stairs, that's another $25 per unit. Hooking up will cost $35 for the washer and $50 for the dryer, unless of course you don't already have a vent installed, in which case we need another $50. We don't remove old appliances, and we don't take back cartons."

"Mr. Cutler, would you mind if I ask a question?"

"Certainly not."

"What did you do before you started selling appliances?"

"I was an arms negotiator for the State Department. It was perfect training for a much tougher profession."

Rather than deal with crazed appliance salesmen, voodoo delivery schedules, or rip-off marketing ploys, it's cheaper and easier to find a local appliance dealer who has his own trucks and includes delivery, installation, and trash removal in his price. Although the unit prices from such dealers may seem higher than discount outfits or large department stores, the savings in time, hassle, and agitation may be more than worthwhile. Also, since higher prices may include a host of services and benefits optional elsewhere, the deal with apparently steeper cost may actually be a bargain.

Insurance is needed throughout the investing process, and therefore a good insurance broker is a valued resource.

You don't need an insurance broker to obtain title insurance (the party conducting settlement will supply it or sell it) or private mortgage insurance (that is provided by lenders who do *not* earn a commission for the placement of such coverage). But you need fire, theft, and liability insurance when you purchase property, and if you fix up and refinance, you'll need additional coverage because the property's value will increase.

As a business client, you may find that some insurance agencies will permit you to purchase insurance on credit. That is, they will establish your policy today and bill you tomorrow. This may appear to be very convenient, but a more prudent business idea is to pay in full for insurance by check at the time a policy is first issued. That way, if a question ever arises as to whether or not coverage was actually in place, you have a canceled check to support your claim.

In addition to fire, theft, and liability coverage, investors may also want to get a liability rider. If the fire, theft, and liability coverage goes to, say, $300,000, for a few dollars more you can have liability coverage increased to $1 million or higher. In a litigious society, this is a good idea.

Our litigious society also produces great disputes involving land boundaries. It frequently happens that lot lines are unclear or that outbuildings such as garages are sometimes built over property boundaries. Given these problems, it becomes extremely important to know where property lines are actually located, information that can be obtained from a surveyor.

Surveyors are also needed if you want to subdivide or if you have raw land on which you intend to build. They can assure that you don't build in areas restricted by set-back zones or across seemingly ambiguous lot lines.

Surveyors can be found in the phone book, but the best recommendations are available from settlement providers, builders, and brokers.

Although not strictly members of "your" team, investors should develop a simple contact list at local utilities—the right numbers to call for meter reading and billing purposes. If you rent property, numbers at the gas, electric, and water companies can be passed on to tenants so they can establish accounts.

A final resource is a plain home computer with word processing, spreadsheet, and database programs—tools investors can use to store contract clauses, analyze property, or track sales. For the best bargains, check newspaper classified sections for used machines with complete software packages.

10

Brokers, Agents, and Multiple Listing Systems

Whether you are buying property, selling, or just eyeballing the marketplace, one group of people you are certain to meet are realty brokers, as well as their salespeople and associate brokers.

Brokers play an important role in the real estate marketing process because they are sources of information, negotiators, and marketers. Brokers can be allies or foes, but in either case they must operate within a basic set of principles.

1. Brokers outrank salespeople. There are two types of real estate licenses: those for brokers and those for salespeople, individuals commonly known as "agents." A broker can act independently, assist buyers and sellers directly, and collect a fee for his or her work. Salespeople, in contrast, can operate only under a broker's supervision.

Importance. Brokers call the shots in real estate. Agents listen. Seen another way, brokers are responsible for the agents they supervise.

2. Brokers are agents. In the usual situation, brokers do not sell or buy real estate for their own account, they assist others. When a broker assists a property owner, the seller is a principal or client and the buyer is a customer. If a broker represents a purchaser, then the buyer is the client.

Importance. When a broker acts as an agent, he or she has a "fiduciary" obligation to a client, a big word which basically means that a broker must act as a trustee and place the client's interests first.

What is expected from a broker? As a trustee of the client's best interests, brokers and their agents have four central obligations.

- To use care when handling the client's affairs.
- To follow lawful directions.
- To account for money and papers. For example, as the seller's agent, a broker will typically hold deposit money in an "escrow" or trust account. This money is separate from the broker's funds and cannot be released without permission from both the buyer and seller.
- To act loyally.

Who Are these People?

In real estate it is entirely possible to find a single individual who is an agent, broker, Realtor, and Realtist—all at the same time. Here is a quick guide to real estate players.

Agent. A salesperson who works under the authority of a broker; a broker who works for a client or principal.

Broker. An individual licensed to represent someone else for a fee in the purchase, sale, exchange, management, and leasing of real estate.

Buyer Broker or Buyer Agent. A broker who represents a purchaser.

Client (or principal). Someone, such as a property owner, who hires a broker.

Customer. Someone, such as a buyer, who is not a client.

Listing Broker. A broker who obtains a listing contract from a homeowner.

Realtist. A member of the National Association of Real Estate Brokers, an organization concerned with general housing matters as well as the specific interests of minority brokers and agents.

Realtor. A registered collective membership mark which may be used only by members of the National Association of Realtors.

Selling Broker. A broker who finds a buyer.

Subagent. A broker who gains the right to show a property by operating under the authority of another broker's listing agreement.

Being an agent is complicated by an unpleasant fact. It is possible to become an agent with a written agreement, and it is also possible to become an agent with words and deeds.

Imagine if broker Thompson lists the Reynolds house, but tells buyer Tate, "Look, don't worry about a thing. Reynolds wants $150,000 but I think you should offer $140,000. Trust me, I can help you get a better deal."

In this situation Thompson is an agent for both Reynolds and Tate. He is also in deep trouble.

As an agent, Thompson has an obligation to get the best possible deal for his client, but in this scenario who is his client? He represents the seller, to be sure, but he is helping the buyer by suggesting a lower purchase price. Without prior disclosure or written approval from both the buyer and the seller, Thompson is an undisclosed dual agent who can face lawsuits by Tate, Reynolds, or both.

Is it possible to be a dual agent and not have problems? In a small number of situations brokers can act as disclosed dual agents. For example, if a broker arranges an exchange of properties and has written permission in advance to work for both parties, then a dual agency can be acceptable.

There are often agents and subagents in real estate. Many real estate transactions involve not one broker, but two.

To understand how this works imagine a movie or play where most actors have one role, but some play two parts.

- If broker Mason lists the Webster home, Mason is Webster's agent. Mason is also the listing broker.
- If broker McDonald knows a buyer and wants to show the Webster home, he can work with Mason. MacDonald is the selling broker. He is also a subagent.

What's a subagent? Mason has a contract to sell the Webster property so there is a direct connection between Mason and Webster. MacDonald may never have met Webster; his authority to sell the property comes from whatever listing Mason has with the owner.

Importance. Because of subagency, a newly formed real estate company can join a local multiple listing service (MLS) and immediately have the right to sell properties listed by competing brokers. In comparison, you don't see Sears and Kmart trying to sell each other's inventory.

3. All deals are unique. In a free and open market a property's selling price is determined at one point in time under specific conditions through the agreement of an informed buyer and a knowledgeable seller. At any other point in time, with other conditions, or with different buyers and sellers, the selling price can be different.

Importance. Since all deals are unique, and since all properties are different, there is no way to prove that broker Jones can sell a property faster or for a better price than broker Smith. There is also no way to establish that one particular selling concept is better than another.

4. All deals must be on paper. It is entirely possible to have an oral real estate contract, a deal from the Old West where Slim says to Luke, "I'll sell the back 40 for $200."

But what if Slim and Luke later forget their exact agreement? Was it the back 40 east of the river, or west? Was that $200 in cash, or will Slim need a loan? Rather than argue and debate, real estate deals must be in writing to be enforceable.

Importance. First, because real estate agreements are written, only commitments made in writing count. Oral promises should be regarded as worthless.

Second, since brokers routinely supply form documents used in realty transactions, the fine print contained in such forms can create concessions or advantages worth thousands of dollars, depending on how the forms are written.

Third, because real estate agreements are contracts, precise wording is required, a job often reserved for attorneys.

5. Because of their police powers, states have the right to regulate real estate brokerage. Brokers and agents in all states are licensed, since regulation is believed to protect the public interest.

Importance. With licensure requirements, states can establish educational standards for brokers and agents, create operating rules and standards, and punish brokers and agents who abuse the public and other professionals. Also, states can insist that brokers are either bonded or compelled to contribute to a recovery fund so that consumers can be compensated if a broker acts illegally.

6. All fees and commissions are negotiable. There is no rule, anywhere, requiring that brokers charge a particular fee for their services.

Importance. There are no standard, usual, regular, or normal fees. If one broker will not negotiate fees, buyers and sellers have a right to go elsewhere. Conversely, brokers may not be restrained from offering their services at any price they elect to charge.

7. Broker interests must be disclosed. A broker cannot buy, sell, appraise, or rent property for himself or his immediate family without full written disclosure.

Importance. Brokers and agents are believed to have a marketplace advantage by virtue of their training, experience, and education. Stating that someone has a license gives notice to everyone else in a transaction that they are dealing with a professional. In the case of appraisals, a broker or agent cannot appraise a property in which they have a current or potential interest, or where a fee is based on results.

8. Discrimination is illegal. Federal and state laws make discrimination illegal, and create substantial penalties for those who discriminate. Beginning with the Civil Rights Act of 1866, federal, state, and local laws have prohibited many forms of housing bias, including discrimination based on race, religion, national origin, gender, familial status, disability, and age.

Importance. The greatest possible access to the housing market suggests the greatest number of deals, something everyone should welcome.

9. You need a license to collect. There is no rule that prevents individuals from buying or selling without a broker, but there are laws that prohibit individuals from acting as brokers. To prevent unlicensed individuals from competing, fees for brokerage services are simply uncollectable without a license. In other words, if Gentler helps Woods sell his home and then asks for a fee, the owner owes nothing if Gentler is unlicensed.

Importance. There is money to be made in brokerage, but being "in brokerage" requires a license.

LISTING AGREEMENTS

To make money when selling homes, a broker must act as an agent for a principal. To show that he or she works for a principal—and to collect a fee—a broker needs a special piece of paper called a "listing" agreement.

A listing is nothing more than an employment contract that defines the broker's job. It shows that the broker is an agent, that the broker has certain rights, and that when the broker meets the precise requirements outlined in the listing agreement, he is entitled to full payment for his services.

In the usual case, sellers hire residential brokers to find a buyer "ready, willing, and able" to purchase property at a particular price and terms. If the Conklin house is listed at $185,000, and broker Eldridge finds a buyer who makes an offer for $185,000 and has the financial capacity to purchase the property, then Eldridge has done his job.

The "usual" case, however, is rarely so simple. Suppose buyer Gittens offers $185,000 but as part of his offer demands that Conklin repaint the living room. Unless Conklin offered to repaint the living room in the listing agreement, Gittens' offer does not meet the precise terms of his contract with the broker.

Or, Gittens can offer $184,999. It's surely a good offer but it doesn't meet the listing agreement's exact terms. To deal with alternative offers, listing agreements are typically written so that a commission is due once an owner accepts any price and terms, even if they vary from the original listing contract.

What happens if Gittens offers Conklin $185,000, meets all the conditions of the listing agreement, has money to buy the property, and then owner Conklin decides not to sell? In this scenario broker Eldridge found a buyer ready, willing, and able to purchase the property, fulfilled his employment contract, and is owed a commission.

What happens if the buyer changes his mind and decides not to go through with the deal? Sale agreements normally say that if a buyer won't finish a deal, then the deposit will be lost. The seller and broker divide the deposit equally up to the value of the broker's commission; everything above the broker's fee goes to the owner.

Around the country various listing forms are specially designed to meet state and local requirements. Such forms typically show a property's street address (1401 Norton Street) as well as the legal address (Lot 2, Block 6, Ford Subdivision). They must have a starting date, a termination date, a commission arrangement, and a specific offering price.

In addition, well-written listing agreements are likely to contain a number of other important clauses.

Advertising. A broker will want the right to advertise the property, including the right to place a sign on the front lawn.

Commission. How much is the broker to be paid? Residential brokers are commonly paid a percentage of the sale price, but it is also possible to be paid by the project or on an hourly rate.

Deposit. When making an offer, buyers normally put down a cash deposit to demonstrate their intent to go through with the deal. A listing contract can show the minimum amount that a seller will accept as evidence of good faith.

Description. What is being sold in terms of bedrooms, baths, parking, kitchens, and other features? A full description defines the property and provides valuable sales information. Listing contracts are often printed on a single sheet of paper along with a lengthy checklist of features.

Financing. Is the seller willing to provide (take back) financing for a would-be buyer? If so, how much and under what terms? Take-back clauses depend—or should depend—on the seller's satisfaction with the buyer's credit.

Fixtures. What is being offered with the property? The stove, furnace, or central air-conditioning system? Sure. But what about the washer and dryer? They can be moved, so are they included in the sale or not? If offered in the listing agreement, the broker can include the washer and dryer as well as other items when describing what is for sale.

Lock Box. Lock boxes are devices that hold house keys and can be attached to doors. Brokers have a common key that opens such boxes and thus gives them access to a property. A lock box clause generally gives brokers permission to use a lock box and limits their liability if lock box keys are used to enter a home illegally.

Nondiscrimination. The property will be made available to any interested buyer, regardless of race, creed, national origin, religion, or other factors irrelevant to a real estate sale.

Ownership. A listing will show whether the property offered for sale is a condominium, a cooperative, or fee-simple real estate. The form of ownership is important because different types of ownership represent more rights than others and are therefore considered more desirable.

Points. A listing form may ask how many "points" a seller is willing to pay. One point is equal to 1 percent of the mortgage, say $1,000 with a $100,000 loan. Points are paid to lenders at closing to hold down interest costs for borrowers, so homeowners are usually loath to pay such fees.

The issue of seller-paid points is complicated by the fact that if you pay points to sell a private residence they are generally deductible as a sales expense. The result is less profit and therefore less income to tax. But, since the tax on profits from the sale of residential real estate can often be sheltered by the rollover-replacement rule and the one-time, over-55 write-off, there may be no tax to pay anyway.

With investment property, seller-paid points are generally deductible as a sales expense. Since the over-55 deduction and the rollover rule do not apply to investment property, money paid for points might otherwise be taxable.

While writing off points is good news, the tax rate is always less than 100 percent. This means that while a tax deduction may reduce the effective cost of points, points still represent a sale-price reduction.

For the latest information regarding points be sure to speak with a tax professional.

Protection Period. Listing forms routinely contain a clause saying that if someone saw the property during the listing period but buys within a certain time after the listing ends—say 45 days—then the listing broker is entitled to a fee. If the property is listed with another broker, then the protection period should end automatically.

Special Conditions. A listing can contain amendments to meet the precise needs of both investors and brokers. There might be an instruction not to show the property on Saturdays or to beware of the dog. Or settlement may be contingent on the seller's ability to buy and close on a new home. Another common condition is to sell something in "as is" condition, perhaps because the outdoor light on the front lawn doesn't work. There is no limit to the number of special conditions that can be included in a listing agreement.

EXCLUSIVE VERSUS NON-EXCLUSIVE

From the broker's standpoint, the most important feature of a listing agreement is the rights received from a seller. How much authority has the broker obtained? Will he be the only broker selling the home, or will competing brokers be involved?

Open. With an "open" or "general" listing a broker has the authority to sell a property but little else. An owner can sell by himself and not pay a brokerage fee, or an owner can hire 20 brokers simultaneously with open listings.

Suppose owner Grenoble doesn't want to list exclusively with any particular broker, but broker Lane says he has a buyer.

In this situation Grenoble can agree to an open listing with Lane. If Lane's customer buys the property, Lane can collect a fee. If Lane's buyer doesn't like the property, Grenoble will keep selling.

With open listings it is important to assure that such contracts not only have a termination date, but also that they end automatically if the property is either sold or listed exclusively with a broker.

Exclusive Agency Agreement. Rather than an open listing, brokers greatly prefer "exclusive agency" arrangements. The attraction of an exclusive agency deal (at least for brokers) is that during the listing period the seller agrees to work with only one broker.

With an exclusive agency agreement the owner still has the right to sell directly and without paying a fee, but this right can create conflicts. If broker Fuentes has an exclusive agency agreement to sell the Nash home and Nash finds a buyer, can we be certain that Nash found the buyer directly? Is it possible that Fuentes' signs and advertisements alerted the buyer to the property?

If Fuentes' marketing "introduced" the buyer to the property, did it set off an unbroken chain of events that led to the sale? If there was an unbroken chain, was Fuentes the procuring cause of sale and therefore entitled to a commission even though the buyer dealt only with the Nash the owner?

Exclusive agency agreements are more attractive to brokers than open listing contracts because they at least allow the broker to have a competitive advantage. Still, exclusive agency agreements leave an area of ambiguity. With exclusive agency contracts it is possible for a broker to spend time, talent, and money marketing a property only to find that the seller has legitimately made a direct sale and that no commission is due.

Exclusive Right to Sell Agreements. For brokers the best possible arrangement is the exclusive right to sell agreement. The beauty of exclusive right to sell contracts is that many issues disappear with this arrangement. Simply stated, if a property is sold during the listing period—whether by the broker, the owner, the owner's brother, or another broker—the broker who lists is the broker who collects.

Net Listings. Banned in many states, net listings allow a broker to be paid the difference between a benchmark price and a sales price. For example, a seller might want $100,000 for a property and agree to pay a broker anything above that amount. If the property is actually worth $150,000 then the broker will receive a $50,000 selling fee. Since sellers rely on brokers for pricing and marketing advice, net listings allow brokers to take advantage of ignorant sellers, not a good arrangement in a system where client interests are supposed to come first.

Oral Listings. In theory it may be possible to create an oral listing, a situation where a seller says sell and then pays a fee if the broker succeeds. If, somewhere, brokers are allowed to take oral listings, the inherent problem with such arrangements is that they are unenforceable.

If a listing is oral, then what is the listing price? What is the rate of commission? When did the contract begin and when does it end? Both seller and broker may agree, but if they don't, then how can a broker collect? If the broker says the list price was $100,000 but the seller says, no, it was $125,000, who is right?

BUYER LISTINGS

The listing forms above all secure a broker's right to sell property. But brokers can act also as agents for purchasers, an arrangement known generally as buyer brokerage, buyer's brokerage, or buyer agency.

With a buyer agency agreement, a purchaser will outline basic interests such as price, location (say, a particular subdivision or street), size, condition, and specific financial terms (Smith will buy only if a seller pays all closing costs). As with property listings, a buyer-brokerage agreement must have a beginning date and a termination date, and it must show the broker's fee.

Buyer-agency listings parallel traditional seller contracts.

Open. Both the broker and the buyer look for a property. If the broker finds one and the buyer purchases it, a commission is due. If the buyer finds a property independently, no fee is earned. The buyer can have open buyer-brokerage agreements with as many brokers as he or she wants.

Exclusive Agency. With this form of listing the purchaser agrees to work with only one broker during the listing period. The buyer cannot hire another broker during the listing period (unless he wants to pay two brokerage fees), but he still has the right to look independently. If a property is found without the broker's help, no fee is due.

Exclusive Right to Buy. In this case the listing will provide that if a purchaser buys within the listing period then a fee will be due, whether the property is located by the purchaser or the broker.

Net Listing. Net listings between brokers and clients are commonly banned.

Oral Listings. It may be possible to create an oral buyer-agency agreement, but why bother? All the problems that make oral listings unattractive for brokers and sellers apply to brokers and purchasers. Oral listings, as the expression goes, are worth the paper they're written on.

Consulting. While brokers traditionally list homes, buyer brokers are less wedded to a given piece of property and thus the need for compensation based on performance.

It can make sense to retain buyer brokers as consultants paid by the hour. A model deal might work like this:

Investor Harper hires broker Winslow to provide negotiating advice and pricing information. Winslow works six hours and is paid $100 per hour. From Harper's perspective, $600 may be a minor expense in the context of a property purchase. From the broker's point of view, the $600 is earned, due, and payable whether Harper buys or does not buy.

MULTIPLE LISTING SYSTEMS (MLS)

One of the most important selling tools in real estate is nothing more than an organized collection of information known as a multiple listing system (MLS). Showing past sales and current listings, such networks allow brokers to price property, determine market trends, and locate suitable properties for would-be buyers.

An MLS can also be something more than a database. Some MLS networks, but not all, create an instant and immediate subagency option when a property is entered into the system.

Suppose broker Klein lists the Roswell property. Klein enters his listing into the local MLS and by doing so he automatically makes a "blanket offer of subagency." With a blanket offer of subagency, any broker who is a system member now has the right to show the Roswell property.

Klein made an "offer" of subagency, so other member brokers may accept or reject the offer. In the usual case there is no reason for member brokers to reject the offer unless they represent buyers.

Subagency has been common for many years, but more and more MLS systems are dropping subagency for separate agency—one broker to serve a buyer and one broker to serve a seller. Separate representation ends the many liabilities associated with subagency and gives both buyers and sellers the individual representation they need and deserve.

Although an MLS may seem fairly simple and straightforward, the agency/subagency system has an enormous impact on the real estate marketplace.

The ability to convey property information quickly to large numbers of brokers clearly benefits homeowners. But an MLS system also does something else; it rewards member brokers with important competitive advantages.

For the cost of an MLS membership, perhaps $500, a broker can gain immediate access to all listed properties, a billion-dollar inventory in many systems. This means that to be successful in real estate, a fledgling broker doesn't need vast amounts of startup capital. Combine a small office with MLS membership, and a new broker—or any broker—can have immediate access to most local properties at the smallest possible cost. Compare startup costs in real estate with virtually any other business and it's easy to see why every community has large numbers of brokerage firms.

MLS networks are also important because they are used not only to market real estate, but also to market real estate services. Individual property owners cannot belong, and in many states only brokers affiliated with particular professional groups may join. An MLS is exclusive, and whatever the values of exclusivity, if homeowners want to use an MLS they need to hire a broker.

Before a property can be entered into an MLS it must first be listed, but not any arrangement is acceptable. Most MLS networks *traditionally* use only exclusive-right-to-sell contracts. The result is that when many or most local listings are entered into an MLS, member brokers have a stronger marketplace position than non-members, non-brokers, and owners.

MLS networks have changed in recent years, however. In a growing number of systems, all brokers may join rather than just those affiliated with select professional groups.

Another important change concerns listing arrangements. Rather than an exclusive-right-to-sell agreement or nothing, many systems now accept exclusive-agency agreements. With such contracts investors can list property with a broker, have the property entered into an MLS, but still retain the right to sell it independently and without a fee.

A third important change is the movement to combine MLS systems to form regional and superregional services. The advantage of such enlarged services is simply more choice—more listings, more areas, more possibilities.

For brokers, however, the switch to regional and superregional MLS services means significant savings and efficiencies. By belonging to a single large MLS rather than ten smaller ones, brokers can substantially reduce marketing costs.

Small MLS systems are generally owned by local real estate organizations. The merger of many small MLS systems into larger services means that not only will the smaller MLS systems disappear, their sponsoring groups will also merge. The result is that we are likely to see fewer, but larger, MLS services and brokerage organizations in the coming decade.

A fourth important MLS change concerns the growing trend away from automatic agency/subagency relationships. Instead, many MLS systems are now equally open to seller representatives and buyer representatives. Such MLS systems are evolving into marketing mechanisms and information exchanges as opposed to sources of agency for selling brokers.

FEE SPLITTING

In a large number of realty transactions it takes more than one broker to sell a home. Since brokerage is not a charitable cause, there must be a glue of sorts to hold a deal together when several brokers are involved. There is a such cement, a basic process called fee splitting.

Suppose the Reeves house is listed and sold for $200,000. Suppose there is a 6 percent commission. Here is how the fee might be divided, depending on how the property is marketed.

- The property is listed and sold by broker Daniels. Daniels receives $12,000.
- The property is listed by agent Cook, who works for broker Daniels. Cook finds a buyer. At closing broker Daniels receives $12,000 and gives part of the fee to agent Cook.
- The property is listed by agent Cook and sold by agent Hart. Agent Hart works for broker Connors. At closing, the commission is split between brokers Daniels and Connors. Broker Daniels then splits with agent Cook, and broker Connors divides the commission with agent Hart.
- Agent Knebel refers buyer Grimsley to agent Cook. Cook sells the property. At closing, broker Daniels receives the commission and gives a portion to agent Cook and a small portion to broker Hartman, the broker for whom agent Knebel works. Broker Hartman splits the referral fee with agent Knebel.

In all cases fees are paid only to brokers. Brokers then split with agents according to such arrangements as they may have in place.

In a situation involving a buyer broker the arrangement is different.

Most buyer-brokerage transactions today are financed this way: Broker Daniels lists the Reeves house for $200,000. Broker Dennis, acting as a buyer's broker, makes an offer on the property which is accepted.

Part of the purchase offer stipulates that if the deal is accepted, then Dennis is to receive the commission amount that would otherwise be paid to a cooperating broker—half the $12,000, fee in this case.

The prevailing method of financing buyer-brokerage fees is both practical and commonplace. It is also flawed, because as the property value rises, so does the fee paid to both the listing broker and the selling broker. In the case of the listing broker, a bigger fee is acceptable because a larger commission is a byproduct of a higher price, precisely what the seller wants.

For buyers, however, higher prices are not a goal. In addition, the listing agreement between the seller and the listing broker is a private matter. Perhaps the property was listed at a discount, say a fee of $500 because the owner is a friend of broker Daniels. A buyer broker who receives half the commission in such a situation may well be surprised.

Rather than fool with overt conflicts of interest (no matter how minor), or with the contractual relationship between sellers and their brokers (no matter how private), a better approach works like this:

Broker Dennis, a buyer broker, submits an offer to purchase the Reeves house. The offer is for a given price and includes a variety of terms and conditions. One condition is that at closing seller Reeves will give a credit to the buyer equal to 3 percent of the purchase price.

If seller Reeves accepts the deal brought in by broker Dennis, then Reeves will have to work out a payment for the listing broker, because the deal will otherwise be too heavy with brokerage fees. Whatever Reeves and his broker work out is a matter between them, something that should have been considered in advance in case a buyer broker entered the picture.

As to the purchaser, he or she is getting a credit at closing, money that can be used to pay a buyer broker, settlement charges, or whatever. If the credit is more than the buyer brokerage fee, then the difference goes to the purchaser.

BEING A CUSTOMER

We have seen how brokers can be retained whether we are buying or selling property. In many cases, however, brokers will be in the deal representing someone else, a position that makes you a "customer" and not a "client."

Given a choice, many investors would prefer to deal directly with a buyer or seller, the theory being that a broker represents an additional cost in the transaction. However, if a broker is involved, investor preferences are no longer an issue. The broker is there and must be addressed.

Can you work with a broker who represents someone else? It's done every day, usually within the context of certain guidelines.

First, understand the broker's obligations. *If you're not paying the broker, assume the broker doesn't work for you.* Once the broker's position is clearly understood, the broker's ideas, comments, and interests can be seen in context.

Second, tell the broker—out loud and in clear language—that you know how the system works and that you understand the broker's obligation to represent the other party.

Third, use those services a broker can ethically provide while representing an owner.

- A broker can introduce you to a variety of prospective properties, detailing their list prices and terms, individual features, zoning, legal description (lot, block, subdivision, square, etc.), and property taxes. If available, the broker can also provide blueprints and a survey.
- If the property is leased, the broker can explain lease terms and options (such as the right to renew), rent schedules, specific areas under lease, plus service and expense provisions—that is, who pays utilities, who pays under the lease if taxes rise (the owner or tenant), etc. Income and expense statements can also be made available. *Note: Lease terms must be honored by a new owner.*
- The broker can provide information concerning any service agreements or warranties that will be in effect after the sale.
- If you're looking at a larger property, the broker can supply a site plan, the latest appraisal report (if available), a list of authorized occupants, a parking diagram, and building plans including information about the electrical, plumbing, heating, ventilation, and air-conditioning systems.
- The broker can describe existing financing, whether or not it's assumable, and the seller's willingness to take back a loan.
- A broker can supply general marketing information when asked. For example, recent sale prices are a matter of public record that can provide some perspective regarding values and demand.
- A broker can transmit written offers to an owner. Be aware, however, that offers are typically made on standardized forms that may require

modification. *Do not confuse the act of "transmitting" an offer with the assumption that a broker is "negotiating" on your behalf.*

- A broker can suggest financing sources, rates, and terms, except when sellers offer to take back loans. With seller take-backs, the broker must try to get the best rates and terms for the owner.
- A broker must respond to investor questions fully and fairly. Material information *known to the broker* which might affect the property's use or value cannot be hidden.
- Be aware that there are certain actions brokers cannot take when representing owners. A broker can suggest no purchase price other than the figure established by the seller, nor can a broker offer specific terms such as the right to occupy the property before closing without the owner's permission.

DUAL AGENCY AND NO AGENCY

Agency relationships are enormously important, as we have seen, and the penalties for a botched agency relationship can be substantial. To reduce their liability, brokers have begun to rethink the agency issue, concluding that in some cases that traditional representation is not attractive.

One alternative is to engage in a *disclosed* dual agency. In this situation the broker effectively tells both buyer and seller, "Look, I will help both of you." The attraction of a disclosed dual agency is that a broker can collect a fee from the seller, the buyer, or both, while limiting liability.

The problem with a disclosed dual agency is that it does not make a lot of sense. If you're an investor and you hire a broker, do you want that person to do anything less than obtain the best possible deal on your behalf? If the broker is getting you the best deal, how can he or she also get the best possible deal representing someone else at the same time and in the same transaction?

Rather than dual agency, some brokers have experimented with *facilitation*, a situation in which a broker represents no one but tries to bring buyer and seller together. Facilitation sounds like a good idea, at least until buyers and sellers realize that the broker is a glorified referee who cannot fight for the best interests of either party.

DISCLOSURE

In a world filled with brokers, agents, dual agents, facilitators, seller representatives, and buyer brokers, it follows that most of the public, most of the time, will be thoroughly confused. To clarify who represents, or does-n't represent, whom, brokers in more than 40 states are now required to disclose their roles.

In most cases, a broker must provide written disclosure at the first sub-stantial meeting with a customer and explain who is being represented and who is not. Disclosure should serve as a big red flag alerting people to the broker's role and obligations, but unfortunately, state disclosure rules vary. For instance, while some states have produced standard disclosure forms that all brokers must use, others states allow brokers to devise their own disclosure forms, forms which may not be equally helpful or revealing.

SHOULD YOU BE A BROKER OR AGENT?

There are probably 2 million licensed real estate brokers and agents across the country out of a total population of perhaps 250 million people. Subtract about 70 million children not yet 18, and in round figures we have one broker or agent for every 90 adults.

Brokers and agents are everywhere, and everybody either knows one or is one. Obviously then, exclusivity is not the reason one gets a real estate license. There must be other attractions.

Brokerage can certainly be remunerative. Sell property worth $1 million in an area with 6 percent commissions, and, bingo, we're talking about $60,000 in fees.

And there's a lot of real estate to sell. Figure about 3.5 million houses a year with typical prices of $110,000 each and you have a gross residential market of $385 billion. With a 6 percent commission, fees worth as much as $23.1 billion will be paid. However, since brokers do not sell all proper-ties, the actual amount of residential commissions will be somewhat less. In addition to residential sales, there are also opportunities for commer-cial, industrial, and farm sales plus more money to be made in leasing, management, and appraising.

By any standard real estate is a big business. It's also a business with few barriers to entry. You don't need an academic degree or seven years as an apprentice. In many states it's possible to obtain an agent's license with 45 to 120 classroom hours of training, less than a single college semester.

Yet as alluring as the numbers may appear, the fact is that few people do well selling real estate. If there are 3.5 million sales and 2 million licensees, then each licensee only sells an average of 1.75 houses. If each house is worth $110,000, fees will total only about $13,200, assuming a 6 percent commission. Subtract licensure fees, auto costs, and other expenses, and suddenly real estate is a tough way to earn a living.

Although 1.75 typical sales will produce fees worth $13,200, it's unlikely that one person will get that amount. Many real estate sales are cooperative ventures where two brokers divide a commission and they, in turn, usually divide their portion with agents who work under their authority. It's perfectly possible that our 1.75 sales will produce commissions to a single individual of just $3,300. (Dividing $13,200 by two brokers means each gets $6,600. If each broker splits with an agent, the commission might be divided in half again and each party will now receive just $3,300.)

The reality is that most licensees do not sell 1.75 houses a year. Many agents sell none. At the other end of the spectrum, some agents and brokers sell dozens of properties annually. Other successful agents have a different approach; they sell just a few properties, but each is worth $500,000 or more. In commercial real estate, it often happens that a broker sells only one property a year, but a single sale may involve real estate worth millions of dollars.

So should investors get a license?

A real estate license should be considered a valued certificate for a variety of reasons.

- There's an opportunity to earn fees and commissions.
- As a licensee you'll learn how the marketing system works from the broker's perspective. Many firms offer extensive training courses that provide important information for investors.
- You'll learn much about local values and trends.
- You can be a part-time agent, and use your license on an occasional basis.
- As a licensee you may receive a commission when you buy or sell property for your own account, in effect earning a discount when you buy and extra profit when you sell.
- As a licensee you'll have an inside track on good loan deals.
- You'll meet other investors, and you'll also meet real estate lawyers, accountants, and other local experts.
- As an agent, you may have a first shot when good deals become available.

But what about problems? Surely brokerage must have some negatives.

The negatives associated with real estate licensure are minimal. It takes time and effort to earn a license, and you'll be required to take continuing education classes in most states to keep your license. Such time and effort, however, can also boost your skills as an investor.

If you're licensed and buy or sell property, most jurisdictions will require that you state in writing that you're a broker or agent when you make an offer. Some buyers and sellers will be more cautious in dealing with you because of your status as a licensee.

If you're interested in VA foreclosures, the Veterans Administration may consider you an "affiliate" and give preference to non-licensees on many foreclosed properties.

If you don't want a license, consider a halfway measure: Take a license preparation course. After the course you can then decide if you want a license or not, but at least you'll have a basic idea of what agents are taught, what brokers do, and an overview of state rules and regulations concerning real estate. Such classes are usually inexpensive, sometimes free, and commonly offered at night and on weekends.

11
How to Find the Right Property

There's a point in every deal when ideas and paper must relate to ground, bricks, and mortar. The greatest financing strategy, the most brilliant negotiating ploy, are worthless without suitable property.

Finding the right property isn't easy, in part because there are so many prospective choices. And while it's good to have a wide selection of properties with a variety of prices, terms, and locations, bad deals abound. Many proposed investments are simply unworkable because of price, poor location, inappropriate design, or unobtainable zoning. And some investments, deals that are otherwise workable, are simply beyond the means or skill of given investors.

What makes a good investment property? The best answer seems to be *unrealized value available at a discounted cost that can be captured by specific individuals.* "Value," in turn, can be defined in such terms as market prices, cash flow, tax advantages, conversion to a higher and better use, or benefits obtained through improved financing or sweat equity.

The search, then, is not just for property per se, but for a very special property, one offering the potential for real profit and the opportunity to create an income stream and tax benefits.

FINDING GROWTH CORRIDORS

Location, not size, is the fundamental source of property value, the very reason 10,000 square feet in downtown Manhattan may be worth far more than 10,000 acres in desolate stretches of the Far West. Location is so critical that even properties on the same block can have vastly different values. In resort areas, for example, property facing the ocean is worth far more than properties of equal size that merely front on a roadway.

Investors are always interested in location. Large investors—the people and organizations who build shopping malls, office parks, and huge factories—may influence property values merely by their decision to select one site and not another. In effect, they have enough economic clout to raise property values just because they own or have optioned certain land or buildings.

Since small investors cannot individually influence general property values, they must latch on to prevailing and prospective trends. But how do you spot such trends?

One wonderful and inexpensive information source is the local paper. News columns are filled with interesting data and insights that, taken with other information, often suggest where the market is heading.

One brief news item, for instance, said engineers were debating whether to replace or expand a certain bridge. Within ten years usage was expected to rise from 30,000 to 75,000 cars, and the present bridge would then be inadequate.

The bridge story—just a few paragraphs—raises some interesting questions. Why are so many additional cars going to use that span? Where do the drivers live now, and where will they live in the future? Where do they work? What businesses and services will be available to all the new bridge users? How much will bridge traffic expand in five years? Which neighborhoods on either side of the river will have the easiest and most direct access?

Local papers often tell us which neighborhoods are hot and trendy this year, information that may suggest which neighborhoods to avoid, because areas in demand are areas where *current* property owners make money. Unless we can get a bargain, hot and trendy is not our style unless the area seems poised for continued growth.

As investors, what we're looking for is not the hottest neighborhood this year, but the area that will be hot next year or the year after. *We want to anticipate growth and development.*

Identifying high-growth areas simply makes our job easier and less risky. If prices in a given neighborhood are rising generally, then the worth of our property is likely to rise with the tide. If prices are stagnant or declining, we are then in the position of fighting market forces, an uncomfortable position at best.

Knowing what's "in" this year may well suggest growth areas in the near future. If Heavenly Acres is a top area for redevelopment now, what about adjoining neighborhoods? Which has the most to offer? Which has the best access? Which is most likely to be the next "in" spot? Many investors have made sizable fortunes merely by purchasing on the cusp of development and moving out as communities grow.

Another good information source is the local planning, zoning, or economic development office. Here you can find community planners, lots of maps, and a variety of land-use proposals. This is where you can learn about prospective development, what's allowed under the current master plan, and very often who owns or controls ground that might be used for a shopping mall, office park, or residential development. It's worth listening to local planners, since they follow community development on a daily basis.

Future growth and demand are obvious in certain situations. A major shopping center typically requires several years to "build out," so if you can uncover a shopping mall in the early stages of development, it's an easy matter to project growth in a given area.

Shopping centers are interesting to investors for other reasons as well.

First, to have a successful center you need a certain mix of people and income within a given radius of the project. However, because the number of major malls left to be built is limited by prior construction, most new malls are on the fringe of today's development and therefore suggest where development will occur tomorrow.

Second, of the mall sites left, those developed first are most likely to succeed. Only a small number of "anchor" tenants—the big stores needed by every major mall—are available, and the first project developed will take as many anchor tenants as possible. The second project gets the leftovers.

Third, when planning a mall, developers rely on marketing, leasing, and demographic experts. By following in the footsteps of a major mall developer, you can effectively benefit from such high-priced talent.

Fourth, the mall development process is so long and so public that it's hard to miss good opportunities for above-average price increases.

Roads are another guide to future development. Planners can tell you which roads will be built, lengthened, or widened—development that will not occur unless growth is anticipated. Or, seen from another viewpoint, improved roads may themselves be a cause of growth.

Other major capital projects also suggest future growth. Hospital expansion, new industry, office development, and government works are just a few examples of large-scale projects that reflect growth trends.

Government works in particular should interest investors. If a community wants to raise $30 million for a project, or just for general financing, it goes to the bond market and borrows money. To borrow money, however, one first must disclose a variety of information in what is often called a prospectus or "Official Statement." Such statements are freely available to anyone who asks and usually contain an extensive section on "demographic and economic factors." Here you can find out about projected construction, population growth, unemployment, income, and transportation throughout the community. In effect, the local government will tell you much of what you need to know about future growth and development, and they'll tell you without cost.

FINDING THE RIGHT NEIGHBORHOOD

Within the path of probable growth we're likely to find a variety of neighborhoods, areas, and small communities worthy of further examination.

It's important to walk or drive through these areas, visit open houses, and speak with local brokers. You want to know as much as possible about each, including such factors as:

Rental Levels. You want to assure that rental levels are sufficient to support a given level of investment. If homes are priced at $150,000 but monthly rentals only total $500, then by definition rentals are not workable.

Property Values. To know how much a property is worth you must also know the value of like properties that have recently sold. For this reason it pays to make careful notes regarding each property you see, even those which are not acquisition candidates.

Recent Sales. Buyers sometimes want to know how much owners paid for their properties, information which is likely to be both dated and irrelevant. What counts are recent sales, those made in the past three to six months that reflect current marketplace realities.

Present Offerings. Homes on the market today compete for buyer attention with like properties. As an investor, you can use such competition as leverage to pressure a seller. ("I really like your place, but the Hudson home on the next block is largely the same and I think they will accept a price that's almost $3,000 less than what you want. Perhaps a combination of better pricing and help at closing could make your home competitive.")

Where People Work. People—whether they own or rent—need access to jobs. If the nearest major employment center is two hours away, then rental prospects are dimmed.

General Economics. Many local communities commission studies to project how they will fare in the future. In the Washington, D.C., area, for example, the local council of governments has issued a report which projects population and job growth during the next 30 years. With the population expected to increase by 1.5 million people and employment by 1.22 million jobs, what will happen to property values, especially in the close-in suburbs?

If we have a choice, we want neighborhoods with a variety of homes and values. If we're looking at a 20-year-old subdivision with 500 homes and three basic models, prices will tend to cluster. "Darwin" model owners will each want the going price, say $100,000, while all recent "Flagstone" sales might be at or near $110,000. We're not likely to break out of the cluster if we sell, so buying in a subdivision becomes attractive only if we can get a substantial discount up front. The same logic applies to like condominium and co-op units in large projects.

In neighborhoods with a variety of residential styles, there's more opportunity to be an entrepreneur. Without standardized properties there can't be cluster pricing. Instead, we're likely to find a range of sizes and physical conditions, and consequently a variety of prices. If the best house in the neighborhood is worth $200,000 and the worst is valued at $130,000, that's fine.

We want to follow the general principle used by all real estate investors; we want *the least expensive property in the most expensive neighborhood we can afford*. This combination gives us the maximum potential for profit and explains why we want the $130,000 house. The best neighborhood house may be a wonderful property, but the current owners are likely to get most of the profit, not us. If someone wants a home worth more than $200,000, the probability is not that the person will buy property in our neighborhood, but rather that he or she will look in a more expensive area where homes worth $200,000 or more are common.

When homes vary in a neighborhood, then individual values are established by the marketplace. If we price a property at $150,000 and a neighbor has a home on the market for $130,000, who's to say one property is overpriced if the size, condition, siting, and other features are different? Each is unique, and if someone wants the package of condition, size, style, and location we're offering, the property will sell. Unlike largely identical properties in a subdivision, values in mixed neighborhoods are less clear, and price must therefore be established by negotiation and marketing rather than past sales of largely similar properties.

Not only do we want a neighborhood with a variety of homes, we want an area which offers other values as well. We want commuter access, nearby shopping and schools, and a continuing stream of property sales, preferably at generally higher prices over time, demonstrating ongoing demand.

We don't want the richest neighborhood in town (it costs too much for entry-level investors to play in this league), nor do we want the poorest (if we fix up, our property may end up as the most expensive in the neighborhood).

We want property in neighborhoods that represent a midpoint between rich and poor, properties in areas where neighbors have enough capital to improve their homes but are not so wealthy that our universe of potential buyers or renters is profoundly limited.

Probably the best justification for the purchase of moderately priced investor properties can be found in a 1987 study of some 20,000 single-family rental properties by what was then known as Epic Realty Services. This survey showed that moderately priced homes generated proportionately higher incomes than expensive properties.

For instance, homes bought for $50,000 had average returns of 10.64 percent. Rentals for $100,000 properties averaged 8.17 percent of the purchase price, while homes at the high end of the market—properties costing $350,000—brought in rentals equal to just 6.09 percent of original acquisition costs.

The conclusion one draws from this survey is that small investors, the folks most likely to buy modest properties, are purchasing within that segment of the real estate marketplace offering the best chance for rental profits. That's a comforting observation.

GENERAL CONDITION

There are homes in every community where the owners have taken meticulous care of their property. Floors sparkle, rugs are immaculate, and every appliance and mechanical system is in top condition. And although such homes are wonderful to own and live in, they generally make poor investments. Such properties are in demand and owners can sell them quickly for top dollar, a price we'd rather not pay.

As investors we want something less. We want property with unmowed lawns, dirty floors, and unmade beds. We want peeling paint, ugly furniture, closets filled with junk, and basements made impassable with boxes and cartons. We want kitchens with old appliances and leaky faucets, and we want bathrooms where new and unknown forms of bacteria grow undisturbed. If possible, we want a large dog to intimidate visitors, preferably a loud animal with big teeth, matted fur, and lots of open sores. If the kids collect spiders and have a large and nicely framed display of local vermin, so much the better.

We want a house so ugly and so profoundly unappealing that other prospective buyers fail to see its value or potential. We want a place which shows so terribly that good plumbing, wiring, heating, and air-conditioning systems are camouflaged. We want a place where the roof doesn't leak, and the basement doesn't flood, but nobody notices or cares because the property is such an appalling mess.

Because when the place is sold, when the dog, the bacteria, the vermin collection, and all the rest are gone, what remains will be a property that needs to be cleaned, painted, and repaired—not unreasonable requirements for the average investor.

FORMS OF OWNERSHIP

The ownership of real estate is traditionally described as a "bundle of rights." The more rights you have, the greater the value of your ownership.

If property is owned on a "fee simple" basis, it means an investor, or several investors together as a partnership or corporation, have all possible rights to the property. Within the bounds of zoning and public safety, an owner can rent it, sell it, finance it, improve it, or ignore it as he or she wishes. A single-family house on a quarter-acre lot is a typical example of fee-simple real estate.

Not every property is owned on a fee-simple basis. Condominium ownership is a form of title where the investor owns a specific property plus an interest in certain common areas and facilities. Unlike the owner of a fee-simple property, a condo owner has to abide with certain restrictions imposed by the condominium association, the body of owners that runs the project. For instance, rentals may be limited to tenants of one year or more. Painting the front door in a color not approved by the architectural committee may create conflicts.

Another condo problem, one that should trouble prospective investors, is the general attitude toward condos shared by many secondary lenders and private mortgage insurance firms. When 30 percent or more of a project's units are owned by investors, these organizations may elect not to originate or purchase condo mortgages except when owner-occupants put down at least 25 percent of the purchase price.

The 30 percent guideline raises a number of problems. If you're an investor trying to purchase a condo and other investors already own 30 percent of the project's units, your chances of getting a loan are just about zero—regardless of your financial strength. If you buy a unit as an owner-occupant, live in it for several years, and then wish to refinance and rent, the 30 percent standard can spoil your plans if the investor threshold has already been reached.

If someone simply wants to buy a condo as an owner-occupant and 30 percent of the units are owned by investors, a buyer with few down payment dollars may not be able to get a loan. Worse yet, a seller may not be able to market his or her property without readily available financing.

While the 30 percent guideline is an important barrier for investors, it is not absolute. As an example, Freddie Mac, the big secondary lender, may not enforce a 30 percent standard for what it calls "Class C" condos. A Class C condo project has been in the hands of the condo association for at least two years and is completely built-out.

A PUD, or private-unit development, is much like a condo project, except that it may be far larger. A "new town" with single-family homes, townhouses, apartments, shopping centers, and office buildings is likely to be a PUD.

Another form of ownership, cooperative ownership, is not truly a direct form of real estate title. With a cooperative, an investor owns stock in a corporation and has the exclusive right to use a particular portion of the corporation's property, such as an apartment or townhouse. It's the corporation, however, that actually owns the property and makes the rules, rules that can include a total ban on rentals and the approval, or disapproval, of prospective purchasers.

It's entirely possible to make money with condo, PUD, and co-op units, but the view here is that fee-simple ownership, with the largest bundle of rights, offers the most flexibility and potential for investors. Unlike with a condo or PUD, you don't have to worry about architectural committees. Unlike a co-op, no one can prevent the sale of your property to the buyer of your choice, nor can your decision to rent be denied.

CONFIGURATION

If we have plans to fix up, divide, or enlarge a home, or if we have an interest in subdividing ground, then we need a property suitable for such development.

Dividing property—perhaps converting an old home into three apartments—raises several issues.

First, zoning laws must be observed. Property cannot be divided without proper zoning, where required. If the property does not have appropriate zoning when offered for sale, then investors can make only contingent offers: "We'll buy your property if we can get appropriate zoning variances by a given date. If such zoning is not available, we have the right to call off the deal and have our deposit refunded in full."

Second, if we're going to divide, then we want a property that lends itself to being carved up. A house with an attic unit that lacks a private entrance won't work. Folks in the lower unit won't have privacy, and the property will be tough to rent, much less rent at a decent price.

Third, if we divide, we want individually metered utilities so tenants can pay such costs directly. In addition to adding separate electrical service boxes and water meters, in a major renovation we may want to replace a central heating system with individual heat pumps. In some areas, gas and electric companies compete to install such units, sometimes offering discounted pricing plus low-cost financing to win your business.

Expanding property creates a different set of problems. If we add a 15 × 20-foot room to a house, we now have 300 more square feet of living space. But what if local zoning laws prohibit building near property lines? Our addition may not be possible without a zoning exception, and such exceptions may not be obtainable.

If our new room is eight feet high, we've also added 2,400 cubic feet of space which must be heated, ventilated, and air-conditioned. Unfortunately, many heating and air-conditioning systems are "sized" at the time of installation. By adding additional cubic area we are now faced with either the cost of replacing or augmenting current systems, or the probability of inadequate performance from our current units.

There are some properties which by their nature are simply unsuited for expansion. A house with a small core area—living room, kitchen, and dining room—may not support the addition of a few extra bedrooms and use by many people.

Expansion may also be impractical if the enlarged structure doesn't fit in the neighborhood. Having a five-bedroom home in the midst of a community with three-bedroom houses will make it tough to get full market value. Such property won't be the least expensive house in the neighborhood, and therefore will be hard to sell.

Subdividing ground is another activity which depends on zoning. Without the right zoning, subdividing may be impossible. In general terms, zoning laws require so many square feet—say 6,000 to 8,000 in some suburban areas—before building will be allowed. In other areas, two to five acres may be required to have a usable lot.

Even with proper zoning, subdividing may be difficult. Some areas have building moratoriums from time to time, a public policy to control growth. Other areas are bedeviled by water shortages, and even with zoning it may not be possible to get water and sewage hook-ups. Thus before subdividing ground, investors must check zoning, local building policies, and the availability of water and sewage. Also, beware of permit costs. Many jurisdictions have discovered that it's politically more attractive to raise permit fees rather than property taxes.

SELLERS

Not only are we interested in the property's physical characteristics, we also want to know something about the sellers.

If our seller just won the lottery, the urge to sell at a discount will be limited. Instead, *we want someone with a need to sell.*

But why would anyone sell property at discount? Would you? In fact, many sellers accept low prices and they do so for a variety of reasons.

- Those with financial problems are often happy to unload property, especially if they can raise cash quickly for other purposes.
- Divorced couples frequently sell at discount, if only to quickly dispel a major bond between husband and wife. Price is sometimes secondary as each side battles the other. More rational couples will wait for the highest possible price so each can benefit.
- Estates may sell property at discount to raise money quickly for taxes.
- Those with new jobs out of town are often a source of discounted properties—they want to sell quickly and relocate.
- Foreclosures, a subject covered in Chapter 23, can be a source of discounts.
- Those who have tax problems. Local tax offices list current assessments and sometimes those owners who are delinquent—data entirely within the stream of public information.
- Tax regulations with specific deadlines can cause owners to sell at discount. As an example, in December 1986, a large number of properties across the country were available at a 20 percent discount. The reason: Selling before December 31st allowed owners to benefit from attractive capital-gains regulations that would end on that date.
- Small investors, discouraged with negative cash flow, problem tenants, or changing plans, will often sell at discount to quickly unload property.
- Properties that show terribly but are not necessarily in bad physical condition often sell at discount.
- Properties that have been on the market for a long time because of generally poor economic conditions frequently go at discount prices.

As this list shows, there's no shortage of properties available at discount. But a discount alone is not enough to make a property attractive. If you can buy a property at discount, that's good. If the property can't be rented, is forever in need of repair, does not increase in value, or is always destined to produce negative cash flow, it may not be a bargain after all.

PRICING, RENTS, AND FINANCING

We know that in general terms we're looking for the least expensive property in the most expensive neighborhood we can afford. But as investors we need more specific guidelines, a better way to analyze prices.

The best way to look at pricing is to consider our intent. What we expect to do with the property will affect our willingness to pay given prices.

Suppose we buy property with the intent of flipping the contract. Here we have a situation where the contract can be assigned to another buyer, and our profit will come from the difference between the owner's sale price and whatever a second buyer will pay.

We want the lowest price possible from the original owner, but *any* price less than a second buyer will pay produces a profit.

If we intend to buy, fix up, and sell, then our pricing computation becomes more critical. In this case we need to look at the purchase price, settlement costs, fix-up expenses, carrying expenses (interest), and marketing costs. These numbers, when combined, must be less than the property's ultimate sale price.

For instance, if Butler buys a property for $100,000, spends $5,000 in closing costs, pays a contractor $10,000 to fix the property, anticipates spending $8,000 for interest and taxes, and projects marketing and closing costs of $10,000, then the property cannot be sold for less than $133,000 if Butler is merely to break even.

Butler must face two questions if he intends to sell:

First, do homes in the neighborhood regularly sell for $133,000? If the top area price to date is just $120,000, he is likely to lose money.

Second, do homes in the neighborhood sell for more than $133,000? If they sell for $150,000, $160,000, or $175,000, the deal looks increasingly attractive.

If we intend to buy, fix up, and rent, then we must analyze each property with care to determine what is a good deal and what isn't.

Suppose we're looking at a four-unit building. If each two-bedroom unit can rent for $850 a month when the property is fixed up, then gross annual rentals should amount to $3,400 a month or $40,800 a year.

Basic Income Analysis for Four-Unit Apartment

Annual rental	$40,800
Less:	
Taxes	$2,500
Insurance	$750
Repairs	$3,000
Vacancies	$3,468
Balance	$31,082
Monthly income	$2,590

If taxes total $2,500, insurance costs are $750, repairs are expected to cost $3,000 a year, and we have an 8.5 percent vacancy factor ($3,468), then our anticipated cash expenses total $9,718. If these assumptions are correct, then $31,082 is available for monthly mortgage payments ($40,800 less $9,718).

With $31,082 remaining after general expenses, it means we have as much as $2,590 per month for mortgage principal and interest. Given these figures, how much should we offer for the property? Since all properties are different, the factors determining a purchase decision may vary. That said, here are some baseline questions to ask.

How secure is the income stream?

We have been told that the property produces a gross rental income of $3,400 per month, but how secure is that money? Are there leases? When do the leases expire? Have any tenants indicated a desire to move? Do the tenants pay on time?

With one-to-four unit properties there can be major headaches when a single tenant moves. The property must be re-let. In addition, while an individual tenant who moves is not a big issue in a property with 200 apartments, a vacant unit in building with four apartments means losing 25 percent of the monthly cash flow, a substantial matter and probably the difference between profitability and poverty for the owner.

Must we worry about rent control?

Rent control is a device that can limit rental increases, require the payment of various fees and charges, exact additional costs when tenants move, and restrict sales and conversions without tenant approval.

If the plan is to raise rates in the future or convert the property to condo or co-op status, then rent control can be a defining factor—one that prevents given strategies or makes them more costly.

What is the property's condition?

Yearly repairs are estimated at $3,000. But have repairs been deferred by the current owner? Such procrastination has the effect of lowering annual expenses, raising cash flow, and producing a bright, shiny balance sheet—at least until the roof must be replaced or the furnace changed.

It is also possible that everything works but that the property needs general updating to attract and hold quality tenants. Better appliances, new paint, and landscaping may be needed and none of these items are likely to be cost-free.

What can we do by ourselves?

There is a substantial difference between an owner who can fix up and repair a property by himself or herself, and an owner who must depend on high-priced professional talent. Especially for entry-level investors, it often makes sense to do some repair and maintenance work directly while leaving harder or more complex jobs to the pros.

How does the local community measure up?

Is the area growing? Attracting jobs? Gaining stores, schools, and roads? Our effort to create additional value will be greatly helped if the neighborhood where we buy is becoming more attractive.

Conversely, our investment will be shaky if people are moving away and the demand for homes declines, or if the local government elects to place a toxic dump a block from our property.

How much cash is required?

Financing is very important to us. If we can buy with little down we can preserve our capital for repairs, improvements, other acquisitions, and alternative investments.

Whether or not we put cash into a property there is an "opportunity cost." For example, in an environment with 8 percent mortgage rates, if we put $10,000 into a property we can save interest worth $800 in the first year, but we lose the use of our $10,000. Alternatively, we can borrow more and keep the $10,000 elsewhere in our pocket. This may be a better choice if we can get a higher rate of return for our capital or if we are simply more comfortable having cash rather than equity.

Some lenders will want us to put down 20 or 30 percent. Alternatively, we may be able to buy with owner financing or money from a pension fund and perhaps put down as little as 10 percent.

How much does it cost to rent money?

We are unlikely to buy for cash, thus we must borrow. But at what rate? High rates force down prices. Low rates make it easy to borrow more at every level of income.

If we buy at a time when interest rates are at 10 percent and they fall to 7 percent, we can refinance and reap additional income or sell. If we buy in a 7 percent market and try to sell when rates are at the 10 percent level, then prices are likely to be depressed relative to what we paid and selling is probably more difficult.

No one knows where rates are headed, especially over the long term. For this reason it is best to engage in a ratcheting process where possible: Seek the best available rates and—should they decline to levels that produce meaningful benefits—then refinance.

What do the numbers say?

There are a number of formulas investors use to gauge property values.

One measure is the "NOI," or net operating income. To calculate the NOI we take gross monthly rentals ($3,400 in this example) and subtract all monthly costs except debt service ($9,718 divided by 12, or $809.83 per month). The result is an NOI of $2,590.17.

If we want a monthly profit of $750, then $1,840 is available for mortgage payments. At 8 percent interest, $1,840 will "buy" 30-year financing worth $250,761.63.

Ideally, we would like to offer no more than $251,000 for the property. In this situation we would put down 10 percent or more and finance the rest. Money from the property would then pay not only for the loan but also for the use of our cash investment, plus a monthly profit of $750. If we put down 10 percent ($25,100) and have an annual net income of $9,000 ($750 × 12), then our rate of return is 35.8 percent. This rate of return is so high that it is improbable.

One catch is that our acquisition cost is not just the down payment. It also includes a variety of closing costs, expenses that depend on where the property is located. If it costs $10,000 to settle the deal, then we have paid out $35,100 up front ($25,100 plus $10,000). Now our rate of return is 25.6 percent. If we put down 20 percent, pay $10,000 in closing costs, and generate $9,000 a year from the property, then the rate of return is 14.9 percent.

A second catch concerns competition. It is unlikely that you will be the only investor out there. If the rate of return is too high, then competition in an open marketplace will drive up the price. If the price is also attractive to the seller, then there is a deal to be made.

What does the seller want?

All deals differ, not only because individual properties are unique but also because seller circumstances vary.

There is a substantial difference between a seller who can take back financing (and help us avoid points), and one who cannot. There is a distinction between an owner who needs to sell, and an owner who is just testing the market.

What needs must we satisfy?

As investors in the buying mode no deal will work unless it meets our needs. What personal preferences must be satisfied? What financial goals are we trying to achieve? What alternatives are available to us?

NEGATIVE CASH FLOW IN PERSPECTIVE

Much is made of negative cash flow—monthly losses that can go on for years with certain properties. For instance, if Wrightman buys a property, rents it for $800 a month but must pay out $900 for the mortgage, insurance, repairs, taxes, etc., he's losing $100 a month or $1,200 a year.

For some households, $100 a month is not significant. For others, it's a very substantial sum, and for this reason part of the investment process is knowing how much you can afford in monthly losses, if anything.

Negative cash flow can also be seen from a different perspective. If you invest in real estate you have certain costs and negative cash flow, in the right circumstances, is nothing more than the expense of being in business, much like an electric bill or mailing costs.

Suppose Wrightman, the buyer in our example, bought his property for $100,000, fixed it up at a cost of $15,000, and spent $7,000 in monthly mortgage payments before refinancing—a total of $122,000. If the property was now worth $150,000 and Wrightman could get 80 percent refinancing, his investment would be $2,000, or a little more than 1 percent of the property's market value ($100,000 plus $22,000 equals $122,000, less refinancing worth $120,000).

Thus, at the end of a year, Wrightman would have "invested" (or "paid," depending on how you look at it) $1,200 in monthly negative cash flow plus $2,000 that was not covered by refinancing. So his cash cost to own this property at the end of a year will be $3,200.

Or is it?

Wrightman, after all, is entitled to tax deductions. If he can write off $2,900 in depreciation plus his $1,200 negative cash flow, he has a tax loss of $4,100. If he's in the 28 percent bracket, his current taxes are lowered by $1,148.

Wrightman thus has an interesting situation. True, his investment is a loser—at least in terms of monthly cash flow. But it's also true that annual tax savings effectively make up for monthly cash losses. If property values rise, however, Wrightman could be ahead very quickly.

Suppose values increase 5 percent a year, a modest gain in many markets. After a year, a property originally worth $150,000 will rise to $157,500. The $7,500 gain, less Wrightman's true cost, $2,052 ($3,200 minus $1,148), puts him ahead by almost $5,500.

Is this $5,500 spendable money? Not directly. Wrightman can get the money out of the property only by refinancing or selling. Closing costs in either case would probably wipe out much or all of his profit. Wrightman's net worth, however, does increase by $5,500, a matter that will please lenders when they consider a loan application.

So far, with timid appreciation, Wrightman is only marginally ahead. But if appreciation continues at 5 percent annually, and rentals rise faster than costs by $25 per month, here's what happens before considering depreciation.

- Year 1: The property is worth $157,500 at the end of the first year. Monthly expenses of $900 less monthly income of $800 leaves a $100 negative cash flow. Total cash cost to date: $3,200 ($2,000 in costs plus $1,200 in monthly losses).

- Year 2: The property is worth $165,375 at the end of the second year. Monthly expenses of $925 less monthly income of $850 leaves a $75 negative cash flow. Total cash cost to date: $4,000 (monthly losses of $75 times 12 months, plus $3,200).

- Year 3: The property is worth $173,643 at the end of the third year. Monthly expenses of $950 less monthly income of $900 leaves a $50 negative cash flow. Total cash cost to date: $4,600 (monthly losses of $50 times 12 months, plus $4,000).

- Year 4: The property is worth $182,325 at the end of the fourth year. Monthly expenses of $975 less monthly income of $950 leaves a $25 negative cash flow. Total cash cost to date: $4,900 (monthly losses of $25 times 12 months, plus $4,600).

- Year 5: The property is worth $191,441 at the end of the fifth year.

Monthly expenses of $1,000 less monthly income of $1,000 leaves no negative cash flow. Total cash cost to date: $4,900.

- Year 6: The property is worth $201,014 at the end of the sixth year. Monthly expenses of $1,050 less monthly income of $1,075 leaves a positive cash flow of $25. Total cash cost to date: $4,600 (monthly profits of $25 times 12 months, subtracted from $4,900).

So, at the end of six years, Mr. Wrightman has had to take $4,600 from his pocket to support an investment that's worth just over $200,000. He hasn't had to pay it all at once, and each year his monthly costs have dropped. In addition, he lowered his tax bill in two ways. First, he had actual operating losses during the first four years of ownership. Second, he was able to depreciate the property each year he owned it.

But Wrightman is a winner on another basis. His $120,000 mortgage, not counting amortization, is at least $80,000 less than the property's market value. His net worth has risen by a substantial amount, and it continues to increase by more than $10,000 a year—more than twice his total investment!

Profits in real estate can be calculated in many ways; indeed, articles suggest various approaches to the IRR (the internal rate of return) all the time. But the view here is that investors must compare costs over time with income and tax benefits, if any. In other words, the "cost" of Wrightman's property was all the money he put into the property during his term of ownership, plus the interest lost on his capital. His benefits include not just the income he received or didn't receive (we have not provided for any vacancies in this example, an unlikely situation) but also the value of tax deferrals. Going further, we could look at Wrightman's profit in terms of buying power, to see if he came out ahead economically as well as in cash dollars.

Wrightman's situation is common in many markets around the country; in fact it's understated because property values often rise far more than 5 percent annually. But the basic point is this: As long as Wrightman can afford to acquire and rehabilitate the property, as long as he can afford a monthly cash loss, he is able to build up his equity and reduce current taxes. Around the country there are many investors who have accepted the reality of negative cash flow during the first several years of ownership in exchange for appreciation, tax benefits, and ultimately monthly income as well. Not a bad trade-off for those who can afford it.

12
How to Bargain Like a Pro

With all the work required to assemble a good investment deal, it's hard to imagine that anyone would skip the most important step. Yet written agreements are frequently regarded as a formality, dull paperwork to be completed once a basic purchase price and terms have been established.

Paperwork may be dull, but without it real estate would be filled with suspense. No one would know if a deal was made, wasn't made, or who agreed to what terms.

Written agreements not only create real estate deals, they also contain a host of provisions which may cost unwary investors thousands of dollars in excess fees, charges, and closing costs.

Every jurisdiction has so-called standardized real estate agreements, but in a sloppy world nice and tidy standardized forms rarely work without modification. Moreover, most jurisdictions have more than one standardized form! Since such forms are not identical, you can bet that seemingly minor differences between them are important. It's a bet you'll win.

Forms should be collected and reviewed *before* entering the real estate market. You want to read whatever forms are used locally, especially those employed by the brokerage community. Such forms, available from brokers, lawyers, and investors, may surprise you.

For instance, forms often describe acceptable financing, say 8.5 percent interest. But if the form also says "or the best available rate," the buyer has agreed to whatever rates are charged at closing. This is a great clause for a seller, the folks for whom brokers normally work, but not so great for buyers or investors. (A similar clause often concerns points. A form may say that buyers will pay one point or the "prevailing market rate." Again, investors who agree to such terms may find that the prevailing market rate, as defined by the lender, is far higher than one point.)

Investors will want to read form agreements, note questions, and then discuss the forms with an attorney, broker, or both. You'll have to pay for consultation services, but this is money well spent, particularly if it later saves you from a costly error.

From the investor's perspective, you want offers that bind the seller but allow you the option to back out of a deal without penalty. This can be done with an offer form that favors your interests, by modifying standardized agreements, or by adding new wording with so-called addenda.

For example, all investor offers should be subject to the availability of acceptable financing—financing detailed in the offer and not whatever rates and terms happen to be available at settlement.

Suppose you offer $100,000 for a property, provided you can find 80 percent financing over 30 years at 8 percent interest and with one point. If the terms change, the deal's economics are also transformed. A deal that makes sense at 8 percent may be a loser at 9 percent or higher.

And why, after all, should you be in a position where you're obligated to accept changing interest rates and thus higher acquisition and ownership costs? The seller isn't obligated to lower his price if interest rates rise, although that would certainly be an interesting arrangement.

In addition to assured financing, contracts can be converted into short-term "options" by making offers contingent on an event or acceptance.

For example, Washburn offers to buy the Clark property for $200,000, contingent on a "satisfactory" property inspection by an inspector of Washburn's choice within ten days. If the inspection isn't satisfactory to Washburn, the deal is finished, and Washburn's deposit will be returned if he wrote a proper inspection clause.

Here Clark is required to sell the property, but Washburn isn't obligated to buy. If Washburn can't locate financing or his needs change, then it's entirely possible that a close look at the property will coincidentally reveal conditions that render it "unsatisfactory."

In principle, the same arrangement can work for any inspection (someone to check the heating system) or review (a contract examination by your attorney). As long as your satisfaction is required, with a properly written form you're in control.

Buying property involves more than just land and a house. You also want as many fixtures as you can get from the seller.

A "fixture" is generally defined as something that's attached to the property and intended to remain with it. A central air-conditioner is a fixture, a window air-conditioner is not.

But with a properly worded agreement, you can create your own list of fixtures. If you offer to buy the Winston house and specifically include the transfer of the window air-conditioners as a part of your offer, they're yours if the Winstons accept the deal.

Other issues which should be considered include these major topics:

Concessions.

Form agreements commonly contain a variety of unnegotiated, but cost-ly, concessions. For example, a form agreement may require the buyer to pay transfer taxes. Why? Who knows? But as an investor you should feel perfectly free to modify this arrangement so that the seller pays all of it, or half of it, or as much as you can get within the context of a workable deal.

Closed offer.

An offer can be arranged so that it terminates automatically at a given time. For instance, if you bid on the Rydells' house, you don't want them to "shop" your offer and look for a better deal. If the offer expires at 5 P.M. Monday or whenever, then the amount of time available to find compet-ing bidders is limited. You, of course, can always submit another offer if the first one ends.

Damages.

Many standardized form agreements provide two types of damages if a contract fails because of an investor. First, the deposit made with the offer is forfeited. Second, the investor is also subject to a lawsuit for claims by both the seller and the seller's agent. As an investor buying property *you want to limit damages to not more than the amount of the deposit, and you want to offer the smallest possible deposit.*

Deposits.

In a typical transaction, it's understood and expected that when the investor makes an offer, that offer will include a deposit. Sellers will want a deposit that rivals Fort Knox in terms of value, while investors might suggest pocket change.

It's sometimes suggested that a "standard" deposit exists, say 5 to 10 per-cent of the total purchase price, but like unicorns, standard deposits are a myth. Investors should offer the smallest possible deposit acceptable to sellers and make certain that if the deal goes through, the deposit is a cred-it toward the purchase price. In other words, if you're paying $100,000 for a property and a $3,000 deposit accompanies your offer, then $97,000 should be due at closing.

If the deal fails because of a contingency (the property fails a structural inspection, financing isn't available, etc.), then investors should be certain their deposit will be refunded in full.

Down payments.

The hallmark of real estate gurus and seers is their avowed determination to buy property with no money down.

However, deals with no money down typically depend on seller financing because lenders will not accept such financing, except with guarantees by the VA. When a buyer has no cash in the deal, there's no security for the seller/lender, since an unhappy or unsuccessful buyer can just walk away from the property.

Worse than no-money-down deals are "equity skimming" frauds, ripoffs that work like this: The buyer gets property with no money down, rents it, collects the rent, and then fails to make any mortgage payments. By the time everyone realizes what's going on, the buyer has fled.

Investors should expect to make down payments and to have additional cash available for closing. At the same time, the smaller the down payment, the greater your leverage, so the obligation to make a down payment should not be seen as a requirement to put down 20 or 30 percent at settlement.

Existing leases.

Owners are bound by existing lease terms, so if a property is rented, investors can only make offers contingent upon their satisfaction with the lease agreement.

Insurance coverage.

Investors are not owners until the moment of recordation, that time after closing when the transaction is placed in local records and title is officially transferred. Since the investor doesn't own the property until that time, the seller can be responsible if settlement takes place on a Monday, the property burns down on Tuesday, and the deal is recorded on Wednesday. Investor buyers, however, can be responsible for the property if the sales agreement confers that obligation on them. Therefore, see what the offer form requires, get appropriate insurance coverage, and make certain the seller has proper coverage as well.

Pre-settlement rights.

As an investor you may want to rent a property as quickly as possible, a goal that will be far easier to achieve if you can advertise and show the property before closing. The right to show, advertise, and erect a "For Rent" sign prior to closing can be specified in an offer.

Price and Terms.

As an investor your goal is to pay as little as possible for property, but "price" includes more than a numerical figure. If you make an offer to buy property for $100,000 provided the seller will pay a 1 percent transfer tax, you've really bid $99,000. It's usually a good strategy to bury costs within a deal so the purchase price appears inflated. For example, if the Cramers want $120,000 for their property it may make sense to pay the $120,000 figure if they'll pay all points, transfer costs, settlement fees, etc. In effect, the price is discounted by the terms of the deal.

Survey.

Usually required by lenders, surveys tell you where the property lines are located and where the house is sited. An offer can be made subject to a survey satisfactory to the investor, a good way to create a short-term option.

Although written agreements are important, there are also intangible factors in the bargaining process that should not be ignored.

When making an offer, always characterize your position in business terms. It's much better to say, "Interest rates and area rents limit what I can offer" rather than "So this is how Egypt looked after the sixth plague." Civil relations, respectful relations, can make difficult dealings more pleasant.

Timing is also important. You don't want to make an offer 20 minutes after a property becomes available. The owner will naturally want full price, and unless full price is a healthy bargain you won't get a good deal. It's best to wait a few days, or a few weeks, depending on the market, and let the owner simmer a bit. Prices and terms become far more malleable once a property has been on the market for a while.

You also need options if a first offer is refused. Do you raise your offer, resubmit it, or go on to the next property? If you raise your offer, what do you get in return?

It's important to listen to sellers and their agents. Why is the property being sold? Is a quick sale important? Have there been other offers? How much remains on the mortgage and is it assumable? How much are gas, electric, oil, and water bills each year? How much are annual property taxes and what's the property's assessed value? How is the property zoned? Does the fireplace work? Has the basement leaked in the past two years? What about the attic?

Negotiating is hard work, fun, rewarding, and exciting. It's also a seductive process that can entrap unwary investors. For your own protection, set limits. There's a point in every deal where prices and terms are so high that even if you got the property, it would be a lousy investment. If you reach that upper limit, if there's no chance for an advantageous deal, thank the seller, shake hands with the broker, be polite, and gently disengage. Tomorrow is another day.

13

Starting Out:
Entry-Level Strategies

There's little doubt that money is the single barrier that separates owners from renters. Take a tenant, add savings and income, and in short order you'll have a proud property owner.

Many people also rent because housing costs have risen faster than earnings. When you see that home prices in some city rose 15 percent in a single year, that's terrific news for the folks who own property—they're vested in the system.

What happens, though, with the young couple who finished college three years ago? They both have jobs, but the probability of their income rising 15 percent in a single year is just about zero. For them, housing is less and less affordable every month.

It's enormously important to become a property owner at the earliest possible age, if only to benefit from inflation and the appearance of rising prices. And in the beginning, as so many investors can tell you, sacrifices are common.

HOW TO RAISE A DOWN PAYMENT

For most investors, real estate deals involve a down payment and closing costs equaling not less than several months' income. The requirement for money up front, cash, is an absolute barrier for many prospective investors.

It's possible to raise funds with gifts from parents and relatives, but the stark reality for most prospective investors is that at some point they must come up with cash from their own pockets.

Cash isn't easy to save. The less you earn, the larger the percentage of your income which must be devoted to basics—food, shelter, and clothing.

Disposable income is minimal, and the idea of saving is like losing weight—something to do tomorrow.

But for those first buying property, for those without the prospect of gifts or grants, the message must be that saving is crucial in the investment process.

How to save? Postpone a new car or buy a cheaper one. Pay credit card bills on time to avoid interest charges. Start a savings account or a money-market fund. Eat in more often. Dress conservatively—find styles to last for more than a season or a year. Look for free or low-cost amusements. See which lenders are offering free checking accounts. Buy at sales and use coupons.

If the idea of saving and sacrifice seems tedious and unfair, don't worry. Other than a few fortunate exceptions, if you look at the history of most successful people, you'll see there was a point in their lives when they worked very hard to build the foundation for later profits and wealth.

Doctors with high incomes today were once med students and residents working 80, 90, or 100 hours a week. Immigrants who work at two or three jobs to raise capital and then buy small businesses where they put in 14- and 16-hour days are legendary. And many successful realty investors began with limited capital and a willingness to paint walls and clean toilets. They knew that to have more, to be successful, saving was essential and sacrifice unavoidable.

RAISING EXTRA INCOME WITH BOARDERS, MINGLES UNITS, AND ACCESSORY APARTMENTS

As difficult as it may be to raise a down payment, monthly mortgage bills are an equally tough problem for most entry-level investors. Even with a gift from parents or others to meet a down payment, even when investors meet lender income requirements, monthly costs are often so high that would-be buyers are condemned to a "house poor" existence, a situation where so much income is devoted to monthly mortgage payments that nothing is left over. In some cases it's actually possible to find large homes with beautiful lawns and no furniture.

Shared housing is a realistic solution to the monthly income problem faced by many entry-level investors. But to have a successful arrangement, investors must look for properties that are not only in the path of future growth, properly priced, and graced with the potential for appreciation, they must also find properties that lend themselves to shared living arrangements.

To have a solid arrangement with a boarder, the tenant's territory must be defined, preferably space with a separate entrance such as a first-floor room or a basement area, which allows privacy to both renter and landlord.

In addition to space, there are other matters to be determined. Will the tenant have a separate bath? How are kitchen privileges handled? How much is the rent and when is it due? (Check the classified ads for local prices.) Does the tenant pay a portion of the utilities? How much notice is required to terminate the rental? If you have a boarder and live in a rent-control area, are you subject to controls? What about pets? Loud music? Waterbeds? Visitors? Parking?

To see the value of a boarder, consider how monthly mortgage payments are supplemented. Suppose your tenant has a basement room with bath, shares a kitchen, and pays $350 a month in a suburban setting. At 8 percent interest, $350 a month will support a 30-year conventional mortgage worth more than $47,500. In addition, as we shall see below, there are tax advantages which may shelter some of the monthly income you receive.

There's growing recognition that housing costs today are so high that individual ownership is very difficult for young adults, the elderly, and those with limited incomes. One approach to these problems is a so-called "mingles" apartment—condominium units with two master bedroom suites separated by a central living room, dining room, and kitchen. Mingles units have clearly defined common areas as well as private space. As an alternative to mingles units, single-family homes with two master bedrooms can work equally well.

The idea of a boarder assumes that certain common facilities will be shared, most notably the kitchen. A somewhat different approach is to buy or create an "accessory" unit within a single-family house. An accessory apartment with a kitchen, bath, and sleeping area is at least the equivalent of an efficiency apartment.

But accessory apartments may be prohibited under local zoning. Generally when you have an area of single-family homes, zoning prevents the installation of a second kitchen. Many jurisdictions, however, have now begun to license accessory apartments, in part because they want utility hookups for gas, electric, and water lines to meet local codes and also because area housing costs may be so high that without accessory units there would be a housing shortage. Check local rules for accessory apartments, particularly those relating to townhouses (they're often not allowed) and new owners (if an accessory unit is not licensed when you buy, there may be a waiting period, perhaps as long as a year, before one will be permitted).

When buying property, beware of any representations that "of course, you can rent the basement unit. We get $400 a month." If the property isn't zoned correctly, objections by a neighbor could quickly end such arrangements. Also, look out for euphemisms. An "English basement" in some areas is simply a code phrase for an unlicensed apartment.

If you have a boarder or accessory apartment, you must report all rental income. However, you may also deduct a proportionate share of utilities and depreciate the tenant's portion of the house. Beware that when you sell the property, not all of it will qualify as a personal residence if a portion has been rented. Speak to a CPA or tax attorney for details.

SWEAT EQUITY: MAKING USE OF TIME ON YOUR HANDS

Would you pay $100 to fill your car's tank with gas? Not if you can help it, but there are people who pay that much, and more.

But if gasoline sells for $1 a gallon or so, how can anyone possibly pay $100 to fill a tank, even one that holds 25 or 30 gallons?

Filling a tank includes both the cost of gasoline and the value of the driver's time. If a top lawyer billing $400 an hour takes five minutes to drive to a gas station, five minutes to fill his tank, and five minutes to settle the bill, his 15 minutes represent $100 in lost earnings—plus he's had to pay for the gas.

If our lawyer takes two hours to paint a room in his house, he's effectively paid $800. It's very much cheaper for him to hire a professional painter.

Entry-level investors not yet established in their business, profession, or work are unlikely to have this problem. For them labor is cheap. Hiring a professional is costly and perhaps impractical if cash is in short supply.

Thus many entry-level investors are in a position where they can benefit from properties that require labor-intensive improvements. Painting, landscaping, minor repairs, and cleaning up are all tasks where investors can do their own work.

In addition, there are situations where given properties may be attractive to entry-level investors but unappealing to wealthier individuals who rely on high-priced professional contractors. In some situations, a deal may only make sense if investor labor is available.

The argument here is not that investors can do an equal or better job than professionals, or that professionals should not be used for certain tasks, but rather that beginning investors often have an abundance of cheap labor that they can use productively. In addition, by doing their own work, entry-level investors can have a better understanding of repair needs, valuable information for future projects.

STATE PROGRAMS

Many entry-level investors simply want property to occupy rather than rent out, a situation which may entitle them to participate in various state and local housing programs.

In general terms, such programs work as follows: A government agency, such as a county housing authority, sells bonds to investors. Because governments represent little risk, and because the interest income from some bonds may be tax exempt, the housing authority pays a low interest rate to bond holders, say 4 percent at a time when mortgage rates are at 7.5 percent.

The housing agency then takes the money raised in the bond market and lends it to local home buyers. The home buyers might pay 5.5 percent interest, less than commercial lenders charge for loans but somewhat more than the housing authority pays bond holders. In effect, the local government encourages local homeownership by providing low-interest mortgages, bond holders earn interest, and the housing authority incurs no cost because the interest paid by home buyers covers that expense. Everyone is happy.

Bond-backed programs are not designed for investors per se, they're oriented toward owner-occupants. But if you're going to live in the property, have never owned property before or have not owned in the past three years, and have an income within certain limits, then you may qualify for preferential financing at interest rates 2 to 3 percent below conventional financing. On a $75,000 mortgage, the difference in monthly payments for a 30-year loan at 7.5 percent ($524.41) and one at 5.5 percent ($425.84) is $98.57—almost $1,200 a year.

MORTGAGE CREDIT CERTIFICATE (MCC) PROGRAMS

With bond-backed mortgages we saw that qualified borrowers could shave monthly cash costs, but there is another approach to lower ownership costs which also works nicely for entry-level buyers.

Under the federal Mortgage Credit Certificate (MCC) program, each state is allowed to grant home buyers a tax credit equal to a percentage of their annual interest.

A tax credit is a much more valuable benefit then a tax deduction. For instance, if you're in the 28 percent tax bracket and can write off interest worth $1,000, your taxes will be reduced by $280. If you have a tax credit worth $1,000, then your tax bill can drop by $1,000.

To see how MCC programs work, suppose that Sutton buys a home and obtains MCC financing. Suppose his interest cost is $5,000 and he is allowed to claim as much as 20 percent of his entire interest bill as a tax credit. When April rolls around, Sutton can write off $4,000 in mortgage interest as an itemized deduction, and deduct $1,000 directly from his tax bill.

While the MCC program is attractive, it is not without problems.

If you refinance to get a lower rate, the MCC benefit may end. If you buy and sell at a profit, you may be subject to a recapture provision, depending on the specific state program. "Recapture," in this case, means the state gets some or all of the profit from the sale. Rentals may be limited or prohibited.

Alternatively, if you need a first home and realize that it may take several years to save for house No. 2, an MCC plan may work very nicely.

Then there is the problem of demand. MCC loans are attractive and many people would dearly love to obtain such financing. Alas, there is much demand and little supply. The result is that MCC financing will be unavailable once yearly state allocations are exhausted.

To find out more about bond-backed and MCC financing, speak with local brokers, lenders, and community housing specialists. As well, visit a local library and check sections 25 and 143 of the Internal Revenue Code for programming details and limitations.

14
Rolling Over with Little Risk

Whether one is an entry-level investor or a buyer with cash and established credit, the easiest, safest, and most plausible real estate investment of all is the property in which we live.

Think about the problems investors usually face. Need financing? Lenders will readily provide 90 percent loans to owner-occupants. Worried about vacancies and tenants? No problem for owner-occupants. Concerned about taxes? The rollover residence-replacement rule allows you to buy a new home of equal or greater value every two years and defer profits. And what about retirement? When you get to be age 55 or older, you have a one-time opportunity to write off up to $125,000 in real estate profits from the sale of a prime personal residence.

But as investors we want something more than any place with four walls and a roof. As discussed in Chapter 11, we want a special property, something in the path of future growth, something we can improve with sweat equity, something to serve as a stepping stone to larger properties, something with excess value we can tap.

Consider the Wilmonts. They bought a two-bedroom bungalow ten years ago for $48,000. They painted and patched, fixed the lawn, and two years later sold for $60,000. They then bought a three-bedroom property for $65,000 and repeated the process. Three years later, they sold the second home for $85,000 and bought a four-bedroom house for $90,000. By now the Wilmonts were good at painting and skilled enough to add bathroom vanities and a new kitchen countertop. House number three sold for $115,000, and the Wilmonts bought another four-bedroom house for $120,000. That property has just sold for $155,000, and now the Wilmonts are searching for a house in the $160,000 range.

What makes the Wilmonts interesting is that while they were fixing up each home, they were also working. They had income, and they had several other advantages as well.

- Convenience. When they went home after work, their tools were available; they didn't lose time commuting to the job site.
- Advantageous financing. Because the Wilmonts are owner-occupants and not "investors," they obtained two major benefits: Their interest rates were lower than rates paid by investors and their loan-to-value ratio was higher than the ratios usually available to investors. By investment standards, their financing was exceptional.
- Pacing. The Wilmonts went at their own speed, doing jobs on a schedule that meshed with their other activities.
- Cashing out. The government's rollover replacement rule says owner-occupants must buy new properties of equal or greater value to defer taxes. It doesn't say *cash* from the old property must be invested in a new home. The Wilmonts financed each property with 90 percent mortgages, a strategy which allowed them to pocket a large amount of cash after each sale. That cash, almost $86,000 after four sales, could be invested or used for still another house.
- Simultaneous settlements. To prevent a situation where the Wilmonts would own two houses at once—and more important, to prevent a situation where the Wilmonts might face two mortgage payments at the same time—each purchase was contingent on the sale *and* settlement of their current property. By making a deal depend on both sale and settlement, the Wilmonts were protected in case a purchaser failed to close on their property.
- Cash preservation. The Wilmonts agreed in each case to a somewhat higher purchase price in exchange for having points and closing costs paid by sellers.
- Tax benefits. The Wilmonts were able to write off interest costs and use the rollover residence-replacement rule to shelter profits when they sold.
- Anticipated growth. Because they selected properties in the path of future growth, the Wilmonts found it unnecessary to make large-scale improvements. Much of the increased value they enjoyed came from generally rising values plus the minor fix-up and repair work they did.
- Do-it-yourself. By sticking to basic improvements and repairs, the Wilmonts were able to do much of the work themselves, thereby avoiding high labor costs.

At the end of ten years the Wilmonts owned real estate worth more than three times as much as their original home, and in addition they had accumulated $86,000. Altogether, their low-risk approach to real estate investing brought them preferential tax treatment, terrific mortgage financing, great convenience, and little risk.

BUYING UP AND RENTING OUT

The Wilmonts were able to avoid income taxes from the sale of their properties by rolling over to new and more valuable homes each time they sold. The Fultons have also moved up and avoided taxes, but with a somewhat different strategy.

Rather than sell each time they move, the Fultons rent. Over a ten-year period they took the following steps.

They bought a small frame home for $52,000 with 90 percent financing. They fixed it up, and two years later it was worth $70,000. Monthly payments for principal, interest, taxes, and insurance totaled $575.

At this point the Fultons leased their property for $600 a month, subject to their buying a new home. They bought a second property for $75,000, again with 90 percent financing.

The $7,500 down payment needed for house number two was raised with a 15-year, self-amortizing second trust on the first house. In the sense that no additional cash was required out of pocket, the second home was a deal with no money down.

Three years later the Fultons bought a third property, this one for $95,000. By this point the first house was worth $80,000 and produced a monthly rent of $675, and the second property was worth $90,000.

To buy the third property the Fultons needed $9,500 down. They had an $80,000 property, their first, with a $46,800 first trust and a $7,500 second trust. They got a new second trust for $17,200 (80 percent of $80,000 equals $64,000 less the value of the existing first and second trusts). They paid off the original $7,500 second trust and used the remaining $9,700 as a down payment for the third house.

The second house, meanwhile, was now worth $100,000 and had a

How the Wilmonts Created Additional Equity

House	Purchase Price	Sale Price	Original Mortgage	Sale Expenses	Cash Balance
#1	$48,000	$60,000	$43,200	$4,800	$12,000
#2	$65,000	$85,000	$58,500	$6,800	$19,700
#3	$90,000	$115,000	$81,000	$9,200	$24,800
#4	$125,000	$155,000	$112,500	$12,400	$30,100
Total					**$86,600**°

° *Cash balance figures do not show an allowance for loan amortization. Loan amortization will increase cash balance figures.*

$67,500 mortgage. The Fultons rented this property for $800 a month.

At this point the Fultons had three houses. Their first property was worth $80,000, their second was worth $100,000, and their third was worth $95,000, a total of $275,000. They also had mortgages of $221,800 ($46,800, $17,500, $67,500, and $90,000). Their equity—market values less debt—was $53,200, exclusive of marketing costs and loan amortization. In addition, they also had income from the first two houses.

To buy a fourth property today, a home for $150,000, the Fultons merely refinance the second property with a second trust. That property is now worth $115,000 but only has an outstanding first trust of $67,500. With 80 percent financing from a non-conforming lender, the Fultons can take as much as $24,500 from the property (80 percent of $115,000 equals $92,000. That figure, less the original $67,500 mortgage, equals $24,500). Instead of taking out the largest possible loan, however, the Fultons instead opt for the $15,000 they need for their next house.

With their fourth house, the Fultons' portfolio looks like this:

- The first house, bought for $52,000, is worth $95,000 eight years later, a 7.82 percent rate of growth, compounded annually. That property has two loans outstanding, the original mortgage ($46,800) and the current second trust ($17,200). Exclusive of any loan amortization or marketing costs, their equity in this property is $31,000.
- The second house, bought for $75,000 six years ago, is now worth $115,000. The equity on this property is $32,500 after subtracting the original loan ($67,500) and the $15,000 second trust. The compounded annual return on this property is 7.38 percent.

Where the Fultons Got Their Money

1) They bought a home for $52,000. They put down $5,200.

2) They bought a second home for $75,000. They got a $7,500 second trust on the first house and used that money for a down payment.

3) Their third house, bought for $95,000, was financed with a new $17,200 second trust on the first property.

4) The fourth house cost $150,000 and was financed with a $15,000 second trust on house number two.

- The third house, now two years old, was bought for $95,000. It's worth $110,000 today and has an outstanding mortgage of $85,500. The equity in this property totals $24,500, an increase of 7.61 compounded annually.
- The fourth property, just purchased, cost $150,000. The mortgage totals $135,000, and the Fultons have equity worth $15,000 in this home.

So now, after eight years, the Fultons own four properties with a total value of $470,000. Equity, without figuring loan amortization (a plus) or marketing costs (a minus), totals $103,000. Cash investment: $5,200.

The Fultons picked properties where values increased and rents rose. And it's entirely possible that after eight years, they not only had equity worth $100,000, but also a positive cash flow from rentals.

It should be understood that not everyone will be as lucky as the Fultons. Values may not rise. Rents may not keep up with costs. A string of vacancies can deplete savings. A water heater can go cold or a dishwasher might break. Moreover, unlike the Wilmonts, the Fultons need to manage their properties with care. In addition, the equity built up by the Fultons is overstated. If they sell the rental properties, their profits will be taxed, most likely at the 28 percent level.

Who did better, the Wilmonts or the Fultons?

On a cash basis, the Wilmonts are greatly ahead while the Fultons have more equity in their properties. The Wilmonts have no tenant headaches, but also no deductions for depreciation. The Wilmonts' assets are far smaller than the Fultons', an advantage to the Fultons in the face of inflation. The Fultons must pay monthly costs when vacancies occur, and if several vacancies arise at one time, monthly payments might be substantial. In addition, the Fultons may be covered by rent control, a factor that can influence rental rates and property values.

The Fultons have the better financial picture, but the Wilmonts have fewer hassles. They both did better than most homeowners, and certainly their position is vastly superior to someone who merely rented during the past eight to ten years. In essence, the strategy used by either family can be attractive, depending on investor interests and concerns.

15

Getting Started with Multiple Units

In the last chapter we saw how the Wilmonts and Fultons started as low-risk investors using seven central strategies.

- They only bought single-family homes.
- They obtained low-interest financing with high loan-to-value ratios because they were owner-occupants.
- They bought in the path of future growth.
- They bought properties in need of repair.
- They benefited from homeowner tax advantages.
- The Wilmonts took advantage of the rollover residence-replacement rule to postpone taxes.
- The Wilmonts never worried about rent control, because they never dealt with tenants.

Although single-family homes can be extremely attractive investments, when they're empty owners are faced with a 100 percent vacancy factor. In comparison, if you have a vacancy in a triplex, the majority of your income isn't cut off.

Multiple units also offer certain economies of scale. It's usually cheaper per unit, for example, to re-roof a four-plex than a single-family house. It's also usually cheaper per unit to buy properties in quantity rather than one at a time.

Yet the Wilmonts and Fultons are cautious investors. How could they, or you, deal with multiple units, have little risk, and still preserve all or most of the six marketplace advantages cited above?

When the Kents began looking at investment real estate three years ago, they quickly discovered that down payment requirements for investors were far tougher than those for owner-occupants. While owners could buy property with as little as 5 or 10 percent down, investors would be lucky to find non-conforming loans for 20 percent down. For a property valued at $150,000, owners could pay as little as $7,500 at closing, but investors would need at least $30,000. If they used a conforming mortgage, the Kents would need $45,000 at closing.

The extra $22,500 down was a difficult hurdle to the Kents. Also, while the Kents could buy a single-family residence as the Wilmonts and Fultons did, buying a single-family prime residence now meant they would not get rental income or investor tax deductions immediately. Rather than make an either/or choice—either a single-family home or a pure investment property—the Kents compromised. They went for both.

The Kents looked for properties in the path of future growth, in need of repair, and priced below comparable real estate. But instead of single-family homes, they searched for properties with two to four units.

The way many lenders work, if you live on a property and it has four or fewer units, you're an owner-occupant and entitled to rates and terms better than those available to pure (non-resident) investors. That means lower interest costs and a smaller down payment.

In addition, the rental units under your roof provide income to offset basic ownership costs. In the best case, the rental units pay all housing expenses, allowing you to use one unit rent-free.

What the Kents found were several four-plex units near a local university. Although area homes were priced at $150,000, a four-plex in need of repair was available for $240,000—$60,000 a unit.

If the Kents bought a single-family home they would have needed 10 percent down ($15,000). Monthly mortgage costs for principal and interest would be $990.58, assuming a 30-year, $135,000 loan at 8 percent. Add in $125 a month for taxes and $35 a month for insurance, and basic housing costs for a single-family home would total $1,150.58 ($990.58 plus $125 plus $35).

With a four-plex, the Kents would pay $24,000 up front, but their monthly costs—after rentals—would be far lower.

Assuming again that they found a 30-year loan at 8 percent interest, they would finance $216,000 at a monthly cost of $1,584.93. Add monthly costs of $200 for taxes and $50 for insurance, and the basic monthly costs for the four-plex would be $1,834.93 ($1,584.93 plus $200 plus $50).

Unlike the single-family home, however, the four-plex produces an income—$500 per unit in this case. Given a $1,500 rental income, the fourth unit's cost—except for repairs, maintenance, and utilities—is just

$335 ($1,835 less $1,500). And that income, reflected in leases, allows the Kents to easily qualify for a loan.

The four-plex owner's unit does not compare to a single-family home in size or quality, but the Kents were not concerned. Their goal was to build equity and an income stream and while their four-plex was not a castle, it was a place to start.

What the Kents found was that by painting, repairing, and replacing they increased property values. Since they lived on site, the work was easily accessible, and they could fix up at their own pace.

They also discovered that good financing was not the only advantage. They're allowed to depreciate the three units they rent, and if they sell the property, the profits on that portion of the property used as a personal residence can be deferred under the rollover residence replacement rule.

A manager was unnecessary since they lived on the property. However, proximity meant they were instantly on call if a tenant had problems—good news in the event of an emergency, not so good in terms of privacy.

Area rents generally rose 3 percent annually as a result of inflation and demand, but because of their improvements the Kents were able to raise rents 5 percent each year for three years. At the end of this period, their monthly mortgage was still $1,585, but their monthly income now totaled $1,735. In essence, the cost for their own unit at this point is about $100 a month, assuming no vacancies and other good fortune.

More realistically, the Kents can anticipate a vacancy here and there when a unit will be unrented for several weeks at a time. As well, the Kents may find it necessary to make large repairs that require professional assistance.

If the Kents rent their unit and move elsewhere, they will earn another $578.81 each month, a figure allowing them to collect a positive cash flow of about $475 a month exclusive of vacancies and big repairs. Equally important, when the Kents bought they paid $10 for each actual or potential income dollar the property could produce ($500 × 4 units × 12 = $24,000). Now, with a higher income, the same rate suggests that the property is worth $277,830 ($578.81 × 4 = $2,315.24 × 12 = $27,783).

Will the property really support a $278,000 value? If someone paid $27,800 down, there would be a $250,200 mortgage. At 8 percent interest over 30 years, that mortgage will require monthly payments for principal and interest of $1,835.88. With monthly rentals of $1,735, a new owner-occupant will pay roughly $100 for his or her unit plus taxes, insurance, and repairs—about the same deal that the Kents got three years and $38,000 earlier.

About the same, but not quite. The Kents saw the property's value rise at a faster rate than the general market because they benefited from inflation, demand, *and* improvements—repairs, painting, fixing up, etc. But it's unlikely that new owners will be able to make additional repairs and still have a property that's not "overimproved."

After three years the Kents have several choices.

- They can sell the property and collect $62,000 ($24,000 from their down payment plus $38,000 in profits), less marketing costs. They'll have to pay regular income taxes on profits of $28,500 (75 percent of $38,000) because three of four units were used as rentals while one was used as a personal residence. The remaining profit can be rolled over if the Kents buy a prime residence of equal or greater value within two years.
- They can just stay where they are.
- They can remain and refinance. In this situation the Kents are owner-occupants and thus able to obtain financing unlikely to be available to pure (nonresident) investors. For instance, if the Kents refinance with a 90 percent LTV loan, they can raise $250,200 ($278,000 × 90 percent). From this sum they must deduct the original mortgage ($216,000 less amortization) and closing costs. At 8 percent interest over 30 years, a $250,000 mortgage will cost $1,834 a month. With rents now pegged at $1,736.43 ($578.81 × 3) their unit will have an effective rental of roughly $100 a month plus their general costs for taxes and insurance. This option, of course, leaves the Kents with approximately $34,000 in their pockets— $250,000 in new financing less the original $216,000 mortgage.
- After an appropriate period of occupancy once they have refinanced, the Kents may elect to move. If they do, then in general terms they will have four units to rent, a monthly rent roll of roughly $2,315.24 ($578.81 × 4), and a monthly mortgage of $1,834. They will have a monthly cash flow of nearly $500 to offset taxes, insurance, and repairs—enough, in all probability, to have some positive cash flow. A positive cash flow, plus $34,000 from refinancing, will allow the Kents to move on to their next property in good financial shape.

What can they do with $34,000? Buy another small property with multiple units. With 10 percent down, they can afford a $340,000 property as owner-occupants.

(Note: Everyone will understand if the Kents move after a "reasonable" amount of time, whatever "reasonable" might be in light of given facts and circumstances. What the Kents can't do is refinance the property by claiming to be owner-occupants and then rent their unit soon after the loan is settled, because that will suggest that the real intent of the loan was to finance an investment property, something which may cause lenders to recall the loan.)

16
Buying with Others: Partnerships

When Maxwell saw a property that could easily be fixed up for quick resale, he reviewed the numbers. It was available for $100,000, needed repairs costing $10,000 if he did the work himself, and could be resold within six months. In addition, it would cost $1,000 a month to carry the property while it was being repaired and sold. Total cost: $116,000, more or less.

Maxwell was willing to work nights and weekends until the job was done. When finished, the property would be consistent with a neighborhood where homes typically sold for $150,000.

As Maxwell looked at this deal, he saw there was $34,000 in excess value he could create ($150,000 less $116,000) in a short time. Some of that value—say, $9,000—would be used for marketing expenses, but even after selling costs, $25,000 would still remain.

There was only one problem with Maxwell's figures. While his estimates might be correct, they didn't matter. Maxwell didn't have enough money for repairs, much less a down payment or carrying costs.

But Maxwell had a friend, Benton, who could help. Sometimes they talked about buying property together and now Maxwell had the ideal project. Here's what he did.

First, Maxwell tied up the property. He offered $100,000, but with a contingency. By November 4, about ten days after the seller's acceptance, the property had to have a structural inspection that was "satisfactory" to Maxwell. If the inspection wasn't satisfactory, the deal was off and Maxwell would get his deposit back in full. In effect, Maxwell had a no-cost option. If he couldn't get financing, the inspection could be declared unsatisfactory and the deal would end without expense.

Second, Maxwell made certain that he had the right to assign the contract without the seller's permission and without additional cost.

Third, once he had a contingent contract, Maxwell went to Benton and made this offer:

- A 50/50 partnership in exchange for Benton co-signing the loan, putting up $10,000 for the down payment, and $10,000 for repairs plus carrying costs (interest and taxes) of $1,000 a month for six months.
- After the first six months, Maxwell and Benton will equally share monthly overhead.
- Maxwell provided a list of needed repairs, a chart showing the order in which the work would be completed, and the amount of time required. Maxwell also listed those projects which would require professional help, such as an electrician to install several smoke detectors.
- When the property is sold, the order of repayment will be as follows: taxes, the existing mortgage, marketing costs, Benton's down payment, the money provided by Benton for repairs, the money paid by Benton to carry the property for the first six months, and then the money paid jointly by Maxwell and Benton to carry the property. Anything left over will be split 50/50. In effect, Maxwell won't earn a dime until all of Benton's money is repaid.

Maxwell has leverage because he has an effective option on the property and he's willing to do the work. Benton could place a backup contract on the property so that if Maxwell's offer falls through, he could get the house. But the deal's attraction is not owning the property outright; it's the *combination* of ownership and Maxwell's labor that will produce excess value in a relatively short period.

As he reviewed Maxwell's figures, Benton saw that half of the projected $25,000 profit would be $12,500—his share as a partner. If this amount was reduced by 28 percent to account for federal taxes, the annualized return on his $31,750 investment ($30,000 plus interest) would be 57 percent ($12,500 less 28 percent equals $9,000, the return earned over six months).

Benton, however, was cautious. Large profits in real estate were possible, and the deal outlined by Maxwell was fairly realistic. However, Maxwell had not calculated closing costs when the property was purchased ($3,000) nor at settlement when the house was sold ($2,000 above the $9,000 anticipated for brokerage expenses).

In addition, Maxwell projected three months to fix up the property and then three more months till settlement. It's entirely possible, thought Benton, that it will take longer to fix up and sell, especially since there was no way to guarantee buyer interest. Figure a nine-month project, rather than six as Maxwell projected, and carrying costs will rise by $3,000.

If Benton's conservative figures are correct, he has a good deal. If Maxwell's estimates are right, Benton has an even better arrangement. In the worst case there's little risk. If Maxwell will not or cannot make promised repairs, his share of the venture can be used to hire professionals. While professionals are costly, they also speed the redevelopment process, thereby reducing Benton's carrying costs. If it's necessary to sell the property at a break-even level, that price would be so far below neighboring properties that marketing costs could be slashed and selling times greatly accelerated.

For this deal to work, Maxwell and Benton must establish a formal partnership agreement with papers drawn up by an attorney. Major topics within the agreement should include:

First, a precise listing of Benton's and Maxwell's obligations.

Second, a list of needed repairs and improvements showing their costs, which will be made by Maxwell and which will be farmed out to others. Also, this list must provide deadlines showing when the work will be completed. If Maxwell does not do the work, or if the work is unduly delayed, the agreement must allow Benton to hire professionals and charge the expense against Maxwell's interest in the property.

Third, the partners must agree to a buy-out arrangement in case one wants to sell.

Fourth, an order of repayment must be established to show how money will be paid out at settlement.

Fifth, if there's a loss, the loss will be divided equally between the partners.

Sixth, risks should be listed. Among other risks, the property may be more expensive to repair than anticipated, it may take longer to fix than planned, it may not sell quickly, it may not sell at all, etc. The agreement should note that potential risks "include, but are not limited to," whatever potential problems are listed.

Seventh, although Maxwell and Benton were buying together as partners, and although they have a partnership agreement and a partnership name, the property should be bought by them as individuals. The reason for buying as individuals is that lenders will readily make investor loans to "natural persons," meaning you or me. Loans to "unnatural persons" such as corporations and partnerships are typically made by commercial lenders who are used to dealing with large borrowers and complex transactions, not small investors with single-family houses and relatively small loans who are neither a primary business target nor an especially lucrative one.

Creative Partnerships

Partnerships can be used to resolve a variety of small-investor problems by trading equity for money, skills, or services. Here are four brief examples showing how such partnerships might look.

- Weston can afford a $10,000 down payment but not a $250 monthly negative cash flow. He offers Remmington an interest in the property if Remmington will cover the first $10,000 in monthly losses. After Remmington has invested $10,000, all future profits and losses will be divided equally. Weston figures that in 40 months ($10,000 divided by $250) the property will either be sold or rents will increase to a point where he'll have little monthly expense.
- Bennett wants to convert a large home downtown into four condominium units. The legal work will cost $15,000, but rather than pay this sum, he offers lawyer Tully an interest in the property in exchange for legal services.
- Fogarty has a property that's in such poor condition it's unrentable. He agrees to give Sheffield a 20 percent interest if Sheffield will provide all the labor needed to repair the building within six months. Fogarty will supply needed materials.
- Hastings makes $750,000 a year from his medical practice. He offers Williams a 25 percent interest in a small building if Williams will do the repair work, manage the property for at least five years, and build an addition onto each unit. It's cheaper for Hastings to give up equity than to invest his valued time in the building.

A partnership agreement is crucial because there are many ways to create a partnership. How a partnership is structured will determine such issues as individual liability, tax status, and the rights of each partner.

"General partnerships," for example, have two or more partners, and each is fully liable for any losses sustained by the partnership. If Arcola Associates has 10 partners and loses $50,000, *each general partner* may be held responsible for not just a share of the loss, but the entire amount.

Worse yet, general partners may be responsible for enormous debts. Suppose an Arcola worker hits a pedestrian with a truck, and the partnership is sued for $5 million. If the partnership must pay a $5 million judgment, each general partner can be responsible for the entire amount.

Not everyone wants unrestricted liability, which is why "limited partnerships" evolved. Here there are one or more general partners plus a number of limited partners. The limited partners' liability cannot exceed the amount of their investment.

There is a catch. A "limited" partner can be classified as a "general" partner by taking an active role in the partnership's management and decision-making process. And once seen as a general partner, that individual has unlimited liability for the partnership's debts.

But to get maximum tax write-offs, to claim up to $25,000 a year against regular income, investors *must* be active, they must own 10 percent or more of a property, and they must participate in the major decisions affecting the property.

Thus partnerships may present a problem. Investors don't want unlimited liability, but they must be active to earn maximum tax write-offs.

Does this mean limited partners cannot write off any losses against regular income?

The issue of who can, and who cannot, write off partnership losses is complex. A ball of twine has fewer twists and turns than the rules relating to partnership deductions, and so the best course of action is to go immediately to a tax professional for specific advice.

In general terms, here are the major issues to consider.

- To be considered "active" and to qualify for a federal write-off, an individual may be required to act as a general partner, with all the liability such an arrangement entails. IRS rules state that "unless future regulations provide an exception, limited partners cannot actively participate in rental real estate activities."
- You are generally considered an active investor if you participated in the activity 500 hours within the tax year; if you participated as much as any other investor and at least 100 hours during the tax year; or if you "participated in the activity on a regular, continuous, and substantial basis." Note that other standards may also apply.
- It may be possible to be a general partner and still not be regarded as an active investor for tax purposes.
- Individuals, say the IRS rules, "can deduct losses from rental real estate activities (in which they actively participated) from up to $25,000 of nonpassive income. Similarly, they can offset credits from such activities against tax on up to $25,000 of nonpassive income after

taking into account any losses allowed under this exception." (Parentheses theirs.)
- Be aware that at this time, the ability to take losses phases out as incomes rise above $100,000.
- Consider the new activity rules that may allow rental real estate to be a nonpassive activity; that is, the requirement to spend more than half your time, at least 750 hours a year, on real estate matters.

In reviewing the list above, be aware that it is not complete, that other factors may apply, and that facts and circumstances may be important when determining your ability to write off losses. For the latest details, please speak with a tax attorney, CPA, or enrolled agent.

17
Equity Sharing

In the last chapter we explored partnerships and saw how two or more people could pool their resources to create profitable deals. However, the partnership we described was a pure investment; no one with an ownership interest actually lived on the property. It's possible to structure a partnership with at least one owner-occupant, however, an arrangement called "equity sharing."

An equity-sharing agreement might work like this: The Huttons want a place to live, and although they can afford rent, they have no savings for a down payment. Rather than wait several years until they accumulate funds—by which time property values will probably have risen—they ask Mr. Logan if he would buy with them.

They want a small house and agree that if Logan will supply the down payment and closing costs, they'll pay the mortgage, taxes, and insurance. They also agree to repair the property, provided Logan pays for all supplies. Ownership will be split 50/50.

The Huttons and Logan find a house that sells for $120,000 and Logan, the investor, puts up the entire $12,000 down payment. Many lenders, however, will finance deals only when the resident co-owner puts up at least 5 percent of the purchase price with his or her own funds, a condition not met by our investors.

The Huttons now reside in a property with a fair market rent of $1,100 per month. Since Logan owns half the property, they pay him $550 per month. Logan turns around and uses that money to pay off his share of the mortgage, taxes, and insurance. The Huttons use the other $550 to pay their share of the expenses. Note that the Huttons *must* pay a fair market rent to have a valid equity-sharing arrangement.

For tax purposes, the Huttons are treated as owner-occupants. They can write off property taxes and mortgage interest to the extent of their ownership interest. Logan can write off his proportionate share of mortgage interest, taxes, insurance, and depreciation. Since Logan isn't paying utilities, he can't deduct those costs.

What we have is a deal with no negative cash flow because the Huttons are paying all monthly carrying costs. The Huttons also have a place to live and a project to fix up and repair.

Logan, our investor, gets tax benefits and the possibility of appreciation. More important, he has access to owner-occupant, low-interest, high-LTV financing, and he doesn't worry about finding tenants or hiring managers—the Huttons are both.

When the property is sold, the Huttons will treat the sale as owner-occupants and roll their profits into a new property of equal or greater value. Logan will declare his profits as investment income.

In our deal between the Huttons and Logan, we have a situation where Logan provided money up front and the Huttons paid monthly costs. It's no less plausible to structure deals differently, depending on the needs of each co-owner.

- The Huttons can supply the down payment while Logan contributes $200 a month up to $10,000. After that, the Huttons will be responsible for all monthly costs.
- Logan might invest no money. Instead, he exchanges co-signing the loan and the use of his credit for an interest in the property.
- The Huttons can pay a fair market rental and receive an hourly fee for the repairs they make to offset their monthly rent bill. Money the Huttons receive for their labor is income to them personally, while

Equity Sharing with the Huttons and Mr. Logan

Purchase price	$120,000
Down payment	$12,000
Mortgage	$108,000
Monthly rent from Huttons	$1,100
Amount paid to Logan	$550
Amount paid for mortgage, taxes, expenses, etc.	$550
Amount Logan pays for mortgage, taxes, expenses, etc.	$550

cash spent by the partnership for their labor is likely to be deductible.

■ Suppose Logan is the Huttons' uncle. In that case they might pay him by check (so there's a record of the payments) for his proportionate share of the fair market rent, and each month he can give them a gift of equal size. Since the gift is below the $10,000-per-person yearly gift threshold, there's no tax on it, and Logan thus subsidizes his relatives while benefiting from an investment.

The keys to successful equity sharing are the right match of co-investors, financing, the correct property, and a suitable agreement between the co-owners.

Co-investors should clearly understand how the deal is supposed to work, who's responsible for what, and that if the deal fails, all co-investors fail with it.

The property should be a prototype investment choice—something in the path of future growth that needs improvement. While a single-family house is a good option, duplex, triplex, and four-plex units can work well under equity-sharing arrangements. With multiple units, the co-owner lives on-site, pays a fair market rent for his unit, manages the property, and performs required repairs and maintenance.

Units that may not work with equity sharing include condominiums (the monthly condo fee underwrites maintenance costs that could otherwise be borne by the resident co-owner in a freestanding house) or co-ops (co-op rules may not permit off-site ownership interests). Mingles units—apartments with two master bedroom suites—are workable in the sense that a co-owner can live in one suite while the other is rented. However, owner-occupied mingles units tend to be condo arrangements and that form of ownership is not the best choice for equity-sharing deals.

Standardized equity-sharing agreements are available but co-investors should have such forms reviewed by local attorneys (one for each side). Among the issues to cover: What happens if the residents don't pay rent, someone dies, or an owner goes bankrupt? What if one party wants to sell and the other wants to hold? What is the order of repayment when the property is sold? How will a loss be handled? What if the residents want to move; who's responsible for finding a tenant, if one is desired? If the property is refinanced, what gets paid first?

While it is important to have a good property and a good agreement when creating an equity-sharing arrangement, nothing will happen without financing. Not every lender will make an equity-sharing loan, so before spending time or money perfecting an equity-sharing arrangement, it pays to first find a financing source. Folks who can help include loan officers, real estate brokers, and attorneys who have previously handled equity-sharing deals.

Equity sharing is a low-risk approach to real estate ownership. From the investor's perspective, it neatly resolves a number of common headaches—management, financing, and leasing. From the resident's viewpoint, equity sharing speeds the acquisition process and provides a powerful financial backer. All in all, it's a good deal for both sides if done right.

18
Converting Assets

Much has been written about Wall Street's leveraged buyouts. With leveraged buyouts, someone—usually top management—purchases all outstanding shares and then takes the company private. At this point the buyers own not only the firm but also a huge amount of debt. To reduce their debt and streamline the company, the buyers sell off chunks of the old corporate behemoth. When done well, what's left is hopefully far less debt and a highly efficient, and highly profitable, core business.

On a smaller scale, real estate investors can use the same principles to reduce debt and enhance profits. The trick is perception. Where someone sees a single-family house, you see two lots. Where someone sees apartments, you see hotel rooms. Where someone sees an old factory, you see ministorage.

REDEFINING RENTALS

When Franklin bought a four-plex he thought he had a good deal. He'd live in one unit, rent the other three, and gradually repair and upgrade the whole place. In addition, Franklin had another idea.

Each unit had a garage behind the building, four bays in a single, one-story structure. Parking was important because the neighborhood streets were crowded and those with garages were spared the daily trouble of finding parking spaces. But the neighborhood also had many people who didn't drive, who didn't want parking hassles or costs. These people, thought Franklin, can be the basis of an opportunity.

Franklin had been renting apartments with garages for $525 monthly. Now, as tenants moved out, he took a different tack. He rented apartments for $500, and he separately leased parking spaces for $75 a month.

Seventy-five dollars was steep for neighborhood parking while $500 was a good deal for tenants without cars. As a result of his approach, Franklin found it easy to locate tenants but hard to lease parking spaces—just what he wanted.

Local zoning allowed Franklin to use his garage space for parking or light storage. Franklin kept one space for himself and took the other three spaces, an area 20 × 30 feet, called them "ministorage," and rented them out at $10 a square foot. Several nearby businesses leased space from Franklin because at $10 a square foot, it was far cheaper to rent space from him than to use valuable commercial property for storage.

At $10 a square foot, Franklin took in $500 a month from his garages (20 × 30 = 600 square feet; $10 × 600 = $6,000 a year or $500 a month). His rental per space was $166.67 a month ($500 divided by 3) and so his effective rental rose from $525 a month to $667 ($500 for each apartment plus $167 for each space).

By converting garage space to ministorage, Franklin increased his monthly rent roll by $142 per unit ($667 less $525). His annual income rose by $5,112 ($142 × 3 × 12). If investors will pay $10 for each revenue dollar Franklin's property produces, the value of his investment has risen by more than $50,000.

CREATING EXTRA RENTAL UNITS

A similar approach was taken by the Haskells. Their plan was to buy, fix up, and move out. However, the property they bought was larger than their personal needs required. They had excess space, which they converted into monthly income by turning an otherwise empty basement into a legal accessory apartment. The basement had a full bath and paneled rec room already, so to make the extra unit they simply installed a galley kitchen, put in a separate electric meter, and upgraded an outside basement door. The work cost $4,750, but the Haskells were able to rent the unit for $375 monthly. The tenant, of course, also paid all electrical costs.

At $375 a month, it took the Haskells just 13 months to recover their basic investment, excluding interest costs. After 13 months, however, they had additional income to offset monthly mortgage costs as well as a more valuable property. At 8 percent interest over 30 years, $375 a month covers payments on a mortgage worth $51,106.31.

If they should decide to move and rent out their home, the Haskells could lease to one tenant who might then offset his rent with income from the accessory unit, a fact which would allow the Haskells to get a better lease. If they were to sell, the accessory apartment could serve as an income unit or a separate suite for a family member, attractive considerations for many prospective purchasers.

And whether or not the Haskells stayed or moved, the improvements they made enhanced the property's value, a factor lenders will appreciate if the property is refinanced. At the same time, the Haskells may qualify more easily for a loan because rent from the accessory unit increases their income.

Both Franklin and the Haskells used low-cost, low-risk strategies to increase values and income. Perkins used a different approach, but the same principal.

CREATING NEW USES

Perkins bought an old factory, a three-story building on the fringe of what had been an industrial area. With economic changes, much of the industry that was once active in the city had now disappeared, and the old factory remained as a monument of sorts to past enterprise.

Perkins had no machines or equipment to put in the old structure, but he didn't buy it to house a factory. Instead, Perkins saw a building with 16-foot ceilings, huge windows, plenty of parking, and enormous open spaces.

If Perkins rented the building as still another factory, he was unlikely to get more than $3 a square foot. The area had plenty of factory and warehouse space and didn't need more.

But Perkins's idea was to convert the factory into an artists' colony. Each unit would be a combination studio and apartment with a bath and small kitchen. High walls and big windows would be ideal to showcase artwork. Large sculptures could be made and moved because the building had a huge walk-on elevator, a lift that measured 20 by 20 feet.

Perkins didn't need fancy finishes or a doorman. Instead, he whitewashed the building, divided the interior with plain white walls, and installed basic kitchens and baths. Since the ceilings were so high, tenants could build lofts if they wanted more space.

Average units contained 1,000 square feet of space and rented for $800 a month—about $9.60 per square foot. However, because some area was given over to common elements—hallways, stairs, and the front lobby—the effective rent per square foot was somewhat lower.

For Perkins, though, the deal worked well. He had taken property sold as undesirable industrial space and converted it to a more valued use. And when he refinanced, the income produced by the property allowed him to get a far higher mortgage than like properties in the area.

CONVERTING OWNERSHIP

When considering conversions, it's important to see what zoning will allow. For instance, when Andrews bought an old row house downtown, he knew there was little market for a four-story rental unit with nine bedrooms, two kitchens, and four baths. However, the property was zoned as a small apartment and up to five units were allowed.

Because of zoning, Andrews could readily divide the property. But if he had more than four units on one site, he would fall under local rent-control rules, something he wanted to avoid.

To resolve this problem, Andrews had an architect draw up plans dividing the property into five units, each with separate gas, water, and electric meters. He then had a lawyer convert the units into condominiums and sold off one unit. The unit sale paid for the conversion as well as much of the construction and left Andrews with four units, control of the building, and a rent-control exemption.

For Andrews to accomplish the conversion, he needed permission from his lender because when he financed his property, the land and all improvements were pledged as loan security. By changing from fee-simple to condo ownership, and by selling off one unit, Andrews changed the conditions under which his financing had been granted.

The easiest way for Andrews to get a release is simply to pledge net proceeds from the unit sale to the lender—that is, any money left over after construction, marketing, taxes, and closing costs had been paid. This pay-off will reduce Andrews's mortgage balance on the rest of the property and lower the loan-to-value ratio on the remaining mortgage, a condition which most lenders prefer.

But if it turns out that the lender will not allow a conversion, then Andrews needs a different tactic. He must refinance the property when it's converted to condo status and simultaneously pay off the old loan.

Condo conversions can be an interesting adventure in cities with rent control. Local rules, for example, may forbid condo conversions without the approval of a majority of tenants, rules which effectively mean that owners must buy tenant approval with discounted units or other enticements.

By dividing his property, Andrews went from being the owner of a nine-bedroom house, something rarely needed in this era of small families, to a landlord with several units more attuned to modern market conditions and thus more valuable. Also, because small units typically have a higher price per square foot than larger units, his property became more valuable for this reason as well.

BUYING SMALL AND EXPANDING

Purchasing property today and expanding in the future is a popular approach for many investors. The logic of this strategy is that investors who cannot afford a larger property now can add on when they have more money. Although there are cases where this approach makes sense, not all properties are suitable candidates for expansion. As Terhune found out, the economics may not be workable.

The Fairlands area is a neighborhood of three- and four-bedroom homes, where Terhune was surprised to find a two-bedroom cottage. It was the neighborhood's cheapest property and had enough land to expand, so Terhune thought it might make a good fix-up-and-enlarge project.

But as Terhune spoke to builders and architects, he made an interesting discovery. The property could be expanded, but the cost of expansion was so great that it would be cheaper to buy one of the larger area homes.

Terhune could easily add a wing to the house with two bedrooms and a bath. But if he made this addition, where would he feed all the people who might presumably use the additional space? The house had no dining area and only a tiny kitchen.

He could add a second expansion, this one enlarging the kitchen and creating a dining area. But this choice only magnified another problem. The property was built with a heating system and electrical capacity suitable for a small cottage, not a suburban castle. A bigger home would mean more cubic volume to heat. More electrical outlets, in turn, would require new wiring and a larger service box.

As for air-conditioning, because the house had radiators—a very effective and efficient form of heating—there were no ducts for air-conditioning. Terhune would be forced either to build ducts or use room air-conditioners. In either case, he would again need more electricity than was currently available.

When he added up the numbers, Terhune found that by the time the cottage was expanded, it would cost no less than other Fairlands properties—and then only after a great amount of work.

Terhune's proposed expansion was unworkable because neighborhood values didn't justify his costs and because the house was a poor expansion candidate. There are situations, however, where expansion can work.

Edison's three-story townhouse was in the middle of town, an area where ground was very expensive. Unfortunately, Edison didn't have much of it; his property measured only 20 feet wide and 90 feet long.

But with living space pegged at $200 a square foot and construction costs far lower, Edison could make money by expanding his house. And in his neighborhood, where prices seemed to rise weekly, the market would support the extra value he was creating.

But where could he expand? Edison couldn't go forward; the house was five feet from the sidewalk. He also couldn't go backward, at least not directly. If he built behind the property, he would lose two valued parking spaces. Zoning prohibited the addition of a fourth floor.

What Edison could do was go *over* his parking area. He could build a two-story addition to the rear of the house, an extension measuring 15 by 20 feet, providing he didn't add on at ground level.

Like Terhune, Edison had to upgrade his electrical service and HVAC—heating, ventilation, and air-conditioning. He also had to obtain an assortment of building permits and pay a variety of fees.

The work cost Edison $75 per square foot, and since he had 600 square feet ($15 \times 20 \times 2$), his expansion was priced at $45,000. However, with finished space selling for $200 a square foot, he increased the value of his property by $120,000—a $75,000 difference.

FLIPPING CONTRACTS

Perhaps the single most risky form of conversion, and perhaps the most rewarding, is the process of flipping contracts. In basic terms, a contract flip works like this: Walters buys the Gurney property for $150,000 and schedules settlement in 90 days. Before settlement, however, Walters "sells" the property to Higgins for $170,000 and pockets the $20,000 difference between that price and the amount due to the original owner, Gurney.

Looking at this transaction more closely, we see that a number of conditions were required before Walters could make this deal.

First, Walters never "sold" the property. He "assigned" it. Because he never had title to the property, Walters didn't pay transfer taxes or lender fees. What he sold was his *right to purchase* at a certain time, at a particular price, and under certain conditions.

Second, the right to assign the property without seller permission had to be in the sales contract. If seller Gurney's approval was required and he saw that Walters was going to make $20,000, then surely Gurney would only agree if he could pocket $19,000.

Third, when he made his offer, Walters put down the smallest possible deposit. He also made certain that in the event of default, his loss was limited to the deposit and that neither the seller nor the seller's broker could collect additional damages.

Fourth, when he assigned the contract, the assignment agreement stated that Walters was not responsible if the seller did not perform as was required under the original contract.

Fifth, Higgins could not modify or change the terms found in the original agreement between Walters and Gurney. If Walters was required to lease the property for a year under the original contract, for example, Higgins was bound by that provision when he bought the assignment.

If we assume that Walters put up $10,000, then he doubled his money in 90 days. But what if Walters couldn't find a buyer willing to pay $20,000 more than he did? What if Walters couldn't find a buyer at all?

Under the agreement with Gurney, Walters was clearly obligated to go through with the deal. But by limiting damages to his deposit, Walters put $10,000 at risk—a considerable sum but not nearly so large as his risk if damages were not limited.

For Walters to succeed, he needed a buyer who was willing to accept a higher value for the property *and* was able to make settlement on the date established between Walters and Gurney. He needed to consult with an attorney to assure that his rights to assign the property and to limit potential damages were guaranteed. He also needed to restrict his obligations to Higgins, to make certain he was required to turn over his purchase rights and nothing more.

Flipping contracts can be enormously profitable, but entry-level investors may not have $10,000 to lose. An alternative approach, one with less risk, is the use of options.

19
Options, Leases, and Profits

Not every real estate deal depends on property ownership. Instead, it's often enough to have certain rights, such as the right to use the property at a given cost or to purchase at a particular price.

The most basic type of option is the simple purchase offer with a contingency clause. Stevens will buy the Radnor property, *if* a structural inspection made within ten days is satisfactory to Stevens. If the inspection isn't satisfactory, the deal is off, and Stevens's deposit will be returned.

Stevens has an option because he can buy the property at a given price and terms. If he doesn't want it, he can get out of the deal without cost—assuming his offer is properly written.

But suppose that Stevens wasn't ready to buy the Radnor house. He might try a different approach. He might offer to lease the property for a year (or two years or whatever) and then buy it at a given price.

To create the best deal, Stevens must carefully tailor his option with an agreeable monthly rent and an acceptable future purchase price.

Ideally, Stevens will pay nothing for the option, current rental rates for the lease, and today's price for the property even though it won't be bought for a year or two. But seller Radnor is sure to want a better deal. He might want a lump-sum amount up front, an expense Stevens should avoid. Instead, Stevens might offer a lease rate above prevailing market levels, say $900 rather than $850.

Next, Stevens will want to argue that all of his rent should be a credit against the purchase price if he exercises his option. Radnor will counter and say that since Stevens is using the property, he's only paying fair market rates. Stevens, in turn, will contend that at least a portion of the rent should apply to the purchase price. Whatever percentage Stevens suggests will be disputed by Radnor, but Stevens will try to keep some portion of the monthly rent as a purchase credit. In this example, let's say that 30 percent of the monthly rent will be considered a credit.

As to the purchase price, if area values are rising, Stevens might suggest a market worth that's high relative to today's market but lower than anticipated future values. If housing prices are rising by 10 percent a year and the property is worth $100,000 now, Stevens might want an option to buy for $105,000 within the coming year or $110,000 in two years.

So now we have a deal where Stevens is renting property, has the right to buy it at a given price, and is receiving a monthly credit toward the purchase. If he buys in a year, he pays $105,000, less $3,240 in rental credits ($900 × 30 percent = $270 × 12). If the property is worth $110,000, he then saves $8,240. However, Stevens paid an extra $50 a month, so his $8,240 benefit should be reduced by $600 ($50 × 12) to give a fair picture. In effect, Stevens has a profit of $7,640.

If Stevens buys after two years, he pays $110,000 less a rental credit of $6,480 ($3,240 × 2). Since his rental premium is now $1,200 ($50 × 24), his true price for the property is $104,720 ($110,000 less $6,480 plus $1,200). If the property is worth $120,000, Stevens is ahead $15,280.

Investors should be aware the lenders have tightened lease/option standards in recent years. Many now want rental credits maintained as cash in an escrow account and not simply pocketed by owners. For the latest trends, be certain to speak with local lenders before entering into a lease/purchase agreement.

To protect his interest, Stevens needs to take four additional steps.

First, he needs the right to sublet at will; otherwise he will either live on the property or face a very expensive vacancy. Subleasing will allow Stevens to offset his monthly cost with rental income. If rentals rise quickly, he can cover his high rent. Indeed, if rentals truly soar—an unlikely event—Stevens might even generate a positive cash flow.

Second, Stevens needs the right to assign his option. This means that if

Mr. Stevens's Lease-Purchase Agreement

	One-Year Lease	Two-Year Lease
Purchase price	$105,000	$110,000
Rent	$900	$900
Rent credit	30 percent	30 percent
Credit value	$3,240	$6,480
Less rent premium	$600	$1,200
Appreciation	10 percent	10 percent
Market value	$110,000	$120,000
Profit	$7,640	$15,280

someone wants to buy such rights as Stevens holds, they can be sold. In the same way that people flip property contracts or sell second trusts, Stevens will be able to profit from the ownership of paper rather than dirt.

Third, Stevens should record his option among the public land records to alert prospective purchasers to his rights.

Fourth, Stevens should work with an attorney or broker (as appropriate) to prepare both a proper lease and a separate, but related, sales agreement.

The idea of an option is that in exchange for something—cash, a lease, whatever—a property owner gives up certain rights. In the case of Radnor, he gave up the right to withhold the sale of his property in exchange for Stevens's lease arrangement. However, since Radnor is actually the property's owner until Stevens exercises his option, Radnor can depreciate the property and take other tax benefits. (Note that in the case of a long-term lease, say 30 years or more, the lease holder rather than the owner of record may be able to depreciate the property. Speak to a tax attorney or CPA for specific details and advice.)

If Stevens does not buy the Radnor property within the lease term, the lease ends and with it Stevens's right to buy. Whatever money Stevens paid under the option is retained by Radnor.

A more sophisticated option arrangement is the "sale and leaseback" agreement sometimes used in commercial real estate. Here a property owner, perhaps a corporation or association, sells the building it occupies and then leases it on a long-term basis from the new owner.

In such arrangements, what really happens is that by selling the building, the old owner gets financial flexibility from the cash generated by the sale plus use of the building. The old owner then pays rent, but the rental cost is offset by the value of the sale price. The new owner gets a depreciable property, a fully occupied building, and a long-term lease which makes financing easy.

Options can also work with land as well as developed property. If Tilden wants to build a subdivision of 60 homes, he might build with a somewhat complex option from farmer Baxter. It works this way:

Tilden gets an option to buy Baxter's farm in exchange for an up-front payment. The option provides that Tilden has the right to survey the farm, subdivide it, and buy lots individually for a period of five years. If Tilden has not bought the entire farm in five years, his up-front payment as well as all unsold property will be kept by Baxter.

Tilden then subdivides the land, lays out improvements (streets, sidewalks, etc.), and erects three model homes. Each time Tilden sells a house, he buys the lot selected by his purchaser, builds on it, and sells the lot and home as a package to the buyer.

Without an option, Tilden would have been forced to buy the entire farm, put money up front, plus pay monthly mortgage interest. With an option, he reduced his up-front expenses plus he never took out a mortgage. How? Because he scheduled settlement on each lot to coincide with the buyer's closing.

On a smaller scale, investors can take the same approach to tie up property for future development. For example, Veblen can pay $1,000 for the right to buy raw ground owned by Quarters. During the option period, Veblen—if allowed in the option—can have the property surveyed, acquire all the permits necessary for development, and then exercise his option when all preliminary development work is completed. Without an option, Veblen would be forced to buy the property. If he bought and needed permits were not available, he would then be stuck with a piece of ground that couldn't be developed.

20
Subdividing Land

Raw land is frequently seen as an attractive investment vehicle because it's a commodity with many options. It can be rented, subdivided, sold, built upon, combined with other property, or traded.

But for raw land to be profitable, it needs both a current economic use and potential value. A current economic use is important, whether the property is used for victory gardens or downtown parking, because otherwise raw land produces no income to offset taxes, interest, and insurance. And raw land never produces depreciation because in theory land doesn't wear out.

Potential means the ability to convert raw ground into something with a higher value. We see developers who make farms into townhouses, for example, but such projects are not truly feasible for most small investors. There are legal barriers, enormous up-front costs, ongoing expenses, and perhaps even maintenance such as seeding or fencing. But if large-scale projects with raw land are impractical for most investors, there are situations where small parcels of raw land can be profitable.

In every community, property sold as "homes" may in fact offer the potential for raw land development. As an example, you may see an area dominated by subdivisions where properties are zoned for lots with 10,000 square feet. An older house, however, may have substantially more property, perhaps 25,000 or 30,000 square feet, enough land to create an additional lot.

Area alone is not the only criterion for subdividing. A moratorium on sewer hookups can effectively block property development. Zealous neighborhood groups can sometimes be an impediment in the subdivision process. The mere task of acquiring all the permits and licenses required for subdivision may also be a lengthy and expensive procedure.

Financing is another problem. When real estate is financed, the loan is secured with property, and thus the property cannot be divided without a release from the current lender. Some lenders, however, won't give a release, especially if current financing on the property features a low interest rate.

When lenders won't release property, owners must locate new financing. But investors can't get new financing unless the size and shape of the new lots are known. Thus owners must do all the preliminary work required to create the new lot (and revise the old one) before new financing can be obtained.

One approach is to get all permissions and processing completed *but not recorded* in government records, a situation which will not breach the lender's security. Then, when the property is ready for division, both lots can be refinanced, or one or both lots can be sold. However it's done, the old loan is paid off at settlement.

Land use is commonly governed by local zoning laws which might say, for example, that the Tremont residence is zoned for single-family homes with a minimum of 6,000 square feet of property, zoning we'll call "R-60." Now if it happens that the Tremonts have 20,000 square feet in an area zoned R-60, it might seem as though their property could be divided into three lots.

This may be possible if the lot is laid out correctly. If it measures 200 feet by 100 feet with the larger side facing the street, it can be divided into three lots, each 66 by 100 feet.

But what if the Tremont lot is 100 by 200, with the 100-foot side facing the street? If the lot is again divided into thirds, each will measure 200 feet long but just 33 feet wide. If there are side yard requirements, say at least eight feet of space between the side property lines and the house, then a home's maximum width is just 17 feet (33 feet less 8×2)—not good for a single-family residence.

With 100 feet of street frontage, most probably the property will be carved into two lots, one lot on the street measuring 75 by 80 (6,000 square feet) and a back lot with a 25-foot strip to the street, containing 14,000 square feet. Thus both lots will have at least 6,000 square feet plus direct street access. Note that if the property was a corner lot, access problems would be greatly eased.

Once subdivided, Tremont's next step is to create a buildable lot. He'll need sewer and water hookups, building permits from the local government, and the approval of any commission, committee, or agency with authority over construction projects. Depending on the property's location, getting permits could take months or years and cost thousands of dollars.

Once zoning and permit work have been completed, buildable lots by

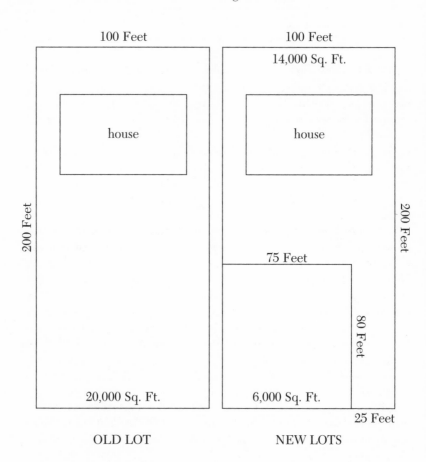

themselves have far more value than raw land. A builder, for instance, is attracted to buildable lots because of the shorter time frame needed to erect a house.

For Tremont, our friend with the lots, the next question is what to do with them.

Suppose Tremont bought the original property for $125,000. If the land under the house is worth 20 percent of the purchase price, it's valued at $25,000. Thus 6,000 square feet of land is worth $7,500 (30 percent of $25,000) plus the value of the time, energy, and money needed to divide the property, get permits, etc.

If we say conservatively the new lot's value is $25,000, we should also ask about the old lot's market worth. It's smaller now, but let's assume that it has the house on it. In this situation we might say that the back lot is worth

$125,000 less the front lot's original value, $7,500, or a total of $117,500.

If Tremont bought his owner-occupied property with 90 percent financing, he has a $112,500 mortgage. However, his mortgage was secured with the old lot, all 20,000 square feet of it plus the house. Tremont must either locate new financing to pay off his existing mortgage or get a release from his lender allowing him to secure his $112,500 loan with the now-smaller property or both lots.

But if the back lot is worth $117,500, a lender won't want a deal where there's a 96 percent LTV (a $112,500 loan, compared to a property value of $117,500). Most probably, Tremont will either find a smaller loan for the back lot, get financing for both lots, or sell one or both properties.

But what happens if Tremont keeps both lots and pays an additional $6,750 to his lender in exchange for a release? Now he can have 90 percent financing on the back lot and a front lot that's free and clear of all debt. If the back lot is worth $117,500 and the front lot has a market value of $25,000, then Tremont has property worth $142,500. If he sells the front lot, he pockets $25,000 plus he still owns the back lot and the house. In effect, he's created $17,500 in additional value.

But Tremont can do better. His property is zoned for single-family housing, so he can build a second house on his new lot. And financing is easy because his free-and-clear lot is worth $25,000. If he gets 80 percent financing, he can use his lot for the 20 percent equity required by a nonconforming lender, put in no additional cash, and finance construction worth up to $100,000.

When homes are sold for resale, they include many costs which Tremont will not face. He has no advertising cost (1 percent), marketing expense (3 percent), land cost (20 percent—but Tremont paid for it when he bought the original property), or someone else's profit (10 percent). Thus a home that sells for $150,000 may actually cost $99,000 in materials, labor, and "soft" expenses (architectural drawings, surveying, etc.).

Whether Tremont builds a house on-site (a so-called stick building), buys a manufactured home, or combines the two building approaches, he can erect a substantial house for $99,000. Given the size of his lot, the probability is that he will construct a home measuring 28 × 44 feet, or 1,232 square feet. Add a full basement, a high value-to-cost choice, and Tremont can have a house with 2,400 square feet, a built-in garage, three bedrooms, and two baths on the main floor, and plenty of excess space on the ground level for his $99,000.

The cost to Tremont for the land and house is unlikely to exceed $106,500 ($99,000 for building and $7,500 for ground). If it's worth $125,000, then Tremont is ahead $18,500 if he sells.

Another choice for Tremont is to rent if property values are rising. If he can generate 8 percent yearly rentals (8 percent of $125,000 is $10,000, or $833.33 a month), that's more than enough to cover the payments on a $100,000 mortgage at 8 percent interest ($733.70 monthly for principal and interest). Combine the monthly mortgage payment with property taxes, insurance, and repairs and the result is likely to be a slight monthly cash loss.

The decision to rent and hold has an advantage for Tremont. Although land can't be depreciated, buildings can, and our owner now has a $99,500 asset to depreciate over 31.5 years, an average tax write-off of $3,158.73 annually. If Tremont is in the 28 percent bracket, his write-off has a cash value of $884.44—about $73.70 a month.

If real estate values are rising, and if rents are rising, then Tremont has an appreciating asset. He is likely to have a minor monthly cash loss, but then his cash investment in the property is fairly close to zero. There were engineering expenses to subdivide the property, and there was a cost for refinancing, but the new mortgage paid for construction and the value of the old house included the land for the second lot. When Tremont goes to buy another property, his net worth will show an asset worth $125,000 and a $99,000 liability—at least at first. Over time, the gap between value and debt is likely to widen in most areas of the country.

21

Profits from
Real Estate Finance

An enormous army of people make money from real estate without painting a room or negotiating with tenants. Their profits come not from real estate itself but from financing, the essential paper and credit that make deals possible.

Compare a real estate sale with a sports deal. Suppose a professional football player receives a five-year contract with the following terms: $200,000 the first year, $300,000 the second year, $400,000 the third year, $500,000 the fourth year, and $600,000 the fifth year. Newspapers will report that the player signed a five-year, $2 million deal. In a sense, the papers are right, the figures do total $2 million. But owners looking at this deal see something different.

If they can earn 8 percent on their money, owners might figure the numbers this way: The first year the owners owe $200,000 to the player, the second year $257,201, the third year $317,533, the fourth year, $367,515, and the fifth year $408,350—a total of $1,569,099. If the owners buy 8 percent securities that mature in two, three, four, and five years, they can save $430,000 in salary costs. The bottom line: There's a time value to money.

Real estate investors need to look at the same concept. Selling football services—or property—for money to be paid in the future represents a certain level of risk. For example, if Boynton sells a house for $200,000 but takes back a $100,000 note for ten years at 8 percent interest, he's wedded to a given rate of return. If during the ten-year period rates rise to 10 percent for investments of equal risk, Boynton's loan is less valuable. Conversely, if interest rates fall to 6 percent, he's ahead.

You don't have to be a loan officer or the manager of a billion-dollar pension fund to make money with real estate financing. Investors can make extra dollars by financing the properties they sell or by dealing in real estate paper, an exotic world of its own.

Logan, for example, can create an income stream using second trusts and wraparound financing. He might purchase a $100,000 home with $15,000 down, and assume an older FHA loan for the balance. He might spend $10,000 for repairs to create a property worth $130,000. And, to maximize profits, he sells with a broker hired as a consultant on an hourly basis rather than a full-fee broker.

Where's the profit? When Logan sold, his buyer—Hentoff—assumed the existing $85,000 FHA loan, Logan took back a $20,000 second trust, and the buyer put up $25,000 in cash. Since there were no points or other major expenses, both Logan and the buyer reduced their closing costs.

Logan's entire cash investment ($25,000) was covered by the purchaser's down payment. His profit came from the $20,000 second trust, perhaps an interest-only balloon note with a five-year term. At 8 percent interest, he received $133 a month plus $20,133 when the loan ends, a total of $28,133. (It's a $20,133 balloon payment, not just $20,000, because interest is paid in arrears—that is, after you use the money—and principal is paid in advance.)

In addition to a second trust, Logan could make a similar deal with wraparound financing. For instance, if his FHA loan was a fixed-rate mortgage at 7 percent and prevailing rates were at the 8 percent level when he marketed the property, he might offer a $105,000 wraparound loan at 7.75 percent to a buyer. The buyer gets a marginally lower rate and avoids points. Logan earns .75 percent on $85,000 ($43.44 monthly) plus 7.75 percent on the $20,000 balance.

Given a few of these deals and Logan would have his starting capital in hand, a monthly income, plus a net worth that grows with each sale. As for his taxes, he pays them on his profits over a period of years; that's because he has an installment sale and pays taxes on the loan interest paid in the year received.

Creating a string of deals such as the one developed by Logan is both possible and complex. There are some pitfalls to consider before using Logan's approach.

- If you are a real estate "dealer," then you cannot take advantage of installment-sale tax rules. Since virtually all small investors are non-dealers, this is good news. Be certain to see a tax professional for complete details before considering an installment sale.
- Not all loans are assumable by investors. As an example, FHA loans issued after December 15, 1989 cannot be assumed by investors. Many

loans are "qualified assumptions," meaning that to be assumed they must meet lender standards, including—sometimes—a requirement for owner-occupancy and the payment of various fees and charges.

Moreover, it should be said that owner financing ties an investor to a property after it's sold, something that may not be wise. As a seller/lender you can have problems if a buyer has warranty claims or complains about defects. If the property is sold and financed by someone else, such claims would be costly to pursue. However, a buyer/borrower has a potent weapon against a seller/lender—the buyer can stop monthly loan payments, a problem which may take months or years to resolve at great cost to the investor.

Rather than become involved as a seller/lender, some investors have a different approach, one that avoids warranty claims: They bank real estate paper.

Suppose Taggart has a second trust on a property. The note pays 9 percent interest, has a $30,000 face value, and is due in five years. In effect, it's an interest-only loan with a $30,300 balloon payment and monthly payments of $225. (Again, it's a $30,300 balloon payment, not just $30,000, because interest is paid in arrears—after you use the money—and principal is paid in advance.)

Taggart wants to convert his note to cash, so he offers to sell it. The value of his note is based on the yield, 9 percent in this case.

If buyers want a 9 percent yield they will pay Taggart $30,000 for his note. However, if they were looking for a 10 percent yield, they would then offer to buy Taggart's note at discount. They will figure that the loan produced interest worth $13,500 (60 × $225) plus a $30,225 balloon payment. In total, the note generates $43,725 over five years. To earn a simple 10 percent return investors will pay $27,000.

There are also situations where Taggart might receive a premium for his note. If interest rates dropped and investors were looking for simple 8 percent yields, Taggart's note would be worth nearly $33,750.

Buying second trusts is not like purchasing corporate bonds; nobody rates small second trusts, and there's no national market where small trusts are individually traded. The value of such notes is based on the borrower's ability to repay the loan, the property's value (if there's a foreclosure, the first trust holder gets *all* proceeds before you receive a dime), and, less directly, the amount of equity the buyer/borrower has invested in the property. The greater the equity, the smaller the lender's risk.

Additionally, investors will want extensive documentation with second trusts. Important papers include:

- The original trust document—*it's negotiable!*
- Insurance coverage on the property sufficient to cover your note and the first trust.
- Evidence that the trust has been properly recorded, such as a receipt from the local records office.
- A copy of the deed.
- Settlement papers showing the property's sale price and the buyer's equity. Also, associated documents such as surveys, termite inspections, and transfer-tax receipts.
- A copy of the first mortgage or first deed of trust.
- An inspection by the investor to assure that the property exists and is habitable.
- The buyer's credit report and at least two recent tax returns.

Because of the high returns available, discounted second trusts can be attractive. However, such notes should be regarded as risky and purchased only with proper documentation and the advice of an attorney where the property is located.

In addition to documentation, investors need to watch second trust properties with care. If there's a foreclosure auction and you don't go, your note can be wiped off the books. If possible, it's good to have a cross-notification agreement with the first trust holder. If the borrower misses payments to either lender, or if either lender begins foreclosure proceedings, the other lender will automatically be notified.

Alternatively, if there's a foreclosure by the first trust holder, then investors may be forced to bid. If you don't bid, the first lender will bid the amount of his loan and walk off with the property without owing other lien holders. If you bid, you have to pay the first trust holder's claims. Good news for the first trust holder, not so good for the investor.

22

Exchanges

Folks who buy a home, sell it, and buy a personal residence of equal or greater value are able to defer taxes from the sale of their first property under the rollover residence-replacement rule. But investors, we know, are not so lucky. When you sell investment property, you pay taxes on the profit.

But what if you don't sell? What if you exchange your property for someone else's investment real estate? And what if their property is worth as much as or more than yours?

In an exchange of investment property, it's possible to postpone taxes, as Barker found out.

Barker had a four-unit property worth $300,000. Although he liked the property, Barker felt there was more money to be made in single-family homes, so he traded with Roberts, one four-plex and $25,000 in cash for three houses.

In this deal, Barker's taxes will be deferred until he sells his houses. Roberts, however, owes taxes, because he received cash in addition to property.

Deals such as the one above may seem simple, but a variety of complications lurk just below the surface. Here are the basic issues that may arise.

What Can Be Exchanged?

You're allowed to exchange "like kind" property used in a business or trade—real estate used for investment purposes rather than as a personal residence or second home, according to Andrew P. Collins, editor and publisher of the monthly newsletter *Exchanging Property* (Suite 331, 916 Shaker Road, Longmeadow, MA 01106). "Like kind" property does not necessarily mean a duplex for a duplex. You might, for example, exchange a single-family rental house for commercial land.

What If No One Will Trade With You?

Try a three-way trade or a four-way trade. Real estate brokers who specialize in exchanges can arrange such deals.

What Are Your Profits on the First Property?

In general terms, your profit is equal to the exchange value of your real estate plus depreciation, less the original cost. In other words, if your property was bought for $100,000 and exchanged for $200,000, and you took $20,000 in depreciation during the term of ownership, the deferred profit is $120,000 ($200,000 plus $20,000 less $100,000).

What Are Your Profits on the Second Property?

Let's assume that the second property is exchanged for $200,000 with the first property. The new property's tax base is now $80,000 ($200,000 less $120,000 in deferred profits from the first investment). If you sell the second property for $300,000, then $220,000 (plus whatever depreciation was taken on the new real estate) will be taxed.

How Do I Determine An Exchange Value?

Look at market values for like properties and then consult with an attorney or CPA for specific rules.

What if the New Property is More Expensive Than the Old One?

Then there's a difference, called "boot," which can be paid in cash.

What if the New Property is Less Expensive Than the Old One, and the Owner Pays You Boot

You'll pay taxes.

Can Mortgage Balances Influence Exchange Values?

Yes. Suppose two properties are exchanged, each with a $200,000 market value. If one property has a $100,000 mortgage balance while the other has a loan with $105,000 outstanding, the difference may be regarded as "mortgage relief." Mortgage relief, in turn, may be construed as a taxable benefit. Again, have a CPA or tax attorney examine the tax consequences of each deal before making any commitments.

Can I Use the Old Depreciation Schedule for the New Property?

No. You must use the schedules associated with the new property.

Can I Sell My Property and Use the Proceeds Later to Buy Another Investment and Still Defer Taxes?

Yes. Such deferred trades are generally called Starker exchanges, after a famous court case. In general terms, a deferred exchange requires that the new property is identified before the 45th day after closing and transferred within 180 days after the first property is sold, and that all the proceeds from the sale are inaccessible to the trader. You'll need a lawyer to do the paperwork and figure out the specifics in each situation.

Note that since the benefits of the original sale—money—must be inaccessible to the investor, there is the issue of who or what holds your cash. Be certain that the money is placed in trust and not commingled with the funds of others. Also, if your money is held by an individual, make certain that person is adequately bonded or that you're protected with a letter of credit from a bank.

Indeed, while an exchange sounds simple, the process requires an enormous amount of documentation, accounting help, and legal time, especially since proposals to revise exchange tax rules are continually proposed. For instance, one idea is to limit exchange deferrals to $100,000. Another proposal limits the exchange process so that "like kind" exchanges would have to be closely related: a single-family rental property for a single-family rental property rather than a small commercial building. Be sure to speak to a tax attorney or CPA for the latest information before exchanging property.

23

Foreclosures and REOs

Folklore is full of stories where handsome princes come along and save damsels in distress. Within the guru industry there are similar tales, only "distressed properties" substitute for distressed damsels and handsome princes (or princesses) are played by dynamic investors who overcome enormous odds (no cash or credit) to find the Holy Grail of great fortune.

It's a hard fact that not every deal works, and not every mortgage is paid in a timely fashion. And the people who fail are not always widows with six children or farmers down on their luck; they're often investors who made the wrong deals or got caught in rough times. In such cases, other investors come along and recycle properties, buying at the lowest possible value and hoping that they'll do better.

We know that among millions of borrowers around the country, some portion will fail. If 1 to 3 percent of all homeowner loans are delinquent—and if there are 60 million outstanding mortgages around the country—then from 600,000 to 1.8 million loans are in arrears at any time. Given such large numbers, we can assume that some tiny portion of those with delinquent loans will be foreclosed. In addition to mortgage problems, some properties will be auctioned off because owners failed to pay local taxes or IRS claims, while others will be sold to pay for deficiency judgments.

Given these numbers, we can safely bet that distressed properties are everywhere, a fact that raises several questions: Where do you find them, how do you get title, and are they good deals?

When mortgage payments are late, borrowers have breached their loan agreements. And while lenders in theory may have authority to foreclose because a contractual obligation has not been met, such actions are rare because borrowers normally have a right to bring payments current and reinstate the loan. Both lender and borrower will be mutually pleased if the loan is quickly brought up to date.

But if late payments turn into no payments, a different sequence of events begins. Whoever "services" the loan must act to protect the note holder or any co-signers, such as private mortgage insurers or government agencies.

Practices around the country differ, but in general terms the borrower is likely to receive a default notice showing how much is due and demanding immediate payment. A borrower may then have a certain period, say 90 days, to bring payments current and, once paid, everyone is usually happy. Indeed, both the VA and FHA will help distressed borrowers, sometimes rescheduling payments or even buying loans from lenders.

However, if the note is not brought current, the owner may then receive a sale notice. This notice is published in local papers and filed in public records. In most cases, it's the first public identification of a distressed property.

If the borrower still does not bring the note current or otherwise satisfy the lender, perhaps by selling the property and making a foreclosure sale needless—or perhaps by merely putting the property up for sale—then the property may be auctioned.

However, if the borrower declares bankruptcy, then an "automatic stay" can halt the foreclosure proceeding. At this point the lender must seek court permission to hold the auction, another time-consuming and costly expense for the lender. (In addition, *after* a foreclosure a bankruptcy court may overturn a sale in some jurisdictions if a property is sold at less than fair market value.)

At the auction the first note holder will make a bid for the property, thereby assuring that the property isn't given away. Ideally, a lender wants to force any "winner" to pay off the entire first trust or mortgage before getting title, but in tough markets lenders may bid below the loan's outstanding value to assure bidder interest.

Folks who hold second trusts, or third trusts, must now make a decision. Assuming that they know about the auction (often they don't), they must make a bid that at least covers the first lender's bid. If they don't, they can lose their equity. Here's how.

Suppose Collins has a $100,000 home with a $60,000 first trust and a $10,000 second trust. Suppose further that Collins defaults, the property goes to auction, and at the auction the first trust lender bids $60,000.

- If no one bids more than $60,000 the lender gets title to the property—something it doesn't want!
- If the winning bid is $60,500, then the second trust lender receives just

$500, because all claims by the first trust holder must be satisfied before *any* money is paid to the second trust lender.

- If the winning bid is $75,000, then the first and second trust holders are paid off and the remaining $5,000 goes to the borrower. In actuality, the borrower may also owe foreclosure fees and legal costs that wipe out this gain.
- If the sale is a tax auction, the property may be sold subject to outstanding liens. In this case if someone bids $15,000 for the property, he will pay that amount to obtain a property with $70,000 in outstanding debt.

After the auction it might seem as though the borrower has lost his property, but that's not necessarily so. In some states there's a "right of equity redemption," which allows owners to recover their property by paying back the loan, auction fees, legal costs, and interest.

Within the process of notification, auction, and redemption, there are several places where investors can be active.

First, when a notice of default is on the public record, investors may contact the owner and offer to buy the property. Investors beware! In some jurisdictions investors may not make "unconscionable" deals with borrowers facing foreclosure. Other rules and regulations may also apply.

If you buy from a borrower, always make the deal contingent on a title examination satisfactory to you and on the availability of title insurance.

Second, investors may bid on properties. The problem here is that the world is teeming with so many seminar attendees and tape buyers that investors may not find room or bargains. However, because bidders must show up with cash or certified checks at most auctions and pay for the property within 30 to 60 days, many of those in attendance are not serious competitors.

Also, because of closing requirements, bidders should have enough cash or credit in hand to cover a purchase. In such situations, lines of credit are enormously valuable.

Third, investors can buy REOs, real estate owned by lenders who take back properties when auction prices are unacceptably low. The attraction here is that the lender has title and may actually finance the deal.

In addition to local foreclosures, investors should also consider a nationwide program run by Fannie Mae. Just dial a toll-free number (800-553-4636), and you can get a printout showing available properties in local areas, the number of bedrooms and baths, list prices, and broker contacts. Such properties are often available at prices marginally below market values, and such prices may be subject to further negotiation. Financing, backed by Fannie Mae, is available through local lenders. Speak to local brokers listed in Fannie Mae printouts for down payment information and other details.

To become involved with foreclosures and REOs, investors should follow public notices in local papers, contact local tax offices, and get on mailing lists which are often available through IRS, VA, and HUD regional offices. Check the local records office to see where sale notices are filed. See what's for sale and who's selling. Attend auctions and see how they're conducted. Speak to trustees and bidders.

Investors should also check with local or regional RTC offices. While the RTC has sold many of the properties in its inventory, there may still be some interesting opportunities in given communities.

In addition, investors may want to consider the use of local tracking services that list upcoming foreclosures. Ads for such publishers often appear in local real estate and business classified sections.

Also, because foreclosures are localized affairs, investors should speak with an attorney to fully understand how foreclosures are handled. Major topics to address include:

- Once a default notice has been issued, how much time do borrowers have to bring loans current?
- Once a sale notice has been filed, how much time do borrowers have to bring loans current?
- In the event of an auction, does the borrower have a right of redemption? If so, how long is the redemption period?
- If you buy property at auction and improve it, is the borrower who redeems the property responsible for repaying your costs? With interest?
- What are the required terms if you bid at auction? In other words, how much time do you have to finance the deal, how much is required in the form of a deposit, what happens if you cannot get financing, etc.?
- Are you a licensed broker or agent? If so, and if you attend a VA auction, you will be regarded as an "affiliate," someone in the business with a marketplace advantage over non-licensees. Given a choice between a qualifying bid from a consumer and a bid of equal value from a licensee, the VA will accept the bid from the non-licensee.
- What rules and regulations apply if you want to contact a borrower who has received a default notice?
- If you buy property from a borrower facing foreclosure, what notices and provisions must be included in the offer? For instance, is there a required right of cancellation?

- If you buy foreclosed property, what form of title do you receive? Beware of deals that involve only quit-claim deeds.
- Quit-claim deeds say that you are receiving whatever title is held by the person offering the deed. It's possible that no title, an incomplete title, or a faulty title is being transferred. Always contact an attorney when dealing with quit-claim deeds.
- If you buy foreclosed property, is it lien-free or will you be responsible for any debts incurred by the owner?
- If the IRS takes back the property, are you entitled to interest on your purchase? If so, how much?
- If you buy a foreclosed property and the original owners are still residing there, how do you get them out?
- What guarantees, if any, are made regarding the property's condition?
- If the property has been vacant for 30 days or more, what steps must you take to get fire, theft, and casualty insurance?

24

How to Get the Best Sale Prices

Much of investment real estate is approached from the buyer's perspective: how to get property and how to hold it rather than how to sell it.

But selling is an integral part of the investment game. In the worst case, selling under duress may be necessary if a deal doesn't work out. In the best case, selling is part of the plan, the time when you'll pocket most of your profit. Either way, every property you own is a potential sale candidate.

As a buyer you looked for certain qualities when you purchased property. You wanted property in the path of future growth (location), real estate that needed basic repairs and upgrading (condition), and a cost that allowed you to capture additional value (price).

It follows that as a seller you'll also be interested in location, condition, and price—albeit from a different perspective.

The property that was in the path of future growth is now, hopefully, in the midst of today's hot market. You've anticipated where demand was headed, and now you have an opportunity to profit.

You benefited from the property's poor condition, but now the peeling paint and old appliances are gone. You've fixed up, painted, landscaped, improved, and cleaned up, so the property you offer for sale is in pristine, move-in or rent-out condition.

Because of the property's original condition and limited demand, you were able to get a price that was below the prevailing cost for like properties when you bought. If neighborhood prices are up generally and your property is now valued at or above like real estate in the same area, you've benefited from your work as well as generally rising values.

To have a successful sale, however, you need more than an attractive property.

Financing must be available to get maximum values. If mortgage interest is pegged at 18 percent, your property can be cleaner than a surgeon's knife and you'll still have trouble selling. And if the local economy is depressed, people are out of work, and farms are closing, demand will be down and so will your ability to collect premium prices.

As investors we naturally want the largest profit from our labor, capital, and entrepreneurial effort. Some investors argue that greater profits can be obtained by selling ourselves as a "Fisbo," or "For Sale By Owner" in brokerage jargon.

But self-selling means marketing costs may be lowered, not eliminated. Self-selling implies that the investor will show the property, advertise it, hold open houses if appropriate, locate financing for the buyer, negotiate, and perform all the functions normally handled by a broker.

If we sell through the brokerage community, we'll pay a fee for services. In return, we'll gain access to the organized real estate marketing system, an efficient, effective method of retailing properties to a large number of prospective purchasers. We'll benefit from the system's seller orientation, proportional commissions, and cooperation. (See Chapter 10 for more information on real estate brokers.)

Seller/broker relationships are created with a "listing agreement," an employment contract that gives a broker authority to sell property at a particular price, under certain conditions, and for a given length of time. With most listings, if a broker finds a buyer "ready, willing, and able" to purchase the property under the conditions established by the listing, the broker is then entitled to a commission. In broad terms there are three major types of listings.

"Open" or "general" listings mean that during the listing period the property may be sold by a broker with an open listing or directly by the owner. More than one broker can have a listing under this nonexclusive format, and if the property sells, the broker who found the buyer gets the commission. If the owner sells it, no broker is entitled to a commission.

Open listings work well when a broker wants to show a property to a particular individual; however, they're unworkable in cooperative deals. If broker Haskell has an open listing and broker Strayer has a prospect, Strayer can deal directly with the owner if he can also get an open listing and avoid splitting a fee with Haskell.

An "exclusive agency agreement" means that during the listing period, the owner or one broker may sell the property. If the property is sold by the listing broker, or by any broker, the listing broker is entitled to a fee. If the property is sold directly by the owner, the broker does not receive a fee.

An "exclusive right to sell" agreement means that if the property is sold during the listing period by anyone, including the owner, the broker will get a commission. This form of listing is the most common and is widely used in multiple listing systems.

A listing agreement, like any contract, is negotiable. Here are the major issues to consider.

- Term: Investors should authorize the shortest *reasonable* term, enough time for the broker to market the property but not enough for months of inactivity to pass. Sixty to 90 days should be sufficient for an initial listing period. If the broker is active and does a good job, the listing can be continued.
- Fee: *Brokerage commissions are absolutely negotiable.* Recognize, however, that real estate fees are commonly shared among brokers and agents, so if the fee is too low, brokers won't be interested in the property.

For example, if area fees are typically 6 percent they will be split 50/50 in a cooperative sale. But what happens with a 5 percent fee?

If the broker who lists the property, the "listing" broker, offers to cooperate with other brokers on a 50/50 basis, then your property will be less attractive than properties of equal value where owners pay a 6 percent fee. The bottom line: If you list property on a discounted basis, make certain cooperating brokers receive a competitive fee, 3 percent in this case; otherwise you'll lose the benefit of the cooperative system.

For instance, if you list at 5 percent in a 6 percent market, make certain that cooperating brokers know that they will receive a 3 percent cut if they bring in a buyer. The listing broker will then get 2 percent if the property sells cooperatively, or 5 percent if he finds a purchaser. The commission's division in the event of a cooperative sale should be shown in the listing contract.

Note also that brokers can be hired by the hour as consultants and on a flat-fee basis—that is, you do some of the work in exchange for a lower cost.

- Price: A fee will be due and payable if a broker finds a buyer "ready, willing, and able" to meet your price. The price you set should be at the top of the market yet within the realm of reason.
- Points: Many standardized listing agreements ask sellers to state the number of points they're willing to pay to assist with a buyer's financing. Since you don't have an offer in hand when a listing is created, you don't

know what a purchaser may offer for your property. If you agree in the
listing contract to pay a certain number of points, you've given away a
valuable negotiating advantage. It's better to offer no points in the listing agreement and then to consider the issue when a signed offer is presented.

- Deposits: Sellers can stipulate in a listing contract that for an offer to be
  acceptable it must be accompanied by a certain deposit. For example,
  an owner might list a property at $200,000 and require a $20,000
  deposit.

Sellers should require high deposits simply to establish a negotiating
position. If a written offer comes in with a smaller deposit, sellers can then
decide whether to accept the offer or not.

- Extras: A listing agreement can, and should, enumerate those items
  either not for sale or which sellers want to use as bargaining chips. For
  instance, the clothes washer and dryer can be excluded from the listing.
  If the buyer's offer includes the washer and dryer, a seller can then
  accept the offer or counter with a demand for better terms.
- Modifications: Listing agreements are typically written by and for the
  real estate community, and it follows that such forms favor broker interests. However, listing agreements can be modified with pro-investor
  clauses as well. A listing might specify how many times a property will
  be advertised during the term of the listing and where the ads will be
  placed. Another clause might require a certain number of open houses
  during the listing term. In effect, listing agreements—like all contracts—can be customized to produce individualized results.

There are many brokers who want your business, good news for
investors because a large number of brokers means a strong degree of
competition.

Investors can certainly hire traditional brokers who charge a given fee
for an inclusive package of services. Alternatively, discount and flat-fee
brokers are now available in most communities.

For investors this means that selling needs can be fine-tuned to meet
your specific requirements. Your range of choices might include:

- No broker. You sell by yourself.
- No broker, some attorney. You sell by yourself and use an attorney to
  provide local forms and check offers before acceptance.

- Some broker. In this situation you sell by yourself but retain a broker as a consultant, paid on an hourly basis or with a given fee.
- Some broker, the menu plan. Here you pick and choose from a list of services offered by flat-rate brokers.
- All broker. A broker takes care of the sale.

It's a good idea to speak to several brokers before marketing your property and to hear how they would sell it, what they think it's worth, and why. Also ask about commitments to advertise, hold open houses (if appropriate), enter an MLS system, and cooperate informally with other brokers. As you listen to each answer, ask if this is the person you want representing your interests in the marketplace.

IV
Rental Properties

The ultimate test of every long-term investment property held for appreciation is rentability. If it can't be rented, it's a financial millstone that can very quickly sink both an investment and its investor.

But as much as we want tenants, not every warm body is desirable. We want responsible people who pay rent, but also individuals who will take good care of the property and who enjoy clean, well-kept households.

Where do we find such people?

Whether we hire a manager or rent by ourselves, properties should be seen as competing with one another for the best renters on the basis of five major criteria.

First, the property must be appropriate. If a renter needs three bedrooms, the property can have no less. The finest two-bedroom house in the world just won't work.

Second, the property must be well-located. Location is defined by tenant needs, not owner preferences or social trends. If a renter requires a place near work, that will be a controlling factor when rental decisions are made.

Third, it helps if the property has amenities that attract tenants. A heavy-duty washer and dryer will be important to a large family with young children. An auto buff will appreciate a large garage.

Fourth, condition is extremely important. A property that's clean, well maintained, and loaded with up-to-date appliances will draw renters.

Fifth, price counts. The lower the rent, the greater the pool of potential tenants. If the prevailing rental for like properties in similar condition is $900 monthly, and you charge $875, more people will consider your unit. If $25 a month leads to a better bottom line because of fewer maintenance problems and reduced vacancies, it's money well spent.

Given the factors above, properties define themselves. Each rental unit has certain advantages that will attract some prospective tenants and eliminate others.

Amenities, condition, and price are within the owner's control. You can do much to make your property attractive and thereby gain the benefit of having better tenants.

It's sometimes argued that rather than improve properties, owners should invest as little as possible—just dab on a little paint. The less you put in, goes this theory, the more money you keep.

The problem with this approach is that it won't attract good tenants or top rentals. It's likely that the property will have more vacancies—and longer ones—than like properties in sound condition. In addition, you need equity to refinance and cash out, something rental properties in poor condition are unlikely to provide.

25
Finding the Right Tenant

Tenants can be found through word of mouth, signs in front of the property, and local housing services. Large companies, universities, and government offices typically maintain housing offices that will list your rental for free.

Paid advertising can also attract tenants, but to get the best results ads must be factual and concise. State the location, type of property (house, condo, farm, etc.), number of bedrooms and baths, special features (full basement, two-car garage, new oven, washer, and dryer, etc.), and the monthly rental. (If the rental isn't shown you may get many calls from people who can't afford the property.) State whether pets are permitted and if they are, what kind ("dogs and cats okay").

How do you judge the prospective tenants who respond to your announcements?

You need to know more about potential renters than the fact that they need space. You need to know something about them, their rental history, and their motivations. To find the information you need, and to outline the basic terms of a possible lease, it pays to develop a basic rental application form that covers a broad range of subjects:

- The location, monthly rental, and preferred lease term should be shown as well as the amount required for a security deposit. Also, the preferred first and last day of the rental agreement should be written out. The rental application should state when the rent is due (1st of the month, 15th of the month, etc.), and that rentals are payable monthly in advance.
- The names and addresses of each tenant and co-tenant, their phone numbers, their social security numbers, and their drivers' licenses.
- Information concerning current employment including, as appropriate, title, the name and phone number of a supervisor, a work address, and length of employment.
- The name, relationship, address, and phone number of the applicant's nearest relative (in case of emergency).

- A list of all residences for the past five years, including if possible the names of managers or landlords and the dates of occupancy.
- A list of income sources including wages, bonuses, overtime, commissions, etc.
- The make, year, and license numbers for all cars, boats, and motorcycles that will be kept on the property.
- The amount of any fee required for a credit check and whether all or a portion of the fee shall be refunded if the application isn't accepted.

In addition to factual information, an application is a good place to set out several understandings that will govern relations between tenant and owner.

First, the owner, or the owner's manager, must have the right to order a credit check at the applicant's expense. As this is written, at least one credit reporting firm will supply one free credit report per year, something that can help both tenants and landlords. Both the owner and manager must be allowed to see the report, but neither will be held responsible for its content.

Second, if the application is accepted, it will be attached to the lease. If it's subsequently discovered that the application contains serious errors, the owner may then cancel the lease at his or her option.

Third, if employment information cannot be verified over the phone, the prospective tenant must be responsible for obtaining written information from an employer.

Fourth, has the prospective tenant's landlord been notified of an intent to move? If not, how should this be handled?

Fifth, why does the tenant want to move? There are many good reasons—better schools, easier commuting, neighborhood preferences, the need for more space or less space, the desire to be near social or employment centers, or simply a preference for something new or different.

Bad reasons to move include property destruction, tumultuous relations with more than one past landlord, and the failure to pay rent.

Sixth, prospective tenants need to understand that an application to rent does *not* guarantee approval. Owners have a right to find the best possible tenant for each property—perhaps the second or third person to apply.

In addition, applicants must be told that while managers and agents may make recommendations to owners, it's the owner who must make the final rental decision, especially in the case of small-property owners. The reason: To be an "active" investor and qualify for special tax benefits, owners must make major decisions concerning their property, and certainly few decisions are more important than the selection of a tenant.

What owners and managers can't do is base rental decisions on discriminatory factors. The Civil Rights Act of 1866 and—a little more than a century later—the Fair Housing Act of 1968 make discrimination illegal. Consider race, color, religion, sex, national origin, disability, or familial status when evaluating a tenant and you may be committing a federal offense. Additional forms of discrimination can also be found in state and local laws.

Investors should take these prohibitions seriously. Not only is discrimination against the law, it's immoral, foolish, and at odds with an owner's best economic interests. Discrimination has the effect of reducing the potential pool of tenants and buyers for any given property, thereby lowering demand and hurting the owner. As investors, our goal is to create the largest possible demand for our properties, something that isn't possible if we exclude major portions of the population.

Given all the information in a rental application, what happens next?

Owners or their agents must verify information with employers and credit bureaus. They must also contact the applicant's current landlord and, if possible, one or more past owners as well.

The reason you want a past landlord is that the current owner or manager may not be an unbiased party. If they've had trouble with the applicant, they're likely to say what a wonderful person the tenant is and how fortunate you'll be to number him or her among your tenants. That way the old landlord can dump the problem on you.

After looking at several applications, which do you choose? There's no absolute answer, but several criteria stand out.

- Look for the applicants with the highest income. They'll have the easiest time paying rent.
- See which applicant has the best rental history. High income doesn't mean anything if a tenant doesn't pay or doesn't pay on time.
- Beware of extremists. If a picky prospect makes a big issue with small matters, forget it. You don't want to deal with a variety of complaints so minor other tenants wouldn't notice.

If you have several application deposits, it makes sense to leave all checks uncashed until a tenant choice has been made. Then, once a renter has been selected, uncashed checks from other applicants—appropriately marked "void" on the front—should be returned as quickly as possible.

Because rental practices are controlled at the local level, owners should work with a broker or attorney to develop a proper tenant application form. In particular, be alert to fee and deposit rules in your community.

26

How to Create High-Profit Leases

Once a renter is selected, it's time to create a formal relationship between owner and tenant, something done through a written lease.

While oral lease agreements may be possible in theory, they're enormously difficult to enforce or interpret. With written agreements everyone knows what the game is and how it's played.

Leases should be seen as a list of understandings which outline both rights and obligations. Leases can include—or exclude—just about everything, but from the investor's perspective there are certain issues which should be addressed.

Acceptance.

Within the lease we need a statement showing that the tenant has examined the property and agreed that it's in satisfactory condition. Unless the owner is notified to the contrary within a brief period, say five business days after the lease begins, it will be assumed that the property's condition is acceptable to the tenant.

Alterations.

Residential properties are designed to meet standardized building codes and safety requirements. The tenant who decides to build a fireplace in the rec room can seriously damage the property's structural integrity, violate local building codes, and negate insurance coverage. For these reasons, a lease must prohibit alterations without the owner's express permission.

Abandoned Property.

Because goods are sometimes left behind after a tenant moves out, an abandoned-property clause allows the owner to keep or dispose of all tenant items after a given time, say three days after the lease expires, without liability to the renter.

Default.

If you've got to sue or evict a tenant, at least make him or her pay some of the cost. A lease should require the tenant to pay a basic legal fee, say $200, for each legal action required. Although $200 won't cover a serious legal tiff, it's a pro-owner clause that gives the landlord additional leverage.

Extension.

When the lease term ends after a year or two, some agreements provide for an automatic month-to-month extension. But lease extensions on a monthly basis may create a problem with lenders, folks who often require leases of at least a year when calculating owner income.

Because investors can be expected to be in the market for financing on a regular basis, the best strategy from the owner's perspective is to raise rents and continue leases on a yearly basis. Annual extensions are not only valuable when dealing with lenders, but also provide a level of continuity for the tenant.

Forfeiture of Deposit.

If the lease is breached—say the tenant doesn't mow the lawn all summer—the owner should have a unilateral right to take funds from the security deposit to correct the problem. Note that security deposits are often subject to special regulations, so speak with a local attorney or knowledgeable broker before touching money held in trust.

Hold Harmless.

This type of lease clause states that the owner cannot be held responsible for injuries, accidents, or damages on the property when the property is under the tenant's control. Speak to an attorney for details and information about this type of clause.

Inspection.

Landlords must have a right to enter the property, and an inspection clause will allow you in the unit for good cause, such as making repairs or showing the property to prospective renters or buyers. As a matter of goodwill and to assure tenant privacy, always make appointments before visiting the property, except in emergencies.

Insurance.

A tenant's insurance obligations can be seen from two perspectives.

First, tenants should do nothing to violate the fire, theft, and liability policy carried by the owner. Operating a commercial auto repair business from a residence, for example, is likely to violate insurance requirements.

Second, tenants should be required by the lease to carry a policy that provides both public liability coverage and personal property coverage. This policy must be in force during the entire lease term and should include public liability coverage of not less than $100,000 and personal-property insurance worth at least $15,000. Such policies protect both the tenant and the owner. If the house is robbed, for instance, insurance will cover much of the damage, thereby reducing any claims a tenant might have against an owner.

Late Charges.

What happens if rent is not paid on time? The tenant has breached the lease, but owners want the *option* of a less drastic penalty than eviction. A provision allowing late charges, say 5 percent of the total monthly rent, is common in real estate. It should be made very clear to the tenant that rents are due on a specific date and that rental payments "in the mail" or otherwise unavailable to the owner cannot be viewed as timely.

One way to resolve the "lost in the mail" problem and other obscure delays is to establish an account with a savings and loan association or commercial bank near the property. The tenant then has the option of mailing rent to this account or making a deposit directly at the institution. The latter choice is particularly convenient when the institution has extended hours and drive-in windows.

If, however, payment is delayed, landlords should vigorously enforce late-payment clauses. Failing one time to use such clauses when rents are late may eliminate the option of charging a penalty in the future. If you don't charge a late fee, at least send the tenant a letter stating that in this particular case you're waiving your right to the fee, something you may not do in the future. As to how large a penalty, while 5 percent may be common, local rules can limit fees. Check with a local attorney to assure that only permissible fees are being assessed.

Maintenance.

Regular and normal maintenance is the renter's responsibility, and the lease should say so. Changing light bulbs, mowing lawns, removing ice and snow, and taking out the trash are jobs for the tenant.

Owners can approach the problem of general maintenance in three ways. One tack is to provide a basic "deductible" threshold for repairs—say $75 per item per incident. Thus, if the toilet is clogged and the bill is $90, the tenant is responsible for the first $75. The problem here is that routine maintenance items may be ignored. Note also that "general maintenance" can be defined so that tenants are not responsible for capital repairs such as a leaky roof or rotted decking.

A second tack is to seek higher rentals and include anticipated repair expenses within the rental budget.

A third strategy is to make the tenant responsible for specific repairs, say the first $100 for any work required on the dishwasher or furnace. This approach allows owners to customize repair agreements to match the needs of each property.

Monthly Rent.

A lease represents an exchange—money for space. How much rent is a matter of negotiation but once established, it should be clearly stated in the lease.

A lease should show the tenant's total obligation over the agreement's entire span, not just a single month's rent. For example, if a tenant leases property at $500 a month for two years, then the contractual obligation should be for $12,000 ($500 × 24). If a tenant stays only 18 months, an owner may be able to collect the remaining rent, assuming the owner makes a good-faith effort to find another tenant.

Owners who want a two- or three-year lease should build rent increases into the original agreement to save yearly negotiating hassles. Long leases with built-in increases are a good way to reduce vacancies while maintaining high rents.

Notice of Termination.

Although a tenancy may continue for many years, at some point all tenancies must end. Leases should require both tenants and owners to give the other party adequate notice when they wish to discontinue a lease, say 30 to 60 days.

Occupancy.

In properties of a given size, owners may have the right to limit the number of occupants to avoid excess wear and tear. Owners must take care that if they establish numeric limits, they do so on the basis of warm bodies and not on the basis of age. If you say that occupancy by two adults and two children is okay but four adults is impermissible, the issue of age discrimination could arise.

Readers should be aware the subject of rentals and occupancy numbers can be contentious. There have been instances where the use of occupancy limitations have led to claims of bias (because large tenant groupings may not have an equal opportunity to rent, as an example). Owners are advised to check with legal counsel for the latest standards regarding numbers.

Group rentals are another approach to occupancy. This is a strategy that can maximize property income in college and urban neighborhoods; however, for group homes to be successful, each tenant must be fully responsible for the entire lease. For instance, if rent is $1,000 and four people share the property, each must be liable for the entire rent, not just $250.

Group-house leases must also provide that new residents will be permitted only with the landlord's approval. Such approval, in turn, should require new residents to sign the lease and be bound by its terms. The approval of new tenants should not be unreasonably withheld.

There may be situations where a prospective renter is below the legal age to make a contract, and in this situation owners lease at their peril. Because minors cannot be forced to honor a contract, always have a parent or guardian co-sign the lease.

Pets.

A lease should clearly state whether or not pets are permitted and, if allowed, the number and type of animals you'll authorize. No venomous animals should be allowed, nor unlicensed animals or those not inoculated as required by local public-health policies.

Tenants should be fully responsible for rug cleaning, fumigating, de-ticking, and the repair of all pet-induced damage during the lease term. Check to see if local rules allow larger deposits or a cleaning fee paid in advance when pets are permitted on the property.

Some landlords permit pets, but insist on highly subjective and largely unenforceable rules. For instance, pets "which can be carried" may be permitted, but not larger animals. The real standard here is not the size of the animal, but rather the carrying capacity of the tenant.

Security Deposits.

Security deposits must be part of every deal, but owners should see if local regulations limit deposit amounts. For example, owners may not be permitted in some areas to charge a security deposit in excess of one month's rent or perhaps two months' rent.

As owners we want the largest possible security deposit. Tenants, however, may not have such funds available. One way around this problem is to charge the tenant monthly rent plus an additional fee that is credited to a security deposit. For instance, if Hobbs is paying a $700 security fee but can only afford $300, it might be reasonable to take the $300 and then charge rent plus $50 a month until the $700 is in hand.

Local regulations may require that tenants receive deposit interest. To resolve the problem of excess bookkeeping, security deposits can be placed in separate accounts *controlled by the owner* but using the tenant's name and social security number. In this way all interest payments are credited directly to the tenant, and the landlord is not responsible for paying the taxes. When the tenant moves, the deposit and all accrued interest are his or hers, less any compensation due to the owner for lease violations. Since interest on the escrow account is added each year, and since the interest will go to the tenant unless you have a claim against the escrow money, it follows that the interest is taxable if collected by the tenant or by you.

The catch is that most people operate on a "cash" basis. They do not pay taxes on money they have not yet received, thus it is probable that neither the tenant nor the owner can pay a tax on dollars which are not yet paid out. In a similar manner, there is likely to be no "income" to report until it is actually given to the tenant or taken from the account as part of a claim. For details and specifics check with a tax professional regarding escrow interest reporting requirements.

An alternative approach to security-deposit interest is to credit the tenant with required interest and keep any excess monies. If the money is in a 5 percent account and deposits must earn 4 percent according to local regulations, landlords may be able to pocket the difference. Check with local attorneys for specific rules.

In addition to collecting the highest possible deposits, owners may also seek rent in advance, perhaps the first month's rent and the last month's rent. Collecting vast sums of rent money up front sounds enticing, but there are three practical problems. First, not every tenant has enough money to cover two months of rent plus a security deposit at one time. Second, your property will be less attractive when compared to other properties that have similar rents but lower tenant costs up front. Third, some jurisdictions may limit tenant pre-payments.

"Rent" money is very different from "deposit" funds. Because deposit money is held in trust, an owner cannot use or "commingle" the tenant's funds with his own. But rent money belongs to the owner and can be used any way he or she likes. Again, however, owners need to check with an attorney to determine if there's a local prohibition to limit the collection of extra rent at the beginning of the lease term.

Smoke Detectors.

Smoke detectors are increasingly required in jurisdictions throughout the country, but whether or not local regulations make them necessary, owners are foolish to ignore the obvious benefits such devices provide. Both electric and battery-operated detectors are available, but electric devices are the better buy. They're more expensive to install, but they don't require tenants or owners to change batteries. Also, electrified detectors represent a capital improvement, something that raises property values.

In addition to smoke detectors, CO_2 detectors are also now available. Such detectors simply plug into an appropriate electrical socket and then test the air every two minutes for the next five years.

The importance of CO_2 alarms is that they may detect a heater malfunction or a similar problem. Since CO_2 is colorless, odorless, and potentially dangerous, all housing units can benefit from such detectors.

Sublets and Assignments.

Under no condition should the property be sublet or the lease assigned without the landlord's written authority. If there's a sublet or assignment to which the owner agrees, the lease should give owners a processing fee for their work qualifying the new tenant. The amount of this fee should be specifically established in the lease.

Note that in some jurisdictions there's a movement by courts to allow sublets even when banned in a lease. The theory is that sublets should not be unreasonably prohibited when qualified tenants are available.

Surrender.

When the lease period ends, the tenant must give up the premises. Landlords, however, don't want the property back with 30 tons of debris, so a surrender clause requires tenants to leave the place broom clean, to remove all trash and garbage, and to leave all mechanical equipment in good operating condition. If these steps are not taken, the security deposit can be used to clean up the property and repair damage.

Tax Increases.

There's no reason why leases cannot contain clear pro-owner clauses, and a good one concerns tax increases. If taxes are raised after the first year of the lease, the increase can be passed through to the tenant on a monthly basis.

Term.

All leases must show a given term, not merely "one or two years," but from a given date to a specific, final date. This way the precise period covered by the lease is clearly understood.

Use.

It may seem obvious that a property with two bedrooms, one bath, and a kitchen will be used only for residential purposes. Some tenants, however, may look at the same property and see everything from an industrial facility to a warehouse. Leases should clearly stipulate that the property's sole function is for residential purposes alone, and that commercial and professional use is prohibited unless otherwise agreed.

Utilities.

In properties with separate meters, the tenant must be responsible for all utilities, including deposits. Be certain all water, gas, and electric meters are read at both the beginning and end of the lease term.

Vehicles.

No campers, buses, motorcycles, or unlicensed or non-operating vehicles should be permitted on the property without the owner's approval. All vehicles must be kept on driveways or in garages so that lawns and gardens are not ruined.

Miscellaneous Items.

Every lease is ultimately a customized agreement between owner and tenant, and you may want to add special language for a variety of reasons. For instance, owners licensed as real estate brokers or agents should say in the lease that they're licensed. Any portion of the property not warranted, perhaps the washer and dryer, should be described in full. If the owner objects to water beds, they can be banned in the lease.

In many jurisdictions, the content of a lease is controlled or regulated by local governments. Owners, for instance, are usually required to hold security deposits in escrow or trust accounts. There may be certain rules regarding maintenance, pets, or cars on the property. Whatever the regulations, recognize that you're not the first person in the community to rent property and that standardized leases undoubtedly exist. You're likely to need help, however, updating, modifying, and customizing such form documents, changes best made with the advice of a knowledgeable attorney and local broker.

27
Should You Hire a Manager?

If you're a small investor and want to get the largest number of tax benefits from your holdings, Uncle Sam requires that you "actively" manage your properties. Just buying a house here and a house there and hiring someone to run them does not qualify you to be regarded as an "active" investor.

Investors should see active management in positive terms. It means owners must be involved in the significant decisions affecting the property's value, issues such as renting versus selling, if and when to refinance, what rent to charge, which repairs to make, and tenant selection.

Active ownership doesn't preclude the use of a broker who acts as a professional manager or agent, someone to oversee day-to-day details. However, old-style management relations are out. Gone are management agreements that give brokers authority to negotiate and execute leases in their "best judgment"—not always such a good idea considering that the best judgment of some brokers includes the woeful notion that the property should rent for less than owners want.

What standards must you meet to be an "active" investor? For the latest specifications, speak with a tax attorney, CPA, or enrolled agent.

Should you have a manager? It's certainly cheaper to manage by yourself, but if your time is valuable then personal management may not make sense. Many small investors hire managers, however, in part because they want management services but also because a good manager is also likely to be a good broker, someone who may know about interesting properties as they come onto the market.

But if you're going to have a manager, it seems very clear that owners—not agents—must ultimately approve all leases. Tenant selection is a core concern for every landlord, and although a manager may sort out inquiries from prospective tenants and assemble applications from highly regarded candidates, it's the owner who ultimately must make the final selection. In this selection process by owners, the views and opinions of a manager should be heard and considered.

As to the lease itself, it should be seen as an agreement between tenant and owner, not tenant and manager. Upon completion of all negotiations, it becomes the owner's decision to accept or not accept the arrangement hashed out between tenant and manager.

Management also involves day-to-day oversight at the property. You want the manager to deal with the tenant, to be available when you're on vacation, to open the property for repairs, collect rent, and keep you informed.

Managers may be authorized to conduct routine maintenance and repairs, but expenditures above a certain threshold—say $50 to $100— should be regarded as significant decisions to be made only with an owner's approval. Once a decision has been made to spend or not spend sums above the threshold, the manager can then be directed to oversee contractors, assure that proper repairs are made, and always keep owners informed.

Even with a threshold, managers still should have authority to order emergency repairs. If it costs $200 for a plumber to stop a flood, and you're not available at 2 A.M., then a manager should surely have the right to order such work.

In addition to clauses that clearly benefit owners, management agreements may also contain several pro-agent clauses that owners need to consider with care.

Buried in management agreements one can usually find a clause which says that if the property is sold to the tenant during the lease term, during any lease extension, or during a certain period after the lease expires—say 90 to 120 days—the broker is entitled to a sales commission of 6 or 7 percent.

This clause is not unreasonable in the sense that the broker did introduce the tenant to the property. However, the commission's size is surely a matter for negotiation, especially since the broker need not expend any money to advertise the property for sale or share the commission with another broker.

A somewhat similar clause gives the broker the exclusive right to sell the property for a set commission, say 6 or 7 percent, if it's offered for sale during the lease term. This clause commits an owner to work with a particular broker, even if relations break down during the lease term, perhaps one, two, or three years into the future. Moreover, by agreeing to a particular commission up front and a certain type of listing agreement, usually an "exclusive right to sell" listing, the owner cannot negotiate sale fees and terms with the broker during the lease term. Major terms have already been established.

In the case of an "exclusive right to sell" agreement, for example, a commission is due to the broker if the property is sold by anyone to anyone during the listing period. Thus, if an owner sells the property to Uncle Max, the broker will earn a commission.

While listing clauses describe the type of listing and fee arrangement, they're remarkably silent on such pivotal matters as the broker's obligation to hold open houses, advertise, or place the property in a local MLS system if the owner desires.

Given these shortcomings, a listing agreement not related to the tenant should be seen as a separate matter to be discussed and negotiated if and when an owner elects to market his property. If the broker has done a good job managing the property, then surely an owner will turn to him when it comes time to sell.

In general terms, the use of managers seems both desirable and necessary for out-of-town property. For properties down the street, the need for a professional manager declines.

However, even if your rental units are nearby, managers still have value. If you vacation, you still need someone to watch over your investments. If you don't like to deal directly with tenants, managers can take on that job. If you don't belong to a credit bureau or if you're not familiar with local rental rules, managers can help. And if you want advice without emotional attachment to the property, brokers are a necessity.

28
Dealing with Rent Control

In perhaps 200 cities, towns, and counties across the country, investors may find that relations between landlord and tenant are governed by rent-control regulations.

Whether rent control is effective or desirable is a matter of considerable dispute. The idea of rent control, according to supporters, is to prevent property owners from charging unconscionable rents, especially when tenants are elderly, poor, or disabled.

Opponents argue that rent control discourages property development, thereby lowering the supply of units and forcing up rents. Moreover, opponents contend that while rents are controlled, property costs are not, particularly items such as fuel, interest rates, insurance, repairs, and taxes. As an alternative, opponents want to do away with rent control, thereby— they argue—increasing the supply of rental units and controlling rates through the marketplace.

Whatever the pros and cons, rent control is a fact in many areas and investors must abide by whatever rules are in force.

Rent control is not a single set of rules used nationwide but rather, localized policies which vary enormously. Investors can find everything from complete rent control to a highly selective set of rules and conditions.

Rents, for example, are likely to be regulated under rent control—no surprise here. In some cases rent increases are limited to set amounts established each year.

But rent-control rules are often less absolute than they appear. "Hardship" increases are often permitted after a hearing. Small landlords, those with four or fewer units in many cases, are often exempt from some or all regulations. Commercial and high-rent properties are typically exempt as well. Repairs and improvements can lead to higher rental rates.

There's also the matter of rent de-control. Some rent-control rules limit rent increases for current tenants. However, once a tenant moves, a landlord can then seek market rents for the property.

Some rent-control regulations address sale situations and not just rents per se. For example, a tenant may have a right of first refusal if a property is offered for sale. If Lincoln wants to sell his rental unit for $100,000 and accepts a $95,000 offer from buyer French, that offer in certain jurisdictions is automatically subject to a tenant's right of first refusal. Making the matter more complicated, the tenant may have a statutory period to match any purchase offer, say 15 days, during which time the owner can't sell and the purchaser can't buy.

Conversion is another rent-control issue. If Lindell wants to convert his ten-unit property into condominiums, in some jurisdictions he may be required to get approval from a majority of his tenants. The tenants, in turn, often have a statutory time to organize and present a united front. How does Lindell get his tenants to accept the conversion? He offers discounts toward the purchase of a unit. This process benefits current tenants while at the same time raising conversion costs. Those higher expenses, of course, are passed on to buyers and mean that fewer people can afford individual units—the direct opposite of rent-control's philosophical intent.

Other matters that might be addressed by rent control include moving allowances (sometimes $500 to $750 per unit to defray moving expenses in the event of conversion), notices (allowing so much time before leases can be terminated), and appeals (the right of a tenant to contest rent increases).

Investors, with the help of brokers and lawyers, should understand their obligations under rent control. Such rules affect property values, rates of return, and relations with tenants. Conversely, investors should also know that rent control is prohibited in a number of states.

29
Additional Information

Successful Real Estate Investing in the '90s is part of a series of real estate books designed to raise ideas, provide information, and suggest strategies that can have value for consumers nationwide.

In addition, you may want to consider other ways to gain real estate information.

First, speak to as many lenders, brokers, and agents as possible. Many will have financing ideas and suggestions that have value.

Second, consider taking a basic, low-cost licensure class. Such classes—which can be available from colleges, universities, real estate organizations, and private schools—will show you how the real estate marketing system works in your jurisdiction and qualify you to take an agent's licensure test.

Third, read local newspapers. Many real estate sections offer solid advice and information, so clip and save the items most interesting to you.

Fourth, visit real estate expositions, particularly those sponsored by local newspapers, real estate organizations, and builder groups. Such expos often have a variety of booths, little or no selling pressure, plus a goodly amount of information.

Fifth, check out personal finance publications such as *Money*, *Consumer's Digest*, and *Kiplinger's Personal Finance* that often carry extensive, timely articles of value to real estate consumers.

Sixth, if this guide has been helpful, then consider the other books in this series: *Successful Real Estate Negotiation* (with Douglas M. Bregman, Esq.), *Buy Your First Home Now*, and *How to Sell Your Home In Any Market—With or Without a Broker*.

Seventh, go electronic. Millions of people have a computer, modem, and mouse—all you need to be a part of the network nation. Local electronic bulletin boards may have real estate information, while a national service such as the real estate forum I host on America Online has an MLS open to brokers and non-brokers, offering current mortgage rates, real estate software, online questions and answers, and much more. For additional information, call 800-827-6364. **Be certain to mention extension 5764 for such free software, online time, and introductory pricing as may be available when you call.**

Lastly, if you do well investing, pass on what you've learned and make the marketplace easier for the next person.

Glossary

THE LANGUAGE OF INVESTMENT

Physicians talk about "myocardial infarctions," garment manufacturers sell goods by the "hundred dozen," and service station owners try to get the highest "pool margin price" for their gasoline. In each case, people within a particular field use words and terms that fellow insiders instantly understand.

Real estate investing is no different. People who buy and sell property, who make loans and who borrow, all work from a common set of phrases and expressions. These terms reflect not only dictionary-style definitions, but also insights, values, and perceptions. To know how the real estate market works, to be successful, one must use and understand the language of investment.

Acceptance.
A positive response to an offer or counteroffer. There are conditional acceptances ("I'll accept if you'll pay another $1,500 for the property"), express or written acceptances, implied acceptances ("I'm not going to say anything if you move in early"), and qualified acceptances ("I'll accept your offer subject to my lawyer liking the deal").

Addenda.
Clauses, documents, or statements added to a contract which alter it in some way. To be enforceable, addenda must be signed or initialed by both buyer and seller and clearly referenced in the contract. For example, a contract might refer to addenda by saying that "Addenda are attached to and made a part of this contract."

Addendum.
Singular of "addenda."

Agent.
Has two meanings in real estate. First, in general terms, someone who acts on behalf of another for a fee, such as a real estate broker or an attorney. Second, a type of real estate licensee who works under the authority of a real estate broker.

Amortization.
As payments are made to a lender each month the mortgage debt, or "principal," declines in most cases. This process is called "amortization." Also, see "self-amortization," and "negative amortization."

Amortization schedule.
A chart showing how each monthly payment is divided into principal and interest during the loan term and how much principal remains after each payment. For a level-payment, 30-year, $85,000 loan at 7.5 percent interest, monthly payments will be $594.33 and an amortization schedule would look like this:

Payment	Interest	Principal	Balance
1	$531.25	$63.08	$84,936.92
2	$530.86	$63.47	$84,873.45
3	$530.46	$63.87	$84,809.58
4	$530.06	$64.27	$84,745.31

Annual percentage rate (APR).
The true rate of interest for a loan over its projected life, say 30 years. May be different from the initial interest rate or the nominal interest rate before compounding.

Appraisal.
An estimate of value produced by an independent appraiser. Typically based on such factors as replacement cost, past sales of like properties, and the ability to produce income.

Appraiser.
A person familiar with local real estate values who estimates the worth of particular properties. Compensation for the appraiser cannot be related to a specific estimate of value ("I'll pay you $500 if you say the property is worth $150,000"), nor can the appraiser have an undisclosed interest in the property ("Come up with a good appraisal, and you can act as a broker in the deal").

"As is" agreements.
Situations where property is sold without warranty and in whatever physical condition it may be in as of the time a contract is signed. Before entering such deals, both buyers and sellers should check state and local regulations and warranty rules to see if and how "as is" sales are affected by such laws.

Assumption.
A situation where a buyer takes over loan payments and obligations from a seller. Both buyer and seller are responsible for repaying the entire debt if the purchaser defaults. Also see "subject to."

Balloon notes.
Real estate loans where some portion of the debt will remain unpaid at the end of the loan term. Second trusts, for example, are frequently short-term loans (say three to five years) where a single large payment is due when the loan ends. Often used with investment property in cases where buyers want low monthly payments.

Blanket mortgage.
A single mortgage secured by several properties.

Broker.
A licensed real estate professional employed by a buyer or seller to assist in a purchase, sale, or management of real property. A broker's duties may include determining market values, advertising properties for sale, showing properties to prospective purchasers, assisting in the preparation of contracts, advising clients with regard to the acceptance or rejection of an offer or counteroffer, and dealing with a wide variety of related matters. While brokers have traditionally represented sellers, they can also be hired by purchasers, a concept known as "buyer brokerage." *For purposes of this guide, the term "broker" is often used in a general sense when either a broker or sales person (or both) might be appropriate in certain situations.* For instance, a sentence saying that "brokers frequently spend many weeks working with prospects" can just as easily apply to sales people.

Buyer brokers.
Real estate professionals paid by, and representing, purchasers alone.

Cash flow.
The difference between expenses and income before depreciation. For example, if a property has an income of $100,000 and expenses of $80,000, it has a $20,000 positive cash flow. If expenses are $130,000 a year, it has a $30,000 negative cash flow. When depreciation is considered, it's entirely possible to have a property that produces a positive cash flow but shows a loss for tax purposes.

Clear and marketable title.
Property that can be sold immediately because all claims, such as existing mortgages, have been paid off, assumed, or otherwise cleared.

Closing.
See "settlement."

Condominium.
When someone owns a condo, he or she possesses an individual property unit as well as a nonexclusive interest in the common areas controlled by the condominium organization.

Cooperatives.
When someone "owns" a co-op, he or she has stock in a corporation that owns real estate and the exclusive right to use a portion of the co-op's property.

Co-owners.
Two or more people with an interest in a single parcel of property. An extremely important issue since the form of co-ownership shown on a title may affect such matters as estates, inheritances, and personal liability in the event of a lawsuit.

Co-signer.
A person who signs and assumes joint liability with another. For instance, Mr. Daly may co-sign a loan with his son. Note that a co-signer may share liability but that such an individual is not necessarily a co-owner.

Contingency.
A provision that makes a contract incomplete until a certain event occurs. For example, if investor Lanham offers to purchase the Hartford property "subject to a structural inspection satisfactory to purchaser," there's no final contract unless Lanham says the structural inspection is satisfactory to him.

Contingent contract.
A contract with a qualification or condition which must be resolved before the contract is final.

Contract.
In real estate, a binding, written agreement between two or more people to attain a common goal, typically the transfer of property ownership in exchange for money.

Credit report.
A report from an independent source which outlines a person's credit-worthiness by listing debts, liabilities, assets, and related information. Used by lenders to assess the credit-worthiness of potential borrowers. (Note: It's always a good idea to check your own credit report regularly to see that it's accurate. Contact local credit-reporting agencies for more information.)

Curtailment.
A payment that shortens or ends a mortgage. For example, if an investor owes $25,000 on a mortgage and pays off the entire debt, the loan is said to be "curtailed."

Damages.
Compensation for loss or injury caused by another. Damages may be recovered by any person who has suffered loss, detriment, or injury through an unlawful act, omission, or the negligent act of another.

Deferred interest.
See "negative amortization."

Deposit.
Usually money delivered by a buyer to a seller to assure that the buyer's contract obligations will be fulfilled.

Deed.
A document that transfers title to real estate from one party to another and is recorded among the governmental land records where the property is located.

Depreciation.
An assumption that property owners will be forced to replace their property improvements after a certain period of time, say 27.5 years for residential investment property, because of normal wear and tear.

Due-on-sale clause (alienation clause).
Language found in loan agreements which requires borrowers to repay loans at the time title changes hands. Such clauses are restricted by federal law in certain cases—for example, when a prime residence changes hands as the result of a death in the family.

Earnest money.
See "deposit."

Easement.
A right to use someone else's property. Beware, sometimes easements are created without an owner's permission or knowledge!

Encroachment.
An intrusion, obstruction, or invasion of someone else's property. For example, if a neighbor just built a fence and the fence is six inches over your property line, it's an encroachment.

Entitlement.
A right due to an individual. Used with VA mortgages. For instance, a $15,000 entitlement would mean that a vet could borrow that sum from a lender and the VA would guarantee its repayment. Since lenders usually want a 4:1 ratio between the value of an entitlement and the loan amount, having a $15,000 guarantee allows a borrower to receive a $60,000 loan.

Equity.
The cash value of property, less marketing expenses, after all liens have been paid off.

Escrow.
When money is held by one party for another it's usually placed in an "escrow" or trust account. For example, when an investor gives a broker a $10,000 deposit to purchase a house, that money is placed in an escrow account. The broker has no right to use the $10,000 for his own purposes.

Fair market value.
The price of a given property at a particular time as a result of negotiation between knowledgeable buyers and sellers.

Fixtures.
Items that usually convey to the buyer in a realty transaction unless specifically excluded from the sale. Fixtures are generally attached to the property and intended to be sold with it. Examples of common fixtures include built-in dishwashers, furnaces, chandeliers, and plumbing.

Gift.
The voluntary transfer of money, property, or anything of value from one person to another without any duty or expectation of repayment. Since gifts in the context of a real estate transaction may be large, donors should check with a CPA or tax attorney before making a gift commitment to assure that all tax consequences are understood.

Hypothecate.
To pledge property as security for a mortgage.

Income-to-debt ratio.
A measure used by lenders to determine if prospective borrowers are qualified for loans of a given size. For example, a lender might allow a borrower to use as much as 28 percent of his total monthly income to pay monthly costs for principal, interest, taxes, and insurance. The income-to-debt ratio is 28 to 100, or 28 percent.

Inspection.
An examination to determine condition or quality.

Installment sale.
A transaction in which the buyer pays the seller in whole or in part after title has been transferred.

Internal rate of return (IRR).
A measure used by real estate investors to judge operating results. In basic terms, the IRR compares annual returns with initial investments. For example, if Henderson invests $20,000 and has a $3,000 cash flow at the end of the year, his

IRR is 15 percent. If the same cash flow took two years to generate, the IRR is 7.24 percent.

Junior lien.
Much like shoppers in a supermarket line, lenders line up to be paid when a property is foreclosed. The order of repayment is established by the loan documents recorded in local governmental offices. The lender with the first claim has the first mortgage or first trust, the lender with the second claim holds the second mortgage or second trust, etc. If a loan is not a first trust or mortgage, it's a "junior" lien.

Language of art (legal wording).
Standardized language with specific legal meanings. A trap for the unwary, legal language may contain definitions, meanings, shadings, and implications not found when the same words are used in everyday conversation.

Lease.
An agreement between an owner and a tenant to rent property for a given amount of time, at a particular price, and with certain conditions.

Leverage.
A general investment concept meaning that you have been able to borrow and thereby use other people's money (OPM). If an investor buys property for $100,000, puts down $20,000 at settlement, and gets an $80,000 mortgage for the balance, his leverage is 1 to 4. If he only puts down $10,000, his leverage is 1 to 9, a better deal—*if* the $10,000 he *didn't* put into the property can earn an equal or better return elsewhere *and* the property's value does not decline.

Lien.
A lien is a claim against property. Not only are mortgages and trusts liens, but overdue property taxes, unpaid repair bills, condo fees, and even water and sewage charges can all be liens. A major purpose of a title search is to be certain that all liens are known as of the day of settlement.

Loan ap.
Industry jargon for "loan application."

Loan origination fee.
A fee charged by lenders to cover loan processing costs, often equal to 1 percent of the loan's value.

Loan-to-value ratio.
Used by virtually all lenders, the loan-to-value ratio, or LTV, compares the market value of a property with the amount of financing being sought. With conventional financing, lenders seek an LTV of 80 percent—that is, property worth $10 for each $8 they lend.

Locking in.
Mortgage rates are widely advertised but the rate you see may not be your final rate at settlement, especially in a market where mortgage costs are rising. To assure a given rate at settlement, borrowers must often "lock in" rates by paying a fee when they apply for financing. Investors should be aware that lock-in arrangements may be subject to conditions that make them valueless—for example, a lock-in agreement that becomes invalid if market conditions change. Market conditions *always* change.

Merge.
To absorb or fuse one document or right into another. In real estate, this usually means the sales contract is merged into or becomes a part of the deed. Once this merger takes place, the real estate contract is no longer in effect. However, if a real estate contract says that a portion of the document—or the complete document—is to "survive," then that material will not be merged into the deed.

Multiple listing system (MLS).
One: a marketing tool used within the real estate industry to disseminate information concerning a given property to a large number of agents and brokers. Two: a system of agency/subagency relationships. For example, if broker Dobbs lists a property for sale, Dobbs is the owner's agent. If broker Courtney sees the property in the multiple listing service and offers the property for sale, Courtney represents the owner as a subagent.

Negative amortization.
A loan where monthly payments are too small to entirely pay for either principal or interest reductions, or both. For example: With a 30-year, $85,000 loan at 7.5 percent interest a self-amortizing loan will require monthly payments of $594.33. If the payments are only $500, the amortization statement will look like this:

Payment	Interest	Principal	Balance
1	$531.25	-$31.25	$85,031.25
2	$531.44	-$31.44	$85,062.69
3	$531.64	-$31.64	$85,094.33
4	$531.84	-$31.84	$85,126.17

Notice.
A declaration or action which conspicuously identifies a condition, action, or non-action. For example, a statement that the basement leaks places a buyer "on notice" that a possibly harmful condition exists. Notice may also be unstated but presumed. For example, if a purchaser sees that the basement floor is wet, and if the seller has not attempted to hide the problem, then the buyer may be effectively on notice.

Offer.
A proposal which, when accepted, will become a contract. In real estate the buyer commonly makes a written offer to purchase property which may then be accepted, rejected, or countered by the seller. Offers may be withdrawn without penalty at any time prior to acceptance, unless the offer provides otherwise. If a proposal is rejected, it may not be resurrected without permission of the person who made the offer.

Option.
A right to act under certain terms and conditions. For example, if Mr. Mullins can purchase the Butler property for $150,000 by June 1, he has an option. If he does not act by June 1, the option is dead. Note that Mullins need not wait for Butler to offer his property for sale or to accept an offer from another purchaser. See "right of first refusal."

Package mortgage.
A single mortgage used to acquire not only property but personal goods such as a microwave oven.

Points (loan discount fees).
An interest fee charged by lenders at settlement. One point is equal to 1 percent of a mortgage. The purpose of points is to raise the lender's yield above the apparent interest rate.

Prime rate.
Traditionally defined as the best rate available to a lender's best customers. Also, the subject of dispute because some borrowers have received rates below prime.

Principal, interest, taxes, and insurance (PITI).
The four basic costs of homeownership that most concern lenders. For instance, a lender might say that a borrower could qualify for financing provided the PITI for a given mortgage does not exceed 28 percent of the individual's gross monthly income.

Quit-claim deeds.
A deed which says, in effect, "whatever title I have, if anything, I hereby give to you." Unfortunately, the seller who offers a quit-claim deed may have no rights or interests to sell. *Always consult an attorney before agreeing to any deal which involves a quit-claim deed.*

Refinance.
To place new financing on a property. The addition of a second trust would be a "partial" refinancing. Replacing one loan with another would be a "total" refinancing.

Release.
Real estate loans are secured by property and an owner may subdivide his ground only with a lender's permission, approval known as a "release." If a release cannot be obtained, the loan must be repaid before the property can be subdivided.

Remedies.
Forms of compensation, such as money or actions, granted in response to a wrongful situation or condition.

Rent.
The economic cost to use someone else's property; or, seen from the investor's perspective, revenue derived from property ownership.

Restructure.
A situation where a loan remains in place but its terms are changed. If you increase your monthly payments by $25 you have *restructured* your loan. By making the additional payments you will reduce the principal debt at a faster rate than originally planned and so will pay less interest and have fewer payments. For example, if you have a $100,000 loan at 10 percent interest, it will take 30 years to repay the loan with monthly payments of $877.57. If the monthly payment is raised to $908.70 the loan can be repaid in a little more than 25 years.

Right of first refusal.
A priority right to purchase property under terms and conditions made by another purchaser and accepted by an owner. For example, if Hains offers $50,000 for the Wilshire property, and Wilshire accepts the offer subject to Kean's right of first refusal, Kean has the right to buy the property for $50,000. Note that a right of first refusal may render a property less salable because marketability is clouded. Also see "option."

Satisfaction.
Acceptance by one or both parties or the completion of an obligation. As an example, Mr. Brody offers to buy the Kent residence if he decides the roof inspection is "satisfactory." If he accepts the inspection report, the contract will be finalized.

Self-amortization.
When monthly payments for principal and interest allow a loan to be repaid over its term without any balloon payment, self-amortization has occurred.

Settlement (closing).
The act or process of adjusting and finalizing all dealings, money, and arrangements for real estate buyers and sellers. At settlement, all debts are paid, all adjustments are made as of settlement, all money is properly disbursed, the deed is prepared with the new owner's name, and the property is conveyed in accordance with the contract and the intentions of the parties.

Subject to.

An offer or contract that depends on a separate condition or action. In real estate, this phrase is usually found in a provision such as, "This property is sold subject to a right-of-way granted to the electric company allowing its electrical lines to cross the front yard."

Subordinated financing.

A second trust is said to be "subordinated" to a first trust; that is, in a foreclosure the first trust must be entirely repaid before any money can be used to pay off the second trust.

Subordination clause.

Allows a borrower to refinance property without repaying a current loan. For example, if Wilkins financed his property with a $50,000 first trust that can be subordinated, he can get another loan, say $25,000, and it can then become the first trust. The old first trust, because it has been subordinated, is now a second trust and markedly more risky. This clause is unacceptable to virtually all lenders.

Substitution-of-collateral clause.

Gives borrower the right to change loan collateral at will and without lender approval. This clause is unacceptable to virtually all lenders.

Survey.

An examination of property boundaries and related matters. A survey can reveal the quantity of land, boundary distances, where improvements are located, ground contours, and other vital information about the property.

Sweat equity.

Additional property value produced by an owner's time, labor, and intelligence. Unlike $100 spent for a carpenter to fix a deck, an owner's efforts are not tax deductible.

Take-back.

An expression that means a loan has been made directly to a purchaser by a seller as in, "Seller Griffin will take back a $50,000 second trust from Buyer Landow."

Taxable income.

The amount of income subject to federal and state income taxes. For example, if a property has annual rentals of $100,000 but annual expenses of $75,000, it's producing a $25,000 cash flow. But if the property also produces depreciation worth $15,000, then taxable income totals just $10,000.

Tenancies.

Interests in real estate defined in the deed. A vitally important matter which shows how title to the property is held.

Tenants.
An individual or entity, such as a business, that occupies someone else's property. Note that while "tenancies" usually describe forms of property ownership, a "tenant" does not own property.

Termites.
Wood-boring insects that can infest and damage homes. Most realty sales require a termite inspection showing the property is free and clear of termites and other wood-boring insects. Such inspections should also list other insect damage, if any.

Timesharing.
A form of activity where a single property is used by multiple owners. Note that "timesharing" does not necessarily refer to real estate ownership; some timeshare units are vacation leases or merely a right to use certain facilities. Note also that since timeshare financing is often in the form of a personal loan rather than debt secured by real property, timeshare interest may be regarded as consumer debt rather than tax-deductible real estate interest.

Title.
The right of property ownership. Such ownership can be held solely, jointly, in common, in corporate, or in partnership form. A person who holds a vested interest in real estate is said to hold title whether he holds it for himself or for others.

Title insurance.
Policies purchased at settlement, which ensure that one's ownership or interest in the property is protected against loss if a title defect is found or if title claims are made after ownership is transferred. Policies differ and may contain exclusions and exceptions. Also, policy coverage may be expanded to include additional protection. Speak to the person conducting settlement for complete information.

Trust.
A loan where the lender's interests are represented by a trustee such as a lawyer, bank, savings and loan association, mortgage banker, etc.

Usury.
In many jurisdictions there's a maximum rate of interest permitted for certain types of loans. If the interest rate is above the limit, it's usury. The usury limit varies not only between jurisdictions but according to loan types. There may, for instance, be one usury limit for first trusts and another rate for seconds. *Investors should be aware that usury rates for owner-occupied housing may not apply to investor loans.*

Warranties.
Guarantees, promises, and protections provided by one party to another. In real estate contracts there are usually warranties regarding the condition of appliances

and certain fixtures. New homes often have extensive warranties covering not only fixtures and appliances but the overall structure as well. There can be "express" (written) warranties and "implied" warranties, guarantees that the parties intended even though they may not have stated them specifically in the contract.

Zoning.
Rules for land use established by local governments.

Appendix I
How to Create
Winning Loan Applications

Borrowers often complain about loan processing. Filling out the right forms and gathering needed—and sometimes unneeded—information is burdensome, dull, and time-consuming.

But such complaints are irrelevant. The fact is that lenders want their paperwork, you want their money, and filling out forms is a necessity. And while home buyers can be excused for not having loan information prepared and available for lenders, investors should know better.

The idea of maintaining extensive records does not mean that every scrap of paper in your files should be submitted to lenders. Many loan programs today, especially when large down payments are involved, require minimal documentation, perhaps nothing more than mortgage and employment verifications plus a basic loan application. Always remember the basic rule for loan applications: Submit only documentation required by the lender. Anything else should be regarded as excessive.

Step One: Get a loan application.
The most basic lender form is a legal-size, two-sided loan application. As a matter of courtesy and good public relations, local lenders will be happy to supply copies if asked.

Step Two: Fill in the blanks.
As you look at the loan ap, you'll discover it asks three types of questions: first, basic data such as your name and address, marital status, number of children, social security number, etc.; second, information you can get, such as credit card numbers and recent account balances; and third, blanks for the lender to complete.

Items in the first category you know and items in the third you don't have to worry about. That leaves information in category two. Before meeting your first lender, create a file with the following information.

- Assets: Show the value of all assets, including cars, furniture, IRA and Keogh accounts, pension funds, savings accounts, stock and bond holdings, money market accounts, real estate, private businesses, partnerships, and the cash-surrender value of insurance policies. *Step to Take:* Assemble information regarding each asset, including names, addresses, and account numbers. Show value for each as of a given date—say the last time a statement was issued.

  Note that the dates for each account can vary. For instance, you can have a Master Card balance from July 1st and a Visa balance from August 15th. The important point is to show the correct balance and to list the date for the balance figure you supply.

- Big questions: Lenders will want to know if you've been bankrupt or had property foreclosed in the past seven years, if you have any outstanding judgments against you, if you're currently involved in a lawsuit, or if you pay alimony, child support, or separate maintenance. They also want to know if any portion of the down payment is borrowed or if you're the maker or endorser of a note. *Step to Take:* If the answer to any of these questions is "yes," then assemble the paperwork to show what happened, when, and how it affects you now. If you're borrowing money for the down payment, provide a copy of the entire loan agreement.

- Citizenship: Lenders will want to know if you're a citizen, resident alien, or a nonresident alien. *Step to Take:* Document your status if you're not a U.S. citizen.

  If you are not a citizen, you may be able to obtain financing on the same terms and conditions as anyone else. Be certain to have Registration Receipt Card I-151 (a "green" card), or a "resident alien card" also known as Registration Receipt Card I-551 with an expiration date; or an Alien Registration Receipt Card I-551 with an expiration date providing you have also filed INS Form I-751; or an unexpired foreign passport stamped "processed for I-551. Temporary Evidence of Lawful Admission for Permanent Residence. Valid until (mm-dd-yy). Employment authorized."

  If you are a legal but non-permanent resident alien, financing may be available, but only with a substantial down payment. See lenders for details.

- Credit references: List lenders to whom you are now in debt or to whom you have previously owed money. Choices can include banks, credit card companies, second trust holders, etc. *Step to Take:* Contact past lenders you intend to name and ask permission to list them as credit references. With large organizations, list contacts by name and title.

- Current housing costs: Show monthly housing costs such as mortgage payments, real estate taxes, insurance, condo or co-op fees, and utility bills. *Step to Take:* Assemble monthly mortgage bills, utility stubs, insurance records, and condo and co-op fee information for the past year.

- Debts: List all debts, including credit cards, mortgages, real estate loans, pledged stock (shares bought on margin or used as collateral for other loans), child support, alimony, and separate maintenance. *Step to Take:* Develop a complete list of all debts showing names, dollar amounts, addresses, and account numbers. Show latest balance for each account as of a given date, and list total credit available. For instance, with Visa you may have a $5,000 line of credit and a $400 debt as of October 15th.

- Government monitoring: Borrowers are asked to indicate their race, national origin, and gender. *Step to Take:* You may or may not elect to provide this information at your discretion. There's no penalty if you decide not to complete monitoring information; however, if you don't respond, the lender may be *required* by federal law to answer monitoring questions on the basis of personal observation and surname.

- Income: Compute gross monthly income. Include wages, *regular* bonuses, commissions, dividends, interest, and net rental income. *Step to Take:* Put two latest pay stubs in the application file. Assemble information to prove monthly income, including records relating to interest and dividends.

  Lenders recognize that if you are buying a property for investment that it will (or should) produce income which can help you obtain financing. The question is: How much income will the property generate?

  If the property is now leased, there is a track record to which you can point. If the property is not leased, then before you make an offer have a broker (if one is involved) provide rental rates for comparable properties in the neighborhood. This information can be used to justify income estimates.

  Be conservative in your rental estimates, point out that they are "estimates" and not fact, allow for vacancies, and show evidence from third parties, such as brokers, to support your estimates. Supply documentation where possible—a lease, broker letters, newspaper ads, etc.

- Name change: Tell the lender if you've been previously known by another name.
- Net worth: Subtract debts from assets.
- New property financing: Estimate your acquisition costs, including the purchase price, settlement expenses, prepaid items (such as lender reserves for taxes), the size of the mortgage you need, additional financing other than the loan for which you're applying, your cash contribution, the value of seller credits at settlement (if any), and the total amount of cash you'll need to close the deal. *Step to Take:* First, get good-faith estimates in writing of closing expenses and credits from the broker selling the property. If there's no broker in the sale, ask the party handling settlement to provide a written list of estimates. Second, give the lender a copy of the full sales contract, including all contingencies and addenda.

- New workers: If you've been employed less than two years, show your old job, where it was, the type of business, your position or title, the period from when you held the position to when you left, and your monthly income. If your previous activity was in school or the armed services, say so. *Step to Take:* Obtain records such as pay vouchers, letters from past employers, college transcripts, and military Form DD 212.

- Other financing: Is the property being purchased with a gift, second trust, or seller financing? If so, you must tell the lender. *Step to Take:* Provide loan agreements and gift letters as appropriate.

- Other income sources: Show other income such as alimony, child support, sep-

How to Improve Your Loan Application

1) Report debts and assets fairly and without exaggeration.

2) Always describe values as "estimates" so lenders will understand that your figures represent opinion and not hard fact. For example, the value of your personal residence is an estimate. You can't know its value unless it's sold or appraised.

3) Use a computer. With a basic spreadsheet program you can update debts, assets, and net-worth figures as bills come in and as debts are paid off. A typical spreadsheet for debts might look like this:

	Total Credit Line	Amount Owed	Date
Master Charge #123-456-789-123 1st National Bank 1 Main Street Center City, US 00000	$2,000	$485.46	June 10
Equity Credit Line #987-654-321 Central Bank 25 Oak Street Center City, US 00000	$55,000	$1,200	June 15
Etc.			

4) Deliver documents by hand to speed processing, but only with lender approval. Some lenders do not want materials hand-carried by borrowers because they fear tinkering.

5) Pay off small debts and close unneeded accounts. Owing $8 on a credit card you rarely use means the lender must verify the account. Unfortunately, the credit card company has little incentive to respond quickly to the lender's inquiry, so everyone benefits if the account is closed before making a loan application.

arate maintenance income, money from a trust or estate, etc. *Step to Take:* Assemble records to show extra income.

Note that borrowers are generally told they're not required to list alimony, child support, or separate maintenance income. However, if these items are shown the borrower will have a larger income and thus qualify more easily for financing.

- Real estate holdings: List all property owned. For investment property show mortgage, insurance, management, maintenance, and tax payments. List rental income. *Step to Take:* Assemble needed information. *Include copies of all current lease agreements.*
- Self-employment: If you're self-employed, lenders will want income tax returns for the last two years and sometimes the last three years. *Step to Take:* Assemble tax returns for the three most recent years. Be prepared to deliver year-to-date financial information—typically a profit-and-loss statement signed by a CPA—in addition to past tax returns.

Step Three: Make photocopies.
Take the forms, records, and data you've assembled, and photocopy the entire file. Sign and date tax return copies in ink. This file can then be made available to lenders, while the original materials are retained for additional loan applications as needed.

Step Four: Develop a cover letter.
Investor loans have traditionally been seen as more risky than mortgages for owner-occupants, so it follows that lenders will expect more from you than a typical homeowner. Don't disappoint them.

In your cover letter explain the circumstances of your purchase, what type of property is being bought, whether or not it's currently leased, and the prospects for appreciation. Detail any improvements or changes you intend to make and offer to provide additional information as required.

Step Five: Add a few extras.
By this time your loan application file may have the feel and heft of a computer manual. Still, you may want to add a few frills. Pictures of the property can give loan officers a better idea of your project. Photos of other property you own, particularly "before" and "after" shots of fix-up projects, can be valuable. Lists of recent neighborhood sales might help, particularly annotated lists comparing other properties with yours. A spreadsheet projecting reasonable increases in costs and revenues during the next three to five years can also have value.

Is it really necessary to have an active loan file, something you keep up-to-date? The answer is "yes." In some deals, for example, the seller may want a lender's assurance that you can get a mortgage loan. To get that assurance, you'll need a lender's letter saying you qualify for a loan. It will be a lot easier and faster to get such a letter if your records are assembled and immediately available to the lender.

Another reason to keep an active loan file is simple self-interest. You'll need this information anyway, so why wait? Like death and taxes, it's unavoidable.

Appendix II
Real Estate and Taxes

Few subjects are more complex then federal taxes, a matter of great importance to real estate investors because property has traditionally been a favored investment medium in the eyes of the federal government.

The good news is that despite the Economic Recovery Tax Act of 1981, the Tax Reform Act of 1986, the Deficit Reduction Act of 1990, and the Omnibus Budget Reconciliation Act of 1993, real estate investments have largely retained a preferential position. This favored status is due to the jobs and economic benefits property investments bring to the economy and because government—by itself—cannot otherwise supply the vast number of housing units now provided through private-sector investment.

There is no question that tax considerations are very important to realty owners. That said, two substantial matters should be mentioned.

First, it does not make sense to buy real estate for tax benefits alone. Buy a particular piece of investment real estate because you think it will appreciate or because you feel it will generate income, but do not buy real estate merely because it offers an assortment of tax advantages. Tax advantages are devalued and sometimes worthless when properties produce real cash losses and price plunges.

Second, beware of books—including this one—that discuss real estate and tax policies. In the best possible case, a book can introduce general policies and practices, and while such information may be helpful, it is not a substitute for professional advice from a tax attorney, CPA, or enrolled agent.

You want advice from a tax professional because books, with their long shelf life, cannot keep up with the latest court cases, regulations, and laws. You also want advice from a tax professional because your particular circumstances and situation may differ from a given example or policy found in a publication.

Having been forewarned, you're now ready to consider where things generally stand—taxwise—as of early 1994.

RATES

Taxes remain stable for lower- and middle-income wage earners in the 15, 28, and 31 percent brackets, but rise for those with higher incomes. There is a 36 percent rate for single people with taxable incomes of $115,000 or more

($140,000 for married couples) and a 10 percent surcharge for singles making $125,000 or more ($250,000 for married couples filing together). In effect, then, the top rate is 39.6 percent. (Note that such categories as head of the household and qualifying widows and widowers may have somewhat different earning thresholds.)

INFLATION

Many benchmark numbers now adjust annually with inflation. Thus, while rates may be set, brackets can change.

INTEREST

You can deduct interest on financing worth up to $1 million to acquire or improve a prime residence, a second home, or both. Since few people own personal property worth $1 million, this limit isn't going to trouble many investors.

In addition, you can borrow up to $100,000 against your prime residence for any purpose and still deduct the interest you pay. If the combination of total debt on a first and second home exceeds $1 million for married couples, interest on loans above that magic figure is not deductible.

PROPERTY TAXES

Deductible on both personal and investment property.

MAINTENANCE EXPENSES

Not deductible at all on personal property. Fully deductible on investment real estate.

CAPITAL IMPROVEMENTS

A capital improvement, such as the addition of a room, may be used to reduce profits when a personal residence is sold. A capital improvement for an investment property may be depreciated over time. In either case, be certain to keep all receipts.

POINTS PAID BY THE BUYER

Points paid for financing used to *acquire* a personal residence are deductible in the year paid.

Points paid to refinance a personal residence, or to acquire or refinance investment property, are only deductible over the life of the loan. Example: if McDowell refinances his business property with a 30-year mortgage and pays points worth $1,500 at settlement, he can deduct $50 each year ($1,500 divided by 30). If he pays off the loan in ten years, the remaining $1,000 in unclaimed points can then be deducted ($1,500 less claims to date of $500 [$50 × 10 years = $500]).

Be aware that the government does not automatically allow deductions for points. Points must represent an interest expense and they must be a typical charge at the time the loan is made.

Also, if you are a buyer, you may be able to deduct points paid by the seller.

POINTS PAID BY THE SELLER

If a seller pays points, the points are deductible in the year paid as an expense of selling.

If a seller pays points to assist the purchaser, the *buyer* may deduct the value of the points paid by the *seller* in the year paid. If the buyer deducts points paid by the seller, the buyer must reduce the sale basis of the property (increase the amount of profit) when the home is sold. This write-off for buyers applies only to the acquisition of owner-occupied prime residences. The new rules do not apply to refinancing, second homes, or investment property.

If you bought a home after December 31, 1990 and had points paid by a seller, you may amend your return to claim an additional deduction. Write "seller-paid points" in the upper right-hand corner of the amended form.

PASSIVE INCOME

All real estate earnings are defined as "passive" income, as opposed to "regular" or "portfolio" income from such mundane sources as employment, stock profits, or interest. Real estate losses and expenses can be subtracted from property income to produce a passive profit or a passive loss. Passive profits are taxed in the same way as other income.

PASSIVE LOSS LIMITATIONS

Realty investments commonly produce both cash flow and tax losses. A property that generates $7,500 in cash flow after expenses, but depreciation worth $10,000, represents a "loss" in the eyes of the government.

For years investors sought to maximize both cash flow and paper losses, but tax reform put an end to many tax-avoidance ploys. Still, three major strategies exist to deal with real estate losses today.

First, passive losses can be used to offset passive profits. The problem is that passive losses in the general case cannot be used to offset income from wages, dividends, and other types of income. Thus some investors may find that they have passive real estate losses which effectively are not deductible.

Second, while passive real estate losses generally cannot be used to offset other forms of income, there is an exception that works well for most wage earners.

Passive write-offs of as much as $25,000 against regular income are available in most cases to "active" investors with adjusted gross incomes of $100,000 or less, and who hold at least a 10 percent stake in the property or properties which produce the loss. Those who qualify are able to offset not more than $25,000 annually in regular income with passive real estate losses, a considerable benefit since few people make $100,000 anyway.

For those souls saddled with adjusted gross incomes in excess of $100,000 a year, smaller write-offs are available. The wealthy subtract $1 from the $25,000 maximum write-off for each $2 in income they earn above $100,000. Using this formula, the rich will no longer be allowed to deduct passive income from regular earnings above $150,000. Special benefits, however, are available to those who invest in low-income housing or rehabilitate historic buildings.

Third, professionals "active" in real estate may now be able to deduct passive losses from regular income.

Who is "active" in real estate? One threshold is those who devote at least 750 hours year to "real property trades or business." A second threshold is that to qualify as active, individuals must spend at least half their working hours in real estate activities such as construction, development, management, or brokerage. A third threshold is that the "professional," if an employee, must have at least a 5 percent equity stake in the real estate activity which generates a loss or profit.

If broker Kent spends 2,000 hours a year acting as a broker and works 2,200 hours a year, then Kent's real estate losses are likely to be deductible from regular income.

If Dobson, a furrier, works 1,100 hours a year as real estate agent and 1,200 hours a year preparing pelts, he cannot claim a write-off as a realty professional because less than half of his hours are spent in the field.

If Bastante, a real estate investor, spends 600 hours a year working on property investments and 500 hours a year working as a printer, she cannot claim a write-off as a realty professional because she has not met the 750-hour standard.

DEPRECIATION
The depreciation schedule has been stretched from 31.5 years for commercial (nonresidential) real estate to 39 years for property placed in service after May 12, 1993. Residential real estate can be depreciated over 27.5 years.

CAPITAL GAINS
The maximum tax rate on profits from the sale of property held a year or longer is 28 percent. This is a substantial benefit for those in the upper brackets.

SECOND HOMES
Both a prime residence and a second residence can qualify for home interest deductions.

For most owners, second-home choices look like this:

- If you have no rental income, it's a personal residence and all qualified interest is deductible.
- If the property is rented less than 15 days a year, the rent is not reportable, but only interest and property-tax deductions that exceed 10 percent of your adjusted gross income are deductible.
- If you rent the place, but spend more than 14 days or more than 10 percent of the days it's rented for personal use, then deductions are permitted up to the amount of rent collected.

The bottom line: You can effectively engineer the tax status of a second property by deciding whether or not to rent it and, if it's rented, how often you use the property.

REHABILITATION CREDITS

There's a 20 percent benefit on historic structures and a 10 percent tax credit for fixing up nonresidential, nonhistoric structures built before 1936.

LOW-INCOME PROPERTIES

If you buy low-income housing you may be able to obtain a 4 percent annual tax credit for up to ten years, provided the property is at least ten years old. For a new property or one that has been significantly rehabilitated it is possible to qualify for a 9 percent annual write-off that can continue over a ten-year period.

AT-RISK RULES—INVESTOR BEWARE

There has long been an idea in the tax code that deductions should not exceed personal liability—except for real estate investments. With other investments you could claim deductions only to the extent you were "at risk," an expression which means you're personally liable for the loan. For instance, suppose you have a $100,000 mortgage, fail to make payments, and the property is foreclosed. If the property only brings $85,000 at the foreclosure sale, the lender can usually go after you for the balance—in this case, $15,000. If non-recourse financing is used, if you have no personal liability, then the lender can foreclose, but only equity in the property can be used to satisfy the debt.

The at-risk rules apply to real estate. If you buy a property for $100,000, put up $20,000 in cash, and finance $80,000 with a loan for which you are not personally liable, depreciation is limited to the amount you're at risk—$20,000 in this case.

When a real estate loan is secured by both property and personal liability, it's called "recourse" financing. If there is no personal liability, then the financing is regarded as a "non-recourse" loan.

ALTERNATIVE MINIMUM TAX (ATM)

To make matters more complicated, in addition to regular tax rates, there is also an alternative minimum tax to assure that those with large incomes—and large deductions—do not escape taxation. The latest ATM rates are set at 26 percent up to $175,000 for married couples ($87,500 for singles), and 28 percent for amounts above $175,000.

Two important points regarding the ATM: First, there is a big up-front exemption for most taxpayers. Married couples, for instance, with an ATM income of $150,000 or less enjoy a $45,000 exemption. As incomes rise, the exemption gradually disappears. Second, itemized deductions used to calculate regular income taxes are not always deductible under the ATM. In effect, they are added back. Mortgage interest is generally a deductible ATM item.

OVER-55 RULE

Owner-occupants 55 or older who have lived in their prime residence for three of the past five years are entitled to a one-time profit exclusion of up to $125,000 at this writing. If a personal residence bought 12 years ago for $25,000 is sold this year for $150,000, the entire profit can be sheltered from federal taxes. If the property brings only $75,000, however, the $50,000 profit can be sheltered but no further profits are protected under this rule, even if another property is later sold at a profit. Why? Because only one claim is allowed.

The over-55 rule does not apply to investment real estate—all profits upon the sale of investment property are subject to tax immediately except for selected installment sales.

MOVING

Individuals moving at least 50 miles from one personal residence to another because of a job change can deduct the expense of moving personal effects and household goods. If there is no job change involved, there is no deduction.

INSTALLMENT SALES

There are often situations where seller/investors elect not only to sell property, but to put up some or all of the financing needed to make the deal work. Since the property is being sold now but paid for later, such deals are called "installment sales."

For example, if Mr. Clark bought a property for $100,000, sold it three years later for $150,000, and took back a $150,000 loan, each monthly payment would represent nontaxable income (the repayment of Mr. Clark's $100,000 acquisition cost), interest income taxed in the year paid (interest on the $150,000 loan), and capital gains income (a tax on the portion of Mr. Clark's $50,000 profit paid each year).

Under current rules, you cannot sell a depreciable property to a relative and have an installment-sale write-off. Other limitations may also apply.

ROLLOVER RESIDENCE-REPLACEMENT RULE

If you sell a personal residence and buy a new home of equal or greater value, taxes can be deferred. Suppose Mr. Barrow bought a home for $150,000 five years ago and sells it for $200,000. He has a $50,000 profit which can be taxed. However, if he buys a new personal residence for $210,000, his tax is deferred. Profits from the sale of personal residences can be sheltered in this manner through a string of sales and purchases, provided the new property value is always equal to or greater than the adjusted net price of the last house. There is no rollover replacement deduction for investment property or second homes.

The rollover exemption can be used once every two years in the general case, but there are exceptions. For instance, if you are forced to move because of employment, and if you qualify for a moving allowance deduction, then it may be possible to use the rollover rule more frequently than once every two years. If you are in the military, then you may have more time to find a new property. See a CPA or tax attorney for specific information.

CASUALTY LOSSES

If personal property is ruined by a sudden disaster—say a hurricane or earthquake—you may be entitled to a casualty loss for damage not covered by insurance if the loss exceeds 10 percent of your adjusted gross income. Investors may be able to deduct all business property losses. Speak to a tax professional for specifics.

HOME OFFICE

If you have a home office you may be entitled to deduct operating costs and depreciation, provided you meet all required rules. In general terms, the area set aside for a home office must be must be used exclusively for your trade or business; it must be used regularly; and it must either be your principal place of business or space required by your employer.

In the past, determining whether home offices could be deducted depended on what was called the "focal point" test; that is, determining if the home office was the principal place of business. Now the latest standard, based on a Supreme Court case involving a Virginia doctor, says that before a deduction can be allowed taxpayers must look at such issues as how much time is spent in the home office and the value and importance of the activities performed there.

If a home office is deductible, then you must consider how much of the house it occupies. If the office represents 10 percent of the home's living area, then 10 percent of the mortgage interest and property taxes can be deducted as business expenses, and 90 percent can be written off as itemized deductions. Expenses for utilities—say 10 percent of the electric bill in this example—can be written off. The portion of the home represented by the office can be depreciated.

When the house is sold, the home office will be treated like investment property while the rest of the property will be treated as a personal residence for tax purposes.

DEALERS

While a variety of tax benefits are normally given to real estate investors, such benefits are not normally available to dealers. In general terms, "dealers" are people who stock real estate for resale, such as builders with many homes to sell. The catch is that investors may sometimes be regarded as dealers, too. If Mr. Downs buys and sells 50 houses a year, given certain facts and circumstances, he may be regarded as a dealer and thus lose a variety of tax advantages.

THE BOTTOM LINE

Real estate offers many opportunities to reduce taxes, but those opportunities are often complex, narrow, and qualified. Determining tax benefits for a given property can be a convoluted process; merging real estate write-offs with other tax matters is generally beyond the patience—and comprehension—of mere mortals. To fully understand your tax situation, consult with a tax attorney, CPA, or enrolled agent before you invest.

Index